The Rehabilitation of Criminal Offenders: Problems and Prospects

Lee Sechrest, Susan O. White, *and*
Elizabeth D. Brown, *Editors*

PANEL ON RESEARCH ON
REHABILITATIVE TECHNIQUES

Committee on Research on Law
    Enforcement and Criminal Justice
Assembly of Behavioral and Social Sciences
National Research Council

NATIONAL ACADEMY OF SCIENCES
Washington, D.C.   1979

NOTICE: The project that is the subject of this report was approved by the Governing Board of the National Research Council, whose members are drawn from the Councils of the National Academy of Sciences, the National Academy of Engineering, and the Institute of Medicine. The members of the Committee responsible for the report were chosen for their special competences and with regard for appropriate balance.

This report has been reviewed by a group other than the authors according to procedures approved by a Report Review Committee consisting of members of the National Academy of Sciences, the National Academy of Engineering, and the Institute of Medicine.

Library of Congress Cataloging in Publication Data

Main entry under title:

The rehabilitation of criminal offenders.

Bibliography: p.
1. Rehabilitation of criminals—United States.
I. Sechrest, Lee B. II. White, Susan O. III. Brown, Elizabeth D. IV. National Research Council. Panel on Research on Rehabilitative Techniques.
HV9304.R4   364.8   79-21707
ISBN 0-309-02895-7

Available from
Office of Publications, National Academy of Sciences
2101 Constitution Avenue, N.W., Washington, D.C. 20418

Printed in the United States of America

PANEL ON RESEARCH ON REHABILITATIVE TECHNIQUES

Members

LEE B. SECHREST (*Chairman*), Department of Psychology, Florida State University

NATHAN H. AZRIN, Behavior Laboratory, Anna State Hopsital

EUGENE EIDENBERG,* Deputy Secretary to the Cabinet and Deputy Assistant to the President for International Affairs

STEPHEN E. FIENBERG, Department of Applied Statistics, University of Minnesota

JACK GIBBS,* Department of Sociology, University of Arizona

GARY GOTTFREDSON,† Center for the Social Organization of Schools, Johns Hopkins University

ALAN E. KAZDIN, Department of Psychology, Pennsylvania State University

JOHN T. MONAHAN,‡ Program in Social Ecology, University of California, Irvine

RICHARD D. SCHWARTZ, College of Law, Syracuse University

GRESHAM M. SYKES, Department of Sociology, University of Virginia

CLAUDEWELL S. THOMAS, Department of Psychiatry, College of Medicine and Dentistry of New Jersey

ANN WITTE, Department of Economics, University of North Carolina

SAMUEL KRISLOV, *ex-officio* (*Chairman*, Committee on Research on Law Enforcement and Criminal Justice), Department of Political Science, University of Minnesota

Staff

SUSAN O. WHITE (*Study Director*), Department of Political Science, Social Science Center, University of New Hampshire

*Resigned from the Panel prior to completion of the report.
†Appointed to the Panel February 1978.
‡Appointed to the Panel September 1977.

iii

Contents

iv

Preface

This report of the Panel on Research on Rehabilitative Techniques is the product of nearly 2 years of effort involving a sizable number of people of very diverse backgrounds and talents. The original schedule of activities was for 1 year of work, but, as so often happens, there were delays in the beginning, more delays in the middle, and delays at the end. But the delays were, for the most part, occasioned by the desire to do just a bit more rather than by inclinations to do nothing for a while. That desire contributed to our realization, early in the life of the Panel, that the magnitude of the task to be undertaken had been misjudged and that far more was involved than had been bargained for. Consequently, plans were developed to extend the life of the Panel.

This report is essentially the report of the first phase of our work. It is addressed primarily to questions concerning the effectiveness of rehabilitation programs within correctional institutions although answering those questions carried us into such fields as benefit-cost analysis and general research methodology. A report on the Panel's second phase of work is expected to concentrate more on noninstitutional rehabilitation programs and on prospects for rehabilitation that have as yet not been tested. That report is expected to be completed in 1980.

As a result of the controversy about rehabilitation over the past few years, many people in the criminal justice field have become strongly identified with rather specific positions. In the interest of examining the issues from a fresh viewpoint, and in the interest of producing a report that would not be merely a compromise between two utterly opposite positions, the decision was made to select Panel members who had taken no public stance on the controversy. Panel members were recruited on the basis of methodological and substantive expertise in their own fields, although several Panel members did have considerable prior experience related to criminal justice. The result was a Panel that had to begin to learn about offender rehabilitation practice and research, but a Panel that was clearly not predestined to take any final position.

In many ways, the results of the Panel's work and deliberations have been surprising to most of us. We failed to anticipate the lack of sound theory, the paucity of good data, the poor management of many programs that were tested, and all the other general disorder in the field. (Why we expected more from the field of offender rehabilitation is a good question to which we have no good answers.) At any rate, over the nearly 2 years the Panel has been working, the members have become considerably better educated and, predictably, see the field and its problems as far more complex than originally imagined. This report reflects what we have learned, much of which is not surprising, e.g., that research methodology should be better than it is, but some of which was surprising to us, e.g., the poor quality control over program implementation.

This report represents the consensus of the Panel, obscuring some disagreements at the margins here and there, reflecting in other places the expertise of individual Panel members to whom the rest deferred. Nonetheless, the report was completed by a group still in substantial harmony.

This volume consists of a report and appendix representing the Panel's own work and five papers commissioned by the Panel. The Panel was fully aware of its limitations from the beginning and planned a conference whose primary function would be to inform its members. Sensing its way as best it could, the Panel commissioned a series of papers to be presented at a conference and invited a number of experts in the field to listen to and discuss the papers. The conference, which proved to be most informative, was held at Woods Hole in July 1977. A list of those who attended the conference is appended to the report.

The Panel was established under the aegis of the Committee on Research on Law Enforcement and Criminal Justice and maintained lines of communication with the Committee. The chairman of the Committee, Samuel Krislov, was a member of the Panel and, during the course of the Panel's efforts, I also became a member of the Committee; hence, communications were simplified and good. Although Committee members were invited to submit comments, the Panel did not formally submit its report to the Committee for approval and thus bears full responsibility for the content of its report and for its recommendations.

Although the editors of the report had major responsibilities for drafting sections of the report and for assembling and integrating contributions of the Panel members, I would like to recognize explicitly the major contributions of the Panel members.

Throughout the course of our work, the Panel and the editors benefited greatly from the consistent and strong support of the staff of the Assembly of Behavioral and Social Sciences, particularly from David A. Goslin, executive director, and from Keith O. Boyum, study director for the Committee on Law Enforcement and Criminal Justice.

Essential and valuable assistance was received from Susan E. Martin and Robin Redner, who are the Panel's current study director and research assistant, respectively. Charles Meyers, a student at Florida State University, gave uncounted hours in library and other assistance to our work. It must also be acknowledged that the original drafts of the report would still be somewhere in limbo had it not been for the outstanding organizational and typing skills and exceptional patience of my secretary, Susan Elliott. Major administrative and secretarial support was also provided by Dorothy Jackson, the Panel's first administrative secretary and by her successor, Juanita Maclin. The penultimate draft of the report was, despite all our efforts, rough in many places and inconsistent in style. Fortunately we were able to call on the Assembly's Eugenia Grohman for help, and her editorial talents are quite evident to those who saw the draft of the report.

Finally, we wish to acknowledge the support we received from the staff of the National Institute for Law Enforcement and Criminal Justice of the U.S. Department of Justice. I wish to thank Blair Ewing for his overall support and Richard Linster and Helen Erskine for their more detailed guidance.

LEE SECHREST, *Chairman*
Panel on Research on Rehabilitative Techniques

REPORT OF
THE PANEL

Summary

The current state of knowledge about rehabilitation of criminal offenders is cause for grave concern, particularly in view of the obvious importance of the problem. After 40 years of research and literally hundreds of studies, almost all the conclusions that can be reached have to be formulated in terms of what we do not know. The one positive conclusion is discouraging: the research methodology that has been brought to bear on the problem of finding ways to rehabilitate criminal offenders has been generally so inadequate that only a relatively few studies warrant any unequivocal interpretations. The entire body of research appears to justify only the conclusion that we do not now know of any program or method of rehabilitation that could be guaranteed to reduce the criminal activity of released offenders. Although a generous reviewer of the literature might discern some glimmers of hope, those glimmers are so few, so scattered, and so inconsistent that they do not serve as a basis for any recommendation other than continued research.

Furthermore, a more penetrating inquiry into the nature of the problem of rehabilitation and the programs and methods that have been tried leads to the conclusion that there is even less in the research than meets the eye. The techniques that have been tested seem rarely to have been devised to be strong enough to offer realistic hope that they would rehabilitate offenders, especially imprisoned felons. In general, techniques have been tested as isolated treatments rather than as complex combinations, which would seem more suited to the task. And even when techniques have been tested in good designs, insufficient attention has been paid to maintaining their integrity, so that often the treatment to be tested was delivered in a substantially weakened form. It is also not clear that all the theoretical power and the individual imagination that could be invoked in the planning of rehabilitative efforts have ever been capitalized on. Thus, the recommendation in this report that has the strongest support is that more and better thinking and research should be invested in efforts to devise programs for offender rehabilitation.

BACKGROUND

The Panel on the Research on Rehabilitation Techniques was formed to complement the work of the Panel on Research on Deterrent and Incapacitative Effects in order to provide the parent Committee on Research on Law Enforcement and Criminal Justice with a fuller perspective on the broad issue of punishment policy. Contributing to the impetus for the Panel's formation was the observation that rehabilitation theory and practice have dominated correctional policy in the American criminal justice system for years although both crime rates and recidivism rates appear to many people to have been increasing. The salience of the issues was increased dramatically by the 1975 publication of a book by Lipton, Martinson, and Wilks that was widely interpreted as supporting the conclusion that "nothing works" in criminal rehabilitation, a conclusion fostered by Martinson in other writings and public appearances. In this context of both public and scientific controversy, the Panel was given the task of reviewing existing evaluations to determine whether they provide a basis for any conclusions about the effectiveness of rehabilitative techniques, clarifying the difficulties of measuring the effectiveness of treatment programs, and recommending methodological strategies for evaluating treatment programs.

THE NATURE AND THEORY OF REHABILITATION

There are numerous varying definitions of rehabilitation, but all definitions involve three aspects considered important to specify in any definition of rehabilitation: the desired outcome of rehabilitation; the intervening variable(s) assumed to be the target of the rehabilitative treatment; and the intervention itself. With the above considerations in mind the Panel arrived at the following definition: *Rehabilitation is the result of any planned intervention that reduces an offender's further criminal activity, whether that reduction is mediated by personality, behavior, abilities, attitudes, values, or other factors. The effects of maturation and the effects associated with "fear" or "intimidation" are excluded, the results of the latter having traditionally been labeled as specific deterrence.*

Although punishment has been conceptually differentiated from rehabilitation and is technically referred to as specific deterrence, the concept of punishment itself is complex. Punishment may operate in various ways to result in a decrease in the frequency or seriousness of criminal activity, and some of those ways are not incompatible with the concept of rehabilitation. However, whether punishment in any way is effective in suppressing criminal activity is an empirical question that has not yet been resolved.

The rehabilitative efforts reviewed by Lipton, Martinson, and Wilks, as well as most others we considered, seem to assume that crime reflects either a specific individual defect or a set of pathological behavior patterns. But theories about the causes of criminal behavior are much more diverse than those efforts and reviews would suggest. The many theories are not necessarily mutually incompatible, and it may even be that they are all tenable, perhaps in different degrees for different cases. If so, it could be important to match rehabilitative efforts with the characteristics of the individuals. In general, unfortunately, most rehabilitative efforts have not taken into consideration the diversity of possible causes of crime; in fact, those efforts have been generally atheoretical, the programs have been narrow in scope, and the interventions have been weak or relatively minor forms of potentially strong interventions.

CURRENT STATE OF KNOWLEDGE ABOUT REHABILITATION

As a first task, the Panel reviewed what research had been done on offender rehabilitation in order to assess the current state of knowledge. The Lipton, Martinson, and Wilks review provided a starting point, but since the literature they covered extended only to 1968, the Panel undertook additional efforts. Moreover, owing to the importance of the Lipton, Martinson, and Wilks review, an importance partly derived from the controversy it sparked, the Panel believed it necessary to undertake an evaluation of that work.

The Panel concludes that Lipton, Martinson, and Wilks were reasonably accurate and fair in their appraisal of the rehabilitation literature. Where they erred it was almost invariably by an overly lenient assessment of the methodology of a study or by a failure to maintain an appropriately critical set in evaluating statistical analyses. Two limitations, however, must be applied to their conclusions: first, inferences about the integrity of the treatments analyzed were uncertain and the interventions involved were generally weak; second, there are suggestions to be found concerning successful rehabilitation efforts that qualify the conclusion that "nothing works." Although the data are far from consistent, there may be some treatments that are effective for certain subgroups of offenders. Recently, interventions involving work and financial support for released offenders seem to hold some promise for rehabilitation.

PROBLEMS OF EVALUATION

For numerous ethical and practical reasons, persons responsible for the delivery of rehabilitation services should be able to demonstrate the effectiveness of those services. There is then the question of how to determine whether rehabilitation services are effective. The Panel believes that the answer can only be found through careful evaluation of services. Although the need for experimentation is sometimes rejected on the grounds that it underestimates what we already know, is expensive, is impractical, and has little influence on policy, it can be shown that often what we think we know is erroneous, current untested procedures are as expensive as experimentation, good experimentation has been done in the past and with effort can be done in the future, and finally, research can be planned to influence policy.

THE CASE FOR RANDOMIZED EXPERIMENTS

Research on rehabilitative techniques for criminal offenders has until now been characterized by weak methodologies, with many projects and reports on rehabilitative effects being virtually devoid of considerations of research design. In addition, sample sizes are often far too small to detect subtle effects such as interactions, further exacerbating methodological problems.

The Panel recommends that true randomized experiments be implemented whenever feasible in evaluating rehabilitation programs, simply because this form of study design allows inferences about causal relationships with a specifiable degree of certainty. Weaker designs may not only allow mistaken conclusions that a program works when it does not, but may also lead to the mistaken dismissal of a program that is effective but is labeled ineffective.

Objections to randomization in social experiments are often based on the assumption that the intervention will work and therefore that some subjects will have been denied beneficial treatment, when, in fact, the experiment has been designed for the very reason that the beneficial qualities of the treatment should not be assumed. A solution to this objection can occasionally be found in an investigation that uses two experimental treatments so that no one will have been denied "treatment." In all efforts, however, the retreat from randomization should be minimized, and systems should be implemented for monitoring and maintaining randomization. If a true experiment cannot be done, only the strongest alternative should be chosen as a substitute design.

Although true experiments are the preferred study design for evaluation of programs, it would be unrealistic to assume that they will become the sole methodology of the future. Possibilities for development of fallback designs, which specify alternatives to the original evaluation plan in case it cannot be fully implemented, should also be explored. In addition, strategies are needed that permit a more continuous interaction between program and evaluation so that programs can be evaluated as they develop and change, with at least some of the change being instigated by the evaluation findings.

MEASUREMENT OF OUTCOMES

Recidivism has been the traditional measure for assessing effectiveness of rehabilitation efforts. As an outcome measure, however, recidivism presents difficulties, not the least of which is that there is no agreement on a definition of recidivism: it is assessed in whatever way is convenient, whether it makes sense conceptually or not. Recidivism is usually measured as if it involves a binary outcome, which results in the loss of considerable information, decreasing the sensitivity of tests for program effects. Attempts to correct for that problem by producing a continuous scale, e.g., by weighting the seriousness of offenses, are probably only partially successful, and they may introduce other problems. Further empirical work on the standardization of measures of recidivism and on the suitability of multiple measures could have a high payoff. Although a decrease in criminal activity is a necessary consequence of a successful program of offender rehabilitation, alternative ways of assessing the effectiveness of rehabilitation programs are needed.

THE BENEFITS AND COSTS OF REHABILITATION

The use of cost-benefit techniques for evaluating rehabilitation programs is still in its infancy. However, analyses done on a work-release program in North Carolina and on a supported-work program in New York City indicate that the procedure can be used effectively, although there are severe problems in estimating the many possible direct benefits, and, even more, the benefits of averted crime.

Limitations on the use of benefit-cost techniques for evaluating rehabilitation efforts result from: generally weak designs in rehabilitation research; the fact that the technique is only applicable when a program is shown to have a positive effect; administrators who hesitate to or cannot value social benefits in monetary terms; the fact that efficiency is the goal of classical cost-benefit analysis while it is often not the goal of administrators; and an inability to specify the time period during which benefits are expected. Despite the limitations of benefit-cost analysis, however, under the right circumstances it provides information of great utility, and further exploration of its applicability to offender rehabilitation programs is to be encouraged.

Economics offers a number of other techniques and analyses, e.g., of cost effectiveness, that could be most useful when combined with traditional evaluative procedures. Although the outcome of a rehabilitative program is of utmost importance, if the outcome is favorable it is critical that decision makers know the costs of achieving that outcome. In the past, this aspect of evaluation has been neglected in research on offender rehabilitation.

WHAT HAS NOT BEEN TESTED

In contemplating the prospects for rehabilitative efforts, it is important to know that what has not yet been tested might offer improvement over previous efforts. The Panel soon came to realize, however, that a major problem lay in determining what actually had been tested because there were so many obvious discrepancies—and undeterminable hidden discrepancies—between what was supposed to have been tested or what was alleged to have been tested and what was, in fact, actually done.

An all-important issue is whether a treatment that was to have been evaluated was actually implemented as described. Even an experiment with an exemplary design will be quite misleading if the treatment was not described, not correctly or fully described, or was not delivered as described. The Panel believes that all three of these situations have been common in offender rehabilitation programs. However, it has not often been possible to get a good grasp of the problems that are involved because documentation of programs is often so inadequate. When it is asserted that "nothing works," the Panel is uncertain as to just what has ever been given a fair trial. If we are to arrive at sound conclusions about the prospects for rehabilitation, future research on offender rehabilitation must pay far more attention to issues of strength and integrity of treatments along with adequacy of experimental designs.

Among the logical possibilities for innovative rehabilitative efforts, several seem especially worthy of consideration for development and evaluation: extensive family interventions; intervention efforts directed at the offender very early in his criminal career (e.g., "quick-dip" sanctions); restitution by the offender; increased support (financial, counseling, etc.) after the prisoner's release from prison rather than before release; employment and vocational programs; and alternative sentencing and confinement. Although some of these interventions may be costly, it may be worth a great deal to show in principle that rehabilitation can work.

LEGAL AND ETHICAL ISSUES

There are important legal issues in offender rehabilitation with respect to the conditions and types of treatment that may be afforded to offenders. One important issue is the degree of persuasion or even coercion that may be used to convince offenders to participate in rehabilitation programs. Some types of rehabilitative programs involve the temporary withholding of some goods or benefits that are ordinarily available, e.g., television privileges, in order to make certain behavioral options more attractive. To what extent may prisoners be subject to deprivations? And does the extent change if it can be shown that temporary deprivation effectively reduces the length of time the offender is required to serve? May officials make rehabilitation programs so attractive that they entice prisoners into participating when they might not otherwise be interested? These and similar questions deserve careful legal scholarship.

Additional legal issues arise out of some of the special conditions required for successful experimentation. Constraints on evaluations of treatments seem to arise out of four basic constitutional and legal issues: due process, which might be interrupted when a research design calls for assignment of offenders to a treatment prior to the offenders' presentation before a court; equal treatment under the law, which could conceivably prohibit the random assignment to different treatments of offenders matched on offense and equal in status; voluntary participation, which may not exist for a prisoner in an institution; and informed consent, which becomes problematic when one considers whether it is ever possible to get truly informed consent from offenders who may have low literacy levels or who may feign understanding for other reasons. Again, careful scholarship is needed to address these issues.

In addition to legal complexities, the techniques and theories of any type of behavior change inevitably lead to consideration of ethical issues in relation to that behavior change, especially when the targets of change are literally captive. While the Panel strongly recommends the use of experiments to ensure that inferences concerning active interventions are valid, care to avoid harm to subjects should be the primary rule and ultimate standard by which research plans are judged. One cannot justify the undertaking of research that could reasonably be expected to be harmful to any subjects of that research.

POLICY RECOMMENDATION

The strongest recommendation that the Panel can make at this time is that the research on offender rehabilitation should be pursued more vigorously, more systematically, more imaginatively, and more rigorously. Specifically, treatments should be based upon strong theoretical rationales, perhaps involving total programs rather than weak or piecemeal treatments. In addition, the strength and integrity of all treatments should be monitored and fully documented, along with documentation of the costs of operation of the treatment. To implement this recommendation it is essential that researchers become more involved in developing appropriate methodologies for evaluation of interventions and that appropriate funding agencies support research on criminal rehabilitation, while making the criteria for funding more rigorous with respect to experimental design, theoretical rationale, and monitoring of integrity and strength of treatment.

1 The Challenge of Rehabilitation

The effectiveness of rehabilitation for criminal offenders and the prospects for effective rehabilitation are currently matters of widespread debate. The debate has been participated in by correctional practitioners, judges and lawyers, criminologists and penologists, philosophers, policy makers, and social scientists. In view of this debate we wish to make clear at the outset of this report why our study was undertaken and what function this report is intended to serve as the debate continues.

THE PROMISE OF THE REHABILITATIVE IDEAL

The promise of the rehabilitative ideal (Allen 1959)—that criminal offenders can be reformed or their behavior changed in such a way that they can live socially productive lives in the larger community without engaging in more criminal activity than most of their fellow citizens—makes the debate about rehabilitation one of the most important of our time.

The appropriate handling of criminal offenders has never been a settled issue in American society. Over the years the dominant purposes of criminal justice have shifted from a strictly punitive goal toward a rehabilitative ideal. In the eighteenth century, felony justice meant corporal or capital punishment; prisons, as places for punishment, did not exist. Prisons were introduced as a more humane way of punishing convicted criminals as well as a way of providing a means of incapacitation. The rehabilitative ideal is a relatively recent addition to these goals. The notion of rehabilitating offenders was initially intended to counter the punitiveness of correctional institutions by introducing a positive "reform the offender" orientation. The growth of the idea of rehabilitation, however, was paralleled by the development of the behavioral sciences, and eventually the rehabilitative ideal became virtually synonomous with the so-called "medical model" of corrections (Allen 1959). According to the medical model, criminal behavior is like a disease that can be cured if the right sort of therapy is applied. This combination of a hopeful outlook toward solving a major social problem with a claim of expertise within the scientific/clinical community dominated the corrections field for many years. More recently, however, widespread perceptions that crime rates are rising and little persuasive evidence that recidivism rates are falling have led to the focusing of critical attention on the effectiveness of correctional institutions and, now, to doubts about the concept of correctional rehabilitation itself. Even though there is no evidence that successful rehabilitation would have a detectable impact on crime rates—and perhaps even in the absence of any reason to believe that there should be an impact—the concept of rehabilitation is under attack.

Part of the disenchantment with rehabilitation stems from ideological or philosophical concerns: some people simply prefer a punitive approach to deviant behavior. This traditionally conservative position has been buttressed by a libertarian argument that the therapeutic approach can be more coercive and dehumanizing than the "just deserts" of punishment (von Hirsch 1976). But the disillusionment stems also from the fact that high recidivism rates seem to give lie to claims for expertise or for behavioral technologies that can indeed reform the criminal offenders receiving the "treatments." Consequently, the medical model itself is criticized because it has not proved capable of accomplishing its own stated goals. Instead of reforming the criminal offender, so the criticism goes, correctional rehabilitation merely masks the reality of a strictly punitive system of control under the guise of doing good.

This critique of the rehabilitative ideal is persuasive for many reasons and particularly because crime and recidivism rates strongly suggest to the public that in general offenders are not being rehabilitated by current programs. Rehabilitation, it is commonly said, is simply not working. But what if it did work? Would the philosophical arguments against rehabilitation be persuasive if recidivism rates were really decreasing as a consequence of rehabilitative efforts? The social benefit to be derived from reforming criminal offenders would be great indeed, provided that the methods used were morally and politically acceptable. Surely the promise of the rehabilitative ideal remains attractive even though it may have been corrupted in actual practice.

Part of the motivation for our study, therefore, is a commitment to determine whether the promise of rehabilitation can ever be realized. This is a very complex question. And on the surface, at least, the evidence for the effectiveness of rehabilitation appears to be weak or nonexistent. But the significance of the goal mandates that the strongest possible effort be made before the rehabilitative ideal is abandoned. We turn, then, to consideration of what we know, and what we can know, about the effectiveness of rehabilitation.

THE KNOWLEDGE PROBLEM

The immediate occasion for the formation of a panel to review the effectiveness of rehabilitation was a widely discussed controversy over whether existing evaluation studies of rehabilitative programs necessitate the conclusion that "nothing works" (see Lipton *et al.* 1975). Unlike the largely philosopical debates, the controversy over the proper inferences to be drawn from evaluation studies raises technical issues about the validity of evidence, about how one measures effectiveness, and ultimately about what can be known in this complex area of human behavior. The Committee on Research on Law Enforcement and Criminal Justice had previously convened a Panel on Research on Deterrent and Incapacitative Effects to consider similar technical questions with respect to the effects of criminal sanctions on crime rates. (The Panel's report was published in 1978 [Blumstein *et al.* 1978].) In light of the importance of this issue and the nature of the questions in conflict, the Committee deemed it appropriate to establish the present Panel on Research on Rehabilitative Techniques. The Panel was asked to clarify the difficulties of measuring the effectiveness of treatment programs, to review existing evaluations to determine whether they can provide knowledge about the effectiveness of rehabilitative techniques, and to recommend methodological strategies for evaluating treatment programs.

A variety of complex, possibly intractable, problems have made it difficult to obtain knowledge about the effectiveness of rehabilitative techniques in corrections. This report is largely concerned with identifying these problems and making clear how they have subverted the validity of prior studies and could contaminate the results of future research. Basically the problems are of two kinds: those having to do with maintaining the integrity of both treatments and experimental research designs within institutions that are dominated by other concerns and those that stem more from methodological problems. We have labeled the first kind problems of implementation and the second kind problems of evaluation. Overcoming both types of problems is essential if reliable information about the effectivenss of rehabilitative techniques is to be developed.

It is the Panel's judgment, explained at length in later chapters, that existing studies cannot yield reliable knowledge about the effectiveness of correctional rehabilitation. This is partly a consequence of problems of evaluation. Not only is there no general agreement among researchers as to appropriate measures of effectiveness, or even as to how one measures recidivism, but it is also clear that the methodological difficulties inherent in studies when simple, straightforward research designs cannot be implemented have defeated most research efforts from the outset. For example, it was impossible in most cases reviewed for the investigator to separate out treatment effects from the effects of other elements of the specific institution. The most telling difficulties, however, have to do with problems of implementation. These include the constraints on program integrity resulting from the pressure of other institutional concerns, the disruption of the research design as institutional needs take precedence over research validity, and the fact that the techniques are normally used across large portions of the prison population without regard to individual needs or individual amenability to particular treatments. Elaboration of these problems can be found in the remaining chapters of this report, along with the Panel's conclusions and detailed methodological recommendations. But one major conclusion deserves to be highlighted at the outset.

The Panel finds little in its review of existing studies, and of the problems involved in implementing and evaluating treatment programs, to allay the current pessimism about the effectiveness of institutional rehabilitation programs as they now exist. Our emphasis is not on the impossibility of rehabilitating criminal offenders, but rather on the difficulty of successful rehabilitation in an institutional setting. This is not to say that well-conceived and properly implemented treatment programs have no effects, for they may well provide helpful therapy and training and generally preserve the sanity of prison inmates. But we should continue to treat as problematic the assumption that long-term behavior in a nonprison environment can be significantly affected by institutional programs.

It should be understood that it is not impossible, nor even very difficult, to change someone's behavior when there is no limit as to what may be done to effect the change. An individual can be rendered physically or mentally incapable of certain acts. The possibilities for modifying both short- and long-term behavior are numerous. But extreme interventions are ethically and legally unacceptable in this society. The real question, therefore, is not whether behavior can be changed, but whether it can be done successfully within the moral and legal limits that the society imposes on the task.

PROSPECTS FOR EFFECTIVE REHABILITATION

If rehabilitation is understood as an attempt to change behavior instead of as a set of programs for reforming the institutionalized criminal offender, a perspective different from that traditionally believed in the field emerges. Rehabilitation is simply a term used to label attempts to "correct" undesirable behavior. It involves problems of inducing behavior change that are similar in critical respects to all problems of behavior change. To put the issue in these terms is not to shift away from a humanistic perspective, for it is certainly no more manipulative than the "coerced cure" that is the goal of correctional rehabilitation today (Morris 1974). Our concern is to move away from a programmatic definition of problems toward a perspective grounded in scientific theories of behavior and a sound understanding of the nature of behavior change.

The first consequence of this approach is the realization that correctional rehabilitation as it is currently practiced (and to the extent that it is practiced at all) seems to have developed out of trends in clinical treatment that happen to be current, regardless of the often tenuous relationship between the particular behaviors involved and the premises of those treatments. And because programs are generally designed for an institutional setting, the connection between the treatment and the individual's life outside the institution that is presumably the target for change is never systematically made.

Conceptually, a number of dimensions are ignored in varying degree in the use of rehabilitative techniques for correctional purposes. Among these are the different effects of the timing of interventions across different stages of an individual's life, the intensity (both frequency and strength) of treatment, the inevitably inhibiting effects of social and institutional constraints on the integrity of treatment, the relative weight of environmental as opposed to dispositional or individual trait factors, and variations in the personality and experiential characteristics of individual subjects.

A sound theoretical approach can both broaden and deepen one's perspective on the effectiveness of rehabilitation. We believe that the prospects for rehabilitation, although pessimistic or at least limited from an institutional point of view, remain an open question. Chapter 5 of this report outlines some of the new directions that should be investigated, including those that the Panel will be exploring in a second phase of its work. Consequently, the current report should not be read as a final statement about the effectiveness of rehabilitation, but rather as a preliminary mapping of the problems and prospects in the field.

THE ROLE OF SCIENCE

It should now be clear how the Panel views its potential contribution to the debate over rehabilitation. While science cannot dictate the issues that are appropriate for national debate in any policy area, it can delineate the empirical questions involved and attempt to focus attention on those questions and the ways in which they might be answered.

In the case of the controversy over the effectiveness of rehabilitation, the Panel believes that the issue has not been stated in a form that is conducive to analysis. Before conclusions can be reached about effectiveness, there must be agreement on a criterion or criteria for success and on how success is to be measured. And before alternatives can be fully explored, the range of knowledge that has been developed about the complexity of human behavior and behavior change should be examined for its potential to provide insight about the problem. This is not to say that public policy should wait on science but it is to argue that science can make an important and sometimes essential contribution to that policy. The paper by Davies (in this volume) makes it clear that the problems involved in devising, evaluating, and disseminating effective programs are not peculiar to the field of offender rehabilitation.

RESPONSIBILITY OF THE SCIENTIST: ETHICAL ISSUES

Important ethical issues are involved whenever scientists attempt to change human behavior. These are magnified considerably when the population of subjects is literally captive. The Panel wishes to emphasize its strong concerns about experimental research using human subjects and to make clear its position on this.

Throughout this report, the Panel recommends research and evaluation strategies designed to produce, for the first time, valid answers to questions about the effectiveness of rehabilitation. This we believe is an essential step toward intelligent decisions on the use of rehabilitative techniques. The research and evaluation strategies often require what is technically termed "experimentation on human subjects," in part because all rehabilitation efforts must be thought of as in the testing stage. But more importantly, we recommend randomized experiments in order to ensure that the resulting inferences are valid and not artifacts of any unmeasured factors in the prison environment.

Recent debate has tended to polarize opinion between those who insist on methodological purity and those who insist on protection of human rights, with the implication that these positions are mutually exclusive. We disagree with this implied dichotomy. We believe that randomized experiments can be carried out with minimal risk to individual rights. We further believe that this minimal risk is justifiable in light of the need for valid information and the potential benefits to society that would result from successful rehabilitation. The promise of rehabilitation is not so important as to outweigh real harm to individuals, but it does justify the use of randomized experiments under the kinds of carefully monitored conditions recommended by the National Commission on the Protection of Human Subjects in Biomedical and Behavioral Research.

We believe it is a mistake to argue that experimentation per se is the issue: experimentation is an indispensable part of a complete research strategy. The issue should be whether individuals are worse off as a result of an experiment. A detailed discussion of the ethics of randomized experiments can be found in Chapter 5. For the present discussion, the Panel wants to make clear its view that the rule "no one worse off" (Morris 1969) must always apply. The history of medical and other research demonstrates that the best information and best judgment of highly qualified researchers cannot always predict the "worse off" condition or even who (treatment or control group) is at risk. In a randomized experiment, those in the control group are presumably not "worse off," although if the treatment is successful they have not received its benefits. Those in the treatment group could be "better off," if the treatment is successful, or "worse off," if the treatment turns out to be harmful. If the best judgment of qualified researchers is that a *prima facie* benign treatment has a reasonable probability of succeeding, it is no less the responsibility of behavioral scientists to test it than it is the responsibility of physicians to do what they believe will most help their patients.

Sometimes the physician is wrong and sometimes the behavioral scientist is wrong. The Panel recognizes this difficulty and calls for the utmost care in choosing treatments, selecting amenable subjects, and structuring experiments. We believe there is an obligation to pursue the promise of rehabilitation and an equal obligation to proceed with the greatest respect for the people directly affected by the work. There are no conditions that would justify the undertaking of research that could reasonably be expected to be harmful to nonvoluntary subjects, whatever the societal benefits, and "voluntary" has to be defined and assessed with extraordinary care when potential research subjects are captives—a subject this Panel will pursue in a subsequent report.

NATURE AND THEORY OF REHABILITATION

Rehabilitation is a complex concept, embodying a number of quite different aspects: its social purpose, its various programmatic interpretations, the behavioral assumptions that underlie it, and the many methodological problems that have plagued all attempts to determine whether it "works." Some of the problems of analysis, therefore, are definitional. Others require a delineation of the various approaches that have been or might be taken in order to identify a particular problem in the more general theoretical context of such problems. Such analytical mapping is the purpose of this section. Its three parts cover questions of definition, a brief discussion of the theoretical bases for correctional rehabilitation, and a description of different types of rehabilitative techniques.

DEFINITION

The term "rehabilitation" can be defined in various ways, which causes confusion in the scientific literature and among those who seek to evaluate the effectiveness of rehabilitation programs. In order to arrive at a definition that will be most helpful for the purposes of this report, it is necessary, first, to clarify the function of rehabilitation as compared to other societal responses to crime; and second, to distinguish the effects of rehabilitative techniques from the effects of other forces that also act to modify criminal behavior.

Seven reasons are commonly given to explain why society sanctions a person who has violated its laws:

1. to deter the offender from offending again by punishment or fear of punishment (without necessarily changing him or her in any other way);
2. to deter others from behaving as the offender has;
3. to incapacitate the offender and thus deprive him or her of the opportunity to offend again for a given period of time;
4. to forestall personal vengeance by those hurt by the offender;
5. to exact retribution from the offender and so set right the scales of moral justice;
6. to educate people morally or socially;
7. to rehabilitate or reform the offender.

Techniques for accomplishing this last goal are the subject of the Panel's study.

We initially defined rehabilitation as *the result of any planned intervention that reduces an offender's further criminal activity, whether that reduction is mediated by personality, behavior, abilities, attitudes, values, or other factors.* Because precise definition of our subject is a prerequisite to the specification of methodological improvements in research on rehabilitation, however, it was clear that some additional distinctions were necessary. In particular, rehabilitation must be carefully distinguished from what is called specific deterrence (reason 1, above) and from the developmental effects of the passage of time on behavior (i.e., maturation).

Definitions of rehabilitation found in writings on the topic appear to differ on at least three dimensions: outcome, intervening variables, and intervention.[1]

Outcome: While most definitions take a reduction in recidivism as their dependent measure, others allude to the *parens patriae* notion of making the offender "better and happier" as an alternative or at least an auxiliary goal.

Intervening variable: The appropriate targets of rehabilitative efforts are given variously as the offender's "intent," "motivation," "character," "wish," "person," "habit," "behavior patterns," "personality," "dynamics," "value system," "needs," or "attitudes."

Intervention: The definitions also vary in how inclusive they are with respect to the mechanisms by which rehabilitation is achieved. Some include as rehabilitation anything done that reduces the probability of an offender's recidivism (e.g., Wilkins 1969, von Hirsch 1976). Others specifically distinguish "intimidation" or specific deterrence from rehabilitation as two separate processes that can result in a decreased rate of future crime in an offender (e.g., van den Haag 1975).

Not too much should be expected of definitions in resolving areas of theoretical controversy, since any definition will involve an element of arbitrariness in setting conceptual boundaries. Different definitions may be required for different purposes. For the methodological purposes of this study, the definition adopted takes a narrow view of what will be measured as the outcome of rehabilitation and of what will count as interventions, while allowing flexibility in the choice of intervening variables by which change is to be achieved.

[1]For a variety of definitions of rehabilitation, see Ogden (1973), President's Commission on Law Enforcement and Administration of Justice (1967), New York Governor's Special Committee on Criminal Offenders (1972, pp. 266–267), Dershowitz (1976, pp. 73–74), von Hirsch (1976, p. 11), van den Haag (1975, p. 58), Wilkins (1969, pp. 17–18), Packer (1968, p. 53), Allen (1959, p. 226), Sommer (1976, p. 22), and Halleck and Witte (1977).

Enough has been written in the past few years on the pitfalls of making people "better" against their will that to adopt offender well-being as the purpose of rehabilitation (outcome to be measured)—or even as a purpose of rehabilitation—appears a hazardous course, one likely to be opposed not only by civil libertarians, but also by offenders, the supposed beneficiaries of the betterment. Reduction in crime, moderated by considerations of justice or moral desert (von Hirsch 1976), appears the more appropriate contemporary goal. It should be added that excluding "beneficial" treatment—that is, treatment that is intended to change an individual in ways other than to reduce his or her offense rate—from the definition of rehabilitation in no sense implies that such treatment, on humanitarian grounds, should not be an integral part of the penal system (Halleck and Witte 1977, Monahan 1977).

To distinguish rehabilitation from specific deterrence is particularly important. The conceptual distinction is sometimes difficult to maintain in practice, and it may be that some forms of "punishment"[2] will turn out to be appropriately rehabilitative as well as effective in modifying behavior. But failure to distinguish, at least conceptually, between specific deterrence and rehabilitation may lead to anomalous conclusions—for example, identifying as "rehabilitative" an offender's fear of returning to a prison in which he was repeatedly homosexually raped. Similarly, one must separate rehabilitative effects from those achieved by the simple ticking of the clock (van den Haag 1975). The fact that a young man convicted of robbery at 19 who serves 20 years in prison does not return to prison after his release at age 39 cannot, in itself, be taken as an index of "rehabilitation." To do so necessarily would lead to the conclusion that lengthy sentences are per se rehabilitative.

Although a narrow construction of the purpose and scope of rehabilitative techniques appears most appropriate, broad latitude should be granted in defining the intervening variables that become the targets of rehabilitation efforts. There is sufficient disagreement within the research community as to whether behavior change is best achieved by altering personal or attitudinal variables, by focusing directly on extinguishing the problematic behavior, by constructing alternative behavioral skills (e.g., vocational skills), or by altering the individual's social or economic circumstances so that any attempt to resolve the issue by definitional fiat is premature.

In light of these considerations, we evolved the following definition of rehabilitation as a guide to our study: *Rehabilitation is the result of any*

[2]The term "punishment" has legal, philosophical, and psychological connotations. The discussion in this report is confined to psychological interpretations. The Panel recognizes the important, and perhaps confounding, legal and philosophical aspects, but does not consider it useful at this time to attempt further definitions.

planned intervention that reduced an offender's further criminal activity, whether that reduction is mediated by personality, behavior, abilities, attitudes, values, or other factors. The effects of maturation and the effects associated with "fear" or "intimidation" are excluded, the result of the latter having traditionally been labeled as specific deterrence. In fact, the effects of rehabilitation, maturation, and specific deterrence are intimately intertwined. Almost none of the attempts to measure the effects of rehabilitation have tried to separate or control for the effects of specific deterrence or its interaction with rehabilitation.

This definition has three features:

1. *Planned intervention.* Excluded is spontaneous reformation such as may occur with an isolated offender in the absence of any organized program.
2. *Eclecticism.* The definition is free of any prior conception of the processes by which rehabilitation may occur or of any specification of physiological, psychological, social, or moral hypotheses.
3. *Future criminal activity.* Criminal behavior, rather than offender growth, insight, or happiness, is the sole criterion against which rehabilitation ultimately must be measured. A favorable effect of rehabilitation may be reflected in a selective reduction in certain types of serious crimes as well as by an overall reduction in criminal activity. Psychological or economic outcomes may serve as intervening variables in pursuit of the goal of reducing criminal activity. Although the definition of rehabilitation excludes treatment in prison that does not have a reduction in future criminal activity as its goal, there is no intent to disparage such treatment since it certainly may be justified on other grounds.

MODELS OF CRIME AND STRATEGIES OF REHABILITATION

The empirical relation (if any) between the nature of rehabilitative efforts and ideas about the origins of crime is not yet clear. Still, ideas about the causes and origins of crime should reasonably have some impact on thinking about what rehabilitative techniques should be tried. Current theories of criminal behavior are diverse, some seeking to explain why people become delinquent and taking nondelinquent behavior for granted. Other theories assume that people would naturally engage in crime if not restrained by society and seek to explain why many people do not become delinquent. Some theories seek to explain the behavior of individuals, and others appear directed to the explanation of differences in rates of delinquency among different social groups (defined, for example, by social class or by location of residence).

These diverse theories sometimes employ concepts such as learning (Bandura and Walters 1963), thinking errors (Yochelson and Samenow 1976), moral development (Hogan 1973, Kolberg 1964, Mowrer 1960), attempts to alleviate feelings of oppression (Halleck 1967), or the absence of shared meanings in groups (Mead 1934). Other theories invoke social disorganization, social stress, or anomie as explanatory concepts (Brenner 1976, Cloward and Ohlin 1961, Merton 1937, 1968). Other theorists use labeling as an explanation (Lemert 1967, President's Commission on Law Enforcement and Administration of Justice 1967), or regard economic gain as an incentive to engage in crime (Baker and Reeves 1977, Ehrlich 1973). One group of theorists seeks to explain delinquency by reference to the conformity to the norms of deviant subcultures (Sutherland and Cressey 1970, Wilkins 1965). In contrast, Hirschi (1969) has articulated a social-psychological theory of social control in which the weakening of a person's ties to society (family, school, career) may result in delinquency. Finally, a number of theorists have discussed the role of human biology in crime and delinquency (Shah and Roth 1974).

These and other views of the origins of crime, diverse as they are, are not necessarily mutually incompatible. We have not attempted to evaluate any of these views, but each may be tenable in varying degree, perhaps in different degree for different cases. Or some may be useful at one level of explanation or aggregation but not at another. If so, there are important implications for rehabilitative efforts, for it will be necessary to match rehabilitative efforts with the characteristics of individual cases (Glaser 1975, Palmer 1975). If the diverse theories are all at least partially tenable, as seems likely, and especially if two or more processes are involved in any person's delinquency, rehabilitative efforts should, to be optimal, be multifaceted. No one rehabilitative effort could be expected to be more than marginally effective, and the task of rehabilitating many offenders might require truly massive interventions.

We shall return to this point later in the this report, but we note here that most rehabilitative efforts that have been tested have been narrow in scope and have involved weak or relatively minor forms of interventions. It is possible that most offenders who are imprisoned for the first time are never imprisoned again (see Glaser 1969, Martinson and Wilks 1977), and issues of rehabilitation do not arise with those offenders. Other data (e.g., Greenwood *et al.* 1977) indicate rather clearly that a relatively small number of criminals account for a large proportion of crimes. This being the case, it should be evident that the problem of rehabilitating criminal offenders is formidable since it often involves repeated patterns of behavior and ways of life that are deeply ingrained. It is the judgment of the Panel that the rehabilitative techniques and programs that have been tested thus far have generally been inappropriate to the difficulty of the task. Work on rehabilitation appears for the most part to have been atheoretical altogether and to have been based on a rather narrow range of views about crime. For the most part it seems correct to say that the medical model is dominant: i.e., present treatment programs assume that crime is a "disease," an individual defect, that can be cured or ameliorated. Even some interventions directed toward improvement of the economic prospects of criminal offenders are based on notions about individual shortcomings such as educational or skill deficiencies. Drawing on a broader theoretical understanding of the origins and nature of criminal activity should provide useful hypotheses for the development of more promising strategies for rehabilitation.

We take special note here of one important theoretical perspective that is indirectly related to rehabilitation. Crime may be viewed as one of the inevitable pathological outcomes of a defective social system, in which case rehabilitative efforts directed toward the individual offender, or even the offender's family, might seem futile. Such a view of crime would lead to an insistence on fundamental social reform such as change in the economic system, elimination of racism or social disadvantage, and the like. Such broad social reforms appear to lie more in the realm of prevention of crime rather than of rehabilitation, and so fall outside the scope of the Panel's study. Nonetheless, the Panel does believe that continuing and serious attention should be paid to the possible role of social structural variables in fostering and maintaining criminal activity, even while efforts to rehabilitate individuals are further explored.

TYPES OF REHABILITATIVE EFFORTS

Rehabilitation of offenders has been the aim of a diverse lot of specific techniques and broad programs. As a continuation of our analytical mapping of the concept of rehabilitation, we offer in this section a brief overview of these various approaches.

If one is to make sense of the whole field of rehabilitation, it is necessary to be able to make distinctions within the myriad of rehabilitative techniques that have been tried. No ready taxonomy of rehabilitative efforts has been developed and accepted, but Lipton et al. (1975) provide a list of 10 types of treatment whose impact on recidivism has been studied. Most of these methods stem from a view of crime as involving either a specific individual defect or as a set of pathological behavior patterns. Extra-institutional methods include probation and parole, both of which are ways of managing offenders outside institutions and have aims in addition to (or perhaps instead of) rehabilitation, e.g., reduction in costs of corrections and surveillance and early detection of violation. Imprisonment is also listed by Lipton *et al.* as a correctional treatment.

Methods usually employed within an institutional setting include individual and group psychotherapy, both directed usually to alleviation of personal problems, although group therapy may also be employed to improve social skills. Skill development is another technique for reducing some personal deficit, usually concerned with work habits and skills. Finally, milieu therapy is a rather ill-defined approach that assumes that a generally good and constructive environment can produce behavior change.

It is of more than passing interest that none of these methods of intervention involves a moral view of crime, but neither does any of them stem in any very direct way from a social structural view of crime. Moral views of crime have been reflected to some degree in the treatment described by Yochelson and Samenow (1976), and the Japanese, among other cultures, have also employed a form of moral therapy with criminal offenders (Lebra 1976).

Nearly all the methods that have been tested to date involve either treatments within institutions or some version of probation or parole. Furthermore, nearly all the methods tested to date have been tested singly. There have been few, if any, comprehensive, multiple-treatment attempts to alter criminal behavior.

It should also be noted that rehabilitative techniques other than probation are rarely tried with first offenders because so very few first offenders come under the purview of the corrections system. Most of the treatments employed within institutions, and especially those employed with adult felons, are being applied very late in the development of patterns of criminal behavior. Even with youths, the genuine first offender is rarely subjected to more than probation and then only in cases where there is a formal hearing.

Beyond what are normally considered rehabilitative efforts, there is also specific deterrence, the inhibiting effect on an individual of being detected in crime, apprehended, and punished. As noted earlier, to some extent the effects of specific deterrence must be distinguished from those of rehabilitation. Although the distinction is only conceptual, it is needed as a reminder that the horrors of prison life should not be regarded as inherently rehabilitative even if they do deter further criminal activity. Nonetheless, to the extent that punishment does result in a decrease in frequency or seriousness of criminal activity, it could be considered to have a rehabilitative effect.

Even though punishment is sometimes thought of as a technique for rehabilitation, however, we have only a rough idea of its specific behavioral consequences. If it is to be used effectively, a much better understanding of just what can be considered to be punishment will be required, and a closer inquiry into the specific effects it has will also be necessary. For example, it may not be the case that prison is invariably viewed as punishment or at least that it may not be responded to in the same way as punishment. As unpleasant as prison might seem to most of us, it may be regarded as no more than a normal occupational hazard by many career criminals. When one considers that people regularly and voluntarily join such organizations as the U.S. Marine Corps and the French Foreign Legion, both of which entail occupational hazards often as bad as or worse than prison, it may be that prison can be regarded as a mere hazard to be endured like many others. Perhaps the occupational hazards of prison, like those of the Marine Corps and the Foreign Legion, are more likely to deter initial entry into the occupation rather than performance once recruited. If so, punishment would deserve a larger role in programs designed for the youthful offender who is part of the population most at risk for further crime involvement. Punishment may be less important in programs for more seasoned offenders who may be inured to punitive methods. This kind of speculation could turn out to be empirically false. In any case, the issue is important and merits careful empirical testing.

The mechanism by which punishment may work to change undesirable behavior is also poorly understood. It may be that the commonly accepted notion that punishment works only because individuals will try to avoid it may not be true for all offenders. As an illustrative analogy, pain is often said to have important survival value as a signal that all is not well with one's body. Similarly, punishment may have an important value as a signal to an individual that his or her relationship to society needs changing. From that standpoint, punishment might have a rehabilitative effect through the information it carries rather than through arousing anxiety about behavior. Punishment may be effective in part because it commands attention and ensures that the message is attended to. If that is the case, then punishment would be expected to have maximal effects at early points of deviation, but it would not necessarily have to be severe; it should, on the other hand, occur in close temporal proximity to the deviation, and its connection to the deviation should be made obvious.

Although the very idea of punishment is repugnant to many and although there are reasons to suspect limitations on its effectiveness in controlling criminal behavior, punishment as a control technique has always been with us and always will be. Our task as a society is to achieve a better theoretical and empirical grasp of the nature and effects of punishment and then to use that knowledge in humane ways to maximize the probability that punishment, whether inflicted out of a sense of outrage or of justice, will have whatever constructive effect might be achieved. We do not want to end up repeatedly punishing those who transgress and in return, and at least as often, suffering the counterblows of those persons who feel themselves irretrievably and morally at odds with the rest of us.

2 The Current State of Knowledge: What Works?

Although concern about the efficacy of rehabilitation goes back many years, the formation and work of the Panel received a strong instigation from the publication of what has come to be known as "The Martinson Report" (Martinson 1974). This was based on work by Lipton, Martinson, and Wilks reviewing a large body of research on the outcomes of various rehabilitative efforts as applied to criminal offenders. Martinson's shorter review was published and widely read, while the larger review volume was not published until the following year (Lipton *et al.* 1975, hereafter cited as LMW). Martinson made use of the materials collected for the book to prepare his lengthy and comprehensive article assessing rehabilitative efforts. There had, however, been previous reviews of a less comprehensive nature that presaged the conclusions ultimately reached by Martinson. The review by Bailey (1966) of 100 outcome studies has been widely cited, but Adams (1975) lists several other smaller or more specialized review studies.

None of these reviews provided very much cause for optimism about rehabilitation, and Martinson's conclusion was also substantially negative: " . . . With few and isolated experiences, the rehabilitative efforts that have been reported so far have had no appreciable effect on recidivism." In a more cautious form, Martinson's conclusion might be stated: it appears that nothing works or at least that there have not been any consistent and persuasive demonstrations of anything that works. The range of interventions dealt with by Lipton *et al.* is quite wide, and it cannot reasonably be claimed that they omitted important categories of intervention efforts from their study. Their report dealt with interventions as diverse as cosmetic plastic surgery, psychotherapy, vocational training, work release, and parole supervision. Therefore, while acknowledging that individual studies may have produced the effect they were designed to show, Martinson noted that no one intervention consistently worked when applied to the problem of offender rehabilitation: the problem of crime and the costs incurred by the public as a result of crime were not being reduced.

Martinson's report, published in *The Public Interest* in the spring of 1974, produced considerable reaction in the corrections field, both positive and negative. Rebuttals began to appear as soon as publication lags permitted. A volume compiled by the National Council on Crime and Delinquency (Matlin 1976) to satisfy the demand for a forum on the efficacy of rehabilitation contained a reprint of Martinson's paper along with critiques by Palmer and Adams and two rebuttals by Martinson. Palmer in particular insisted that Martinson's conclusions were not justified and were probably quite wrong. The basis for Palmer's criticism was that Martinson's focus was inappropriate: instead of asking what one treatment could work for the offender population, the question should have been (Palmer 1975, p. 150): " . . . Which methods work best for *which* types of offenders and under *what* conditions or in what types of settings?" Yet Martinson's conclusions were seemingly widely accepted and even welcomed, bolstered by the views of those who already believed that rehabilitation was ineffective, and they meshed well with other emerging views about appropriate ways of dealing with criminals, e.g., that they should experience the natural consequences of their acts and receive their just deserts (Morris and Zimring 1969). Nonetheless, an important segment of the corrections community found it difficult to accept a conclusion that efforts at rehabilitation were futile, and its members insisted that Martinson was wrong.

In light of this controversy the Panel undertook its review of the evidence on effectiveness of rehabilitation. The Panel as a whole has considered a great deal of evidence in deciding whether Martinson's overall conclusions are supportable. As part of its work the Panel also undertook to review Martinson's work specifically. That task involved an examination of the data base from which he operated, i.e., the annotations and summaries provided by Lipton et al. (1975); also required was an examination of Martinson's use of that data base. To accomplish the first task, Panel member Fienberg and his colleague Patricia Grambsch drew a random sample of the studies reviewed by Lipton et al. and did an independent analysis of the data to determine the accuracy and fairness with which the original review was done (see Appendix).

AN EVALUATION OF THE WORK OF LIPTON, MARTINSON, AND WILKS

Because of the pivotal role that the LMW book has already played in arguments regarding the efficacy of rehabilitation, it was important that the accuracy of LMW be examined with care. The summaries and annotations of prior studies made by LMW had to be assessed for accuracy, placing special emphasis on the research design of the studies and on the statistical analyses reported. The LMW volume contains both a data base (summaries and annotations of selected studies) and a set of conclusions derived from an integration of the components of that data base. A sample of the data base was reexamined to determine (1) whether the conclusions in the source articles are based on reasonable statistical analyses and tests, (2) whether there are important errors or omissions in the LMW summaries and annotations, and (3) if so, whether the errors and omissions affect the conclusions that might reasonably be drawn from the studies.

LMW used five methodological criteria to select studies for inclusion in their report (1975, pp. 4–5):

1. The study must represent an evaluation of a treatment method applied to criminal offenders.

2. The study must have been completed after January 1, 1945.

3. The study must include empirical data resulting from a comparison of an experimental group with control group(s) or from a comparison of a treatment group with some comparison group(s)—that is, the treatment group may be compared with the general inmate population, matched control subjects, base expectancy rates, or itself (a before-after comparison).

4. These data must be measures of improvement in performance on some dependent variables, which include recidivism, parole or probation performance, institutional adjustment, educational achievement, vocational adjustment, personality and attitude change, drug and alcohol readdiction, and cost benefits.

5. Specifically excluded are after-only studies without comparison groups, prediction studies, studies that only describe and subjectively evaluate treatment programs, and clinical speculations about feasible treatment methods.

LMW give a detailed description of the search procedure used to locate studies for possible inclusion in their report. For studies that met the basic criteria, annotated summaries were prepared, and a further screening of the studies took place. This screening led to the exclusion of studies with major research shortcomings, such as: (1) reporting of insufficient data; (2) data that were too preliminary; (3) availability of only a summary of the actual study; (4) findings that were confounded by extraneous factors; (5) treatment or outcome variables that were inadequate or whose measurement was unreliable; (6) conclusions that were unrelated to the data presented; (7) failure to indicate how the sample was chosen or inadequate selection procedures; (8) sample size that was too small; and (9) statistical tests that were inappropriate with insufficient data available to allow reanalysis. Those studies eliminated at this stage were listed in a separate bibliography by LMW.

The selection procedure used by LMW resulted in 231 "acceptable" studies. Our evaluation of LMW focuses only on those acceptable studies. Some have argued (e.g., Adams 1976) that the LMW criteria for inclusion are too stringent. We disagree. In their study of social innovations, Gilbert *et al.* (1975, p. 44) note:

> The review of these studies leads us to the conclusion that randomization, together with careful control and implementation, gives strength and persuasiveness to an evaluation that cannot ordinarily be obtained by other means. We are particularly struck by the troublesome record that our examples of nonrandomized studies piled up. Although some nonrandomized studies gave suggestive information that seems reliable, we find it hard to tell which were likely to be the misleading ones even with the power of hindsight to guide us.

Others studying innovations and treatments in different contexts have come to similar conclusions. For example, the biostatistician Muensch (as reported in Gilbert *et al.* 1977) has a set of "statistical laws," one of which says, essentially, that nothing improves the performance of an innovation as much as the lack of controls. After examining several studies included by LMW, we concluded that their criteria for methodological acceptability were, if anything, not stringent enough. Many of the 231 studies reported are badly flawed and they contribute little to a proper assessment of the efficacy of rehabilitative programs (see also Rezmovic in this volume).

A further issue concerns the criteria to be used for judging whether a particular treatment is successful as a rehabilitative technique. In discussing Martinson's (1974) article, Halleck and Witte (1977) argue that he used extremely rigorous criteria for the success of a treatment program, and that, considering the type of programs evaluated, the failure to achieve dramatic alterations in behavior is certainly not surprising. Palmer (1975) suggests that almost half of the studies described in Martinson (1974) show positive or partly positive results; thus, in our review we tried to determine whether LMW downplay such positive findings in their overall summaries. We find little support for the charge that positive findings were overlooked. In fact, as our review of a sample of studies reported by LMW suggests, by ignoring the problems associated with multiple comparisons and simultaneous inference, LMW and the original authors often make claims for partially positive results that cannot be substantiated by the data they report.

Note should be taken of the contention of one of Martinson's major critics, Palmer (1974), that nearly half of the studies cited by Martinson show an effect favorable to rehabilitation. Palmer's optimistic view cannot be supported, in large part because his assessment accepts at face value the claims of the original authors about effects they detected, and in too many instances those claims were wrong or were overinterpretations of data, such as ignoring the risks of picking one significant finding from among a large set of comparisons.

Thus, the work of Fienberg and Grambsch for the Panel indicates that LMW were reasonably accurate and fair in the appraisal of the rehabilitation literature. Where LMW erred, it was almost invariably by an overly lenient assessment of the methodology of a study or by a failure to maintain an appropriately critical set in evaluating statistical analyses. The net result was that Lipton *et al.* were, if anything, more likely to accept evidence in favor of rehabilitation than was justified (see Appendix).

Were the conclusions of LMW warranted? Within the limits noted below, the Panel concludes that Martinson and his associates were essentially correct. There is no body of evidence for any treatment or intervention with criminal offenders that can be relied upon to produce a decrease in recidivism. Where there are suggestions of efficacy, they are just that—suggestions. They prove to be elusive, not replicable, not quite statistically significant, working now only with one group, then only with another. The Panel does not believe that it would be possible on the basis of the literature available to Martinson—and if he missed something important, no one has stepped forward to reveal it—to put together an intervention that could be counted on to reduce recidivism rates in any group of offenders.

If the LMW review were the only work available, Martinson's pessimistic view might still be discounted. For one thing, the LMW data base extended only to 1968, and a number of important studies have appeared since then. The more recent studies have received a thorough review by Greenberg (1977). His conclusions are essentially the same as those of LMW, and his methodological critique accords closely with that of Fienberg and Grambsch: nothing has been shown to work. Moreover, Brody (1976) has recently reviewed the British and American work on institutional treatment of juvenile offenders and has reached similar conclusions about the ineffectiveness of a variety of rehabilitative efforts. The other reports that are available from foreign countries seldom report actual research results, but those that do indicate that no magic answer is to be found in some far-off place.

This negative conclusion, however, must be tempered by some important reservations. Earlier it was mentioned that Martinson's conclusions were acceptable within some limits. In part those limits have to do with issues concerning the strength and integrity of the treatments that were tested in the studies reviewed by Martinson (see Halleck and Witte, 1976). These issues will be explored in some detail later in this report. Here we simply note that many of the interventions tested seem to have been so weak in proportion to the problem involved that it would scarcely have been credible had any effect been found. Even when interventions of some potential strength were tried, it is not always certain that integrity of the treatments was maintained, i.e., that the treatments were actually delivered as planned. Moreover, the conclusions of Martinson and others are limited to the interventions that have actually been tested. The Panel believes that there may be interventions not yet tested that merit attention and that might prove effective in reducing recidivism rates. Some potentially effective interventions might grow out of approaches now only beginning to be developed, and tests of rehabilitation should not cease simply because efforts to date have been found wanting.

Another limitation on Martinson's gloomy conclusion is that there are some suggestions in recent research reports that interventions involving work and financial support may have a modest impact on postrelease criminal activity. The work-release program in North Carolina appears to reduce the seriousness, although not the amount, of postrelease criminal activity (Witte 1977). Two California programs have also reported some effect of work release in reducing criminal activity (Jeffrey and Woolpert 1974, Rudoff and Esselstyn 1973), although programs in Massachusetts (LeClair 1973) and Florida (Waldo and Chiricos 1977) have not. Reasons for the inconsistent results are not known; they may relate to specific details of the programs or to local employment conditions, among other things. Mallar and Thornton (1978) have reported on a program offering financial assistance to released offenders that appears to reduce the frequency of theft offenses. Although the results available to date do not justify any policy recommendations, they point to a set of interventions that should be thoroughly explored in a systematic research program. The payoff could be high.

The third limitation on Martinson's conclusion involves the question of cost effectiveness of various ways of managing criminal offenders. Although such considerations as retribution and incapacitation may be important in decisions to incarcerate offenders, cost may not be an irrelevant factor. Without giving blanket endorsement to cost minimization as a criterion for evaluating rehabilitative efforts, the Panel does think it worth noting. Although the studies reviewed by Martinson may not support the conclusion that we know how to rehabilitate criminals, the very fact that so many interventions result in equal outcomes (but see Rezmovic's discussion [in this volume] of problems involved in accepting the null hypothesis) means that different ways of treating criminals may be interchangeable. If that is the case, then, assuming that the treatments are equally humane, the less expensive alternative should be chosen. For example, work-release programs should in most instances be cheaper than continuous incarceration (Witte 1977); early release would always be cheaper than later release; and less parole supervision would be cheaper than more parole supervison. Thus, there is in the rehabilitation literature a great deal of potentially useful information about management of imprisonment, even if that information is not useful for achieving the goal of rehabilitation.

The Panel does not wish to be taken as unmindful of the problems involved in working in the area of rehabilitation research. The practical, administrative, and political problems are enormous, and that so many studies have been done at all is remarkable, even if they have not been done as well as is required for sound inference. But that is the point at issue, since the studies as done do not provide a good basis for inference about effects of rehabilitation, and consequently, their net impact is virtually nil. The recommendations made by the Panel concerning methodological requirements for future studies, and those made by Resmovic (in this volume) are conditioned heavily on the realization that the weaker methods employed to date have contributed so little to our knowledge.

There continue to be claims in the literature about rehabilitative efforts that have been successful. One recent report (Murray *et al.* 1978) concerned the Unified Delinquency Intervention Services (UDIS) program in the Chicago area, which dealt with delinquents with high rates of offending. The UDIS program assigned the delinquents to various dispositions, although not on a random basis. One group was incarcerated while another received an array of services, some of which included removal of the youth from the community. The UDIS program found a sharply lower level of postrelease offenses for youths who were incarcerated or removed from the community. The difference in pretreatment and posttreatment rates was not related either to the judged harshness or to the length of the treatment. The UDIS findings, if dependable, are fraught with implications since they suggest that a distinct, sharp intervention, perhaps of short duration, could markedly change delinquent behavior. However, the UDIS findings are not going unchallenged. McCleary *et al.* (1978) believe that the UDIS design, a before-after design, permitted the operation of a regression artifact that could easily account for the findings. Murray and a colleague replied (Murray and Cox 1979), McCleary and his colleagues countered (McCleary *et al.* 1979), and the battle was joined. The brief history of the UDIS program illustrates very well the fate of even a fairly strong finding in the face of an opponent armed with a methodological sword.

To conclude, the Panel believes that there is not now in the scientific literature any basis for any policy or recommendations regarding rehabilitation of criminal offenders. The data available do not present any consistent evidence of efficacy that would lead to such recommendations, but the quality of the work that has been done and the narrow range of options explored militate against any policy reflecting a final pessimism. On the basis of its review, the Panel believes that the magnitude of the task of reforming criminal offenders has been consistently underestimated. It is clear that far more intensive and extensive interventions will be required if rehabilitation is to be possible; even then, there is no guarantee of success.

3 Problems of Implementation

A major obstacle to assessing the effectiveness of rehabilitation has to do with the difficulties of translating knowledge about human behavior into treatment programs. When one looks at actual programs—at what has actually been tried—it turns out that much of what is called rehabilitation cannot reasonably be expected to effect real changes in behavior over time. This chapter reviews these problems of implementation, including the adequacy of program design, the difficulties involved in maintaining program integrity, and issues related to variations in offender types and classification schemes.

ISSUES OF PROGRAM DESIGN

There has been a wide variety of attempts to rehabilitate criminal offenders, as reviews by Lipton *et al.* (1975), Brody (1976), and Greenberg (1977) show. Yet the interventions that have been devised and tested seem in many ways inadequate and narrow. For one thing, the interventions that have been tested often seem inappropriate to the task to which they are directed. They appear to be derived primarily from conventional wisdom, scarcely from any careful analysis of the task to be accomplished or from any carefully thought-out theoretical premises regarding either crime or rehabilitation. Greenberg (1977) has described the theoretical assumptions of many rehabilitative efforts as "bordering on the preposterous." For the most part, the theoretical premises of rehabilitative efforts have remained implicit and have consequently been unexamined.

The premise of many, if not all, interventions is the notion of "curing" criminals of their tendencies, in much the same way as one might aim to cure a patient suffering from, say, bacterial pneumonia by a dose of antibiotics. Such notions of cure by a specific intervention are simplistic and misguided. Criminal behavior is likely to be the result of a complicated set of circumstances, individual characteristics and predelictions, and social conditions. If any analogy is to be drawn with medicine, it probably should involve a condition for which long-term support is required to allow for natural growth and healing.

Viewed in another way, many rehabilitative interventions that have been tested seem to assume that little treatments can produce big effects, thereby implying that with a relatively little nudge offenders can be put back on the right track, and that, once there, inertia will guarantee a straight course. London (1977) calls such a process cumulative convergence, and it appears to be a grossly oversimplified view of the task of rehabilitation. And yet how can one otherwise account for trying to determine effects on recidivism rates of isolated treatments such as group counseling, cosmetic surgery, or even job training?

Despite the wide range of interventions that have been tested at one time or another, within any one study the range has been very limited, usually involving a single type of intervention: e.g., counseling or vocational training or more intensive parole supervision over a brief period of time. Moreover, except for probation and parole, nearly all the tested interventions have been carried out within institutions and with the offender as the direct and sole target. Even work release can be regarded as an intramural program, since it is prison-based. Halfway houses fall somewhere in between intramural and extramural programs, but are oriented toward the just-released offender. Community-based corrections are something of an exception to the focus on intramural programs, but such programs have not been extensively tested except in California, and descriptions of programs that have been tested is often so sketchy that it is difficult to determine just what was involved beyond the diversion of offenders from the prison system (Sechrest and Redner 1979).

It is unusual to find a study in which a combination of rehabilitative techniques has been employed, e.g., psychotherapy plus job training plus work release. There apparently has never been a controlled study that could be regarded as a truly comprehensive effort to achieve the aims of rehabilitation. Such efforts have probably been made with individual prisoners, with what success it is not possible to say.

The range of interventions that has been tried can only be suggested, but the information in Table 1 provides support for the contention that the range is wide and that the focus of specific studies is usually narrow.

Perhaps the greatest lack in the field of rehabilitation has been the failure to develop an adequate conceptual framework for rehabilitation with criminal offenders (Glaser 1975). Such a framework would require a better articulated theory of criminal behavior and a better specification of the processes by which any set of interventions could be expected to change behavior. Not only might a better conceptual framework lead to more systematic intervention, but it might point to as yet untried possibilities. We need as much rigor in our thinking as is recommended for our methods.

ISSUES OF PROGRAM INTEGRITY

In evaluating the rehabilitative techniques that have been tried, the weakest link in the attempt to establish a causal chain relating program to outcome is evidence bearing on the integrity with which programs have been implemented. Although Lipton *et al.* (1975) established methodological criteria by which they determined whether a study would qualify for consideration in their review, no criterion related either to the strength or the integrity of the treatment being evaluated was established. One might argue that strength is not an issue in determining what works because strength of intervention is inferable from the treatment description. But treatment descriptions are frequently fragmentary (Sechrest and Redner 1979), and, furthermore, when one wishes to reach a generic conclusion about whether caseload, for example, is an important variable, it matters a great deal whether the values studied extend over a great or a narrow range. In deciding whether group counseling works, it is important to know whether it has been tested with highly trained counselors working for many hours or only with ill-trained counselors and a few sessions. Few of the interventions tested to date have been implemented at anywhere near optimal or maximum strength.

Lacking a sound theoretical position with respect either to criminal behavior or to the workings of a rehabilitative technique, it is difficult to say what is optimal. For example, by what process could one arrive at a conclusion about an optimal caseload size for a parole supervisor? Or about the optimum conditions for a work-release program? What has been done in planning interventions appears to have been based on intuition and practicality rather than on a rationale stemming from concern to make the treatment as powerful as possible. In fact, many "rehabilitative" attempts may merely seek to make prison life more tolerable by giving offenders something to do. In this sense, "rehabilitation" may be viewed as nothing more than a tool for prison management. Whether any treatment has been tested in its optimum form is questionable.

TABLE 1 What Has Been Tried

Reference	Research Design	Intervention	Outcome	Locus of Effort
Quay and Love (1977).	Experimental.	Vocational counseling, job training and placement, academic tutoring, personal and social counseling.	Significantly fewer arrests for experimental group.	Community.
Witte (1977).	Post-hoc design with a nonequivalent control group. The experimental group was randomly selected from releasees over two time periods.	Work release.	No differences in the recidivism rates of the two groups, but there was a significant decrease in the seriousness of crimes committed by the experimental group.	Prison.
Reinarman and Muller (1975).	Experimental.	Financial assistance to parolees.	No differences in the recidivism rates of the two groups. Data "suggest" there may be differences for subgroups although there is no statistical analysis to support this.	Community.
Mullen (1974).	Experimental.	Individual and group therapy, vocational rehabilitation, family counseling.	No differences in rearrest rates.	Community.

38

Berecochoa et al. (1973).	Experimental.	Parole (early or regular).	No differences in recidivism rates.	Prison.
Sloane and Ralph (1973).	Quasi-experimental.	Behavior modification.	No differences in recidivism rates, although there was a modest gain in educational achievement.	Prison (youth training center).
Ricker and Walker (1976).	Post-hoc design with an equivalent control group.	Therapeutic camping, survival skills, academic tutoring, counseling.	The experimental group had significantly fewer court contacts than the control group.	Community.
Geis (1966).	Experimental.	Parole (normal or residence in a halfway house).	No differences in recidivism rates.	Community.
Robinson et al. (1969).	Experimental.	Probation (officers given varying case load sizes).	No significant differences, although smaller case loads had slightly lower detention rates and higher rates of technical violations.	Community.
Cronin (no date).	Experimental.	Employment counseling.	No differences in recidivism rates at 6, 9, or 12 months.	Community.
Mandell et al. (1967).	Experimental.	Surgical correction of disfigurement, social services.	Significant differences in recidivism rates were found between control and experimental groups of nonaddicts for plastic surgery alone.	Prison.

The issue of treatment integrity has to do with whether the treatment was actually delivered in a manner closely approximating the treatment description (Sechrest and Redner 1979). There are disturbing indications that treatment integrity may not always have been achieved. One of the most widely cited studies of rehabilitation is that of Kassebaum *et al.* (1971), the admiration for which seems largely based on its almost exemplary research design. The results of the study appear to indicate that the value of group psychotherapy in rehabilitation is nil. However, Quay (1977) raises serious questions regarding the legitimacy of the interpretations of the study on the grounds that the treatment as described never occurred. Quay's critique of the Kassebaum *et al.* study and its conclusions is revealing and worth consideration in some detail.

Noting that although group counseling had been used extensively in corrections, its effectiveness as a rehabilitative technique had never been established, Kassebaum *et al.* devised an experiment to test its effectiveness in a California penal institution for young adult males. Inmates were assigned randomly to either counseling or control conditions, and some counselors were given special training beyond the sessions ordinarily scheduled. Counseling was begun and continued for a period of from 6 months to 2 years depending on the inmates involved. Sessions occurred once each week for "an hour or two." Effectiveness was measured by parole outcome at 12, 24, and 36 months. At no point were there any significant differences between counseled and control cases by the recidivism measure employed. The authors did a number of supplementary analyses, addressed to issues such as faithfulness of attendance and stability of group leadership, and they found no variable or combination of variables that would improve upon or alter the conclusion that counseling had no impact.

Quay lists four major issues involved in assessing the integrity of a program: first, whether the intervention can be adequately conceptualized and whether that conceptualization has sufficient grounding in previous empirical evidence; second, whether service is actually delivered, whether it is sufficient in duration and intensity, and whether it is carried out as described; third, whether the personnel delivering the service are qualified, trained, and adequately supervised; and fourth, whether the treatment is actually appropriate for all of those chosen to receive it. Quay indicts the Kassebaum *et al.* (1971) study on all four counts.

On the first issue, Quay notes that the investigators themselves state that the nature of the group counseling process is not easily described and operationalized. Moreover, only about a third of the counselors appeared to think that group counseling might have any effect on recidivism, the major dependent variable. Quay goes on to note that the counselors were not professionals and were poorly trained and supervised and that many seemed to have little personal involvement in the counseling. The counseling was described by Kassebaum *et al.* as often superficial, poorly conducted, and characterized by instability in group leadership. Furthermore, participation in the groups was involuntary for some participants and probably coerced for most others, the groups were quite heterogeneous, and group members did not regard the treatment as meaningful or the counselors as competent to run the groups.

Quay's analysis of what is often regarded as a landmark study upsets the popular view that the Kassebaum *et al.* research provides definitive evidence concerning the effectiveness of psychotherapy for the rehabilitation of offenders. He notes that the study is unusual in the wealth of detail it presents, which, therefore, makes his analysis possible.

Is it likely that other studies that are silent on matters pertaining to program integrity are in fact superior to the one analyzed by Quay? There are at least some other reports that suggest that the question of program integrity is one that needs to be routinely raised and answered (cf. Sarri and Selo 1974, Sechrest and Redner 1979). Lerman (1975), for example, has shown that the community treatment project (CTP), which was supposed to deliver various services to probated delinquents, actually involved extensive social control and detention, i.e., the treatment was not adequately conceptualized. Moreover, the planners of CTP had intended for treatment to be different according to maturity levels of the youth involved, but treatment was administered largely independently of judgments of maturity level. Lerman points to a variety of other ways in which the CTP failed to conform to expectations, and he makes similar points with respect to the California probation subsidy program.

In an institutional study of behavior modification and transactional analysis, Jesness *et al.* (1975, p. 764) reported that:

Counselors at Close were expected to conduct at least two transactional analysis sessions with their clients each week. In addition to the academic contracting, Holton counselors were expected to negotiate at least one behavioral contingency contract each week with their clients. Staff at Close fulfilled two-thirds of their expected quota, Holton staff one-half of theirs.

It is instructive to consider the problems involved in contingency contracting with delinquents: Jesness *et al.* (1975) noted that many field officers were not very successful in implementing the training they had received, some officers being unable to write any contracts at all. Ultimately, contracts were written for only 269 of 1,248 delinquents with identified problem behaviors, and only 104 of the contracts met criteria of adequacy. However effective the contingency contracting program might have been, it seemingly could not be implemented with the personnel available.

These three examples of studies that may be questioned on grounds of failure to maintain integrity of treatment are not the only instances that could be found (cf. Sarri and Selo 1974). There are suggestions, for example, in investigations of variations in parole officer caseloads, that reduced caseloads have not invariably resulted in greater contact with offenders (Glaser 1969).

These three examples do provide convincing evidence, however, of the need for systematic and searching attention to this critical issue when far-reaching policy decisions may be founded on failures of treatment to demonstrate effectiveness.

Quay (1977) noted that one probable reason for the neglect of treatment integrity as an issue, a reason that applies equally to strength of treatment, is that there is no set of criteria, no established set of principles, by which treatment integrity may be judged. There is not, in fact, even any established tradition in the social and behavioral sciences for assessing and describing treatment integrity. And strength of treatment has not been assessed independently of outcome. What is needed in evaluating rehabilitation outcomes is more attention to the type of evaluation usually described as formative (Scriven 1967) or process (e.g., Bennett and Lumsdaine 1975). Campbell (1974) has also written persuasively on the need to document what actually occurs during the course of a program as opposed to what is supposed to have happened.

It is difficult, then, to interpret research findings on treatment effects, or the lack thereof. It is not clear for how many rehabilitation studies interpretations are seriously jeopardized by failure to maintain integrity of treatment. That some of the more widely cited evaluation studies are flawed in this way implies that any conclusion that rehabilitation does not work would be premature. Mark Twain once observed that not only is the thirteenth chime of a clock in and of itself suspect, but it also casts doubt on the validity of the preceding twelve.

ISSUES OF VARIATION IN OFFENDER TYPES

Criminal offenders differ in type and severity of offense, in sex, age, race, and religious belief, in family situation, and in most of the other ways people differ from each other. It seems evident that at least some of these differences should have a bearing both on the probabilities of achieving rehabilitation and on the differential probabilities associated with different methods of doing so. To point to but one example, in a study designed to test the effects of providing discharged offenders with a financial subsidy while they looked for employment, the decision was made to limit the program to offenders who had committed crimes against property, in the seeming expectation—never stated—that a financial subsidy would be of less importance to offenders against persons (Lenihan 1978). To the extent that offenders could be classified in ways that would maximize treatment effects, the interests of rehabilitation would be furthered.

Prisoners are regularly classified, but that classification is often to serve the purpose of prison management and control rather than that of rehabilitation. Still, it is possible, as Fowler (1977) suggests, that the very existence of a classification system may have some rehabilitative effect since it may separate offenders in ways that make imprisonment more endurable and that lower the probabilities of learning new criminal ways. As Conrad (1975) notes, the minimum goal for our prison system should be that offenders do not come out of the prison as worse persons than when they went in, and custody classification may operate toward the achievement of that goal.

The major issue that inheres in the idea of offender types is that there may be some subgroups of offenders who are especially amenable to treatment or who can be matched to a particular treatment in such a way that effects of treatment will be enhanced. We refer to this major issue as the amenability issue. There are additional special questions that may be raised about particular types of offenders and their prospects for rehabilitation. White-collar criminals have often been singled out as a subgroup, as offenders who may pose different problems in rehabilitation than other criminals. The link between mental disorder and crime is also an issue of importance, since the existence of such a link would imply that rehabilitative efforts might well have to focus on treatment for the mental disorder. Within that general issue resides the additional question of whether there is one or several "criminal personalities," a type especially likely to get involved in criminal activity and, hence, perhaps needing personality restructuring for rehabilitative goals to be met. Finally, there is almost universally a distinction made between youthful and adult offenders when consideration is given to appropriate response to and treatment of criminal behavior.

THE AMENABILITY ISSUE

An optimistic note for the possibility of rehabilitation lingers in the claims of some that programs can work if they are tailored to fit offenders who are "amenable" to being rehabilitated (Glaser 1975, Palmer 1975). When an examination of the research on amenability is undertaken, however, it soon becomes clear that the issue of whether "amenable" offenders can be rehabilitated is really addressing the topic of whether rehabilitation itself can "work." The same problems that exist throughout the broader area of assessing the efficacy of rehabilitation are just as prevalent when one addresses the question of whether rehabilitation can work with an amenable population.

The best illustration of these troublesome issues can be found in Lerman's critique (1975) of the most ambitious of all amenability research—the California treatment project (CTP). In that study, the questions of what constitutes recidivism are brought to the fore because different criteria for parole revocation were found for the control and experimental groups of adolescents. Furthermore, the integrity of the program is challenged by Lerman's disclosure that the adolescent offenders in the experimental group did not in fact receive the treatment that the program had purportedly delivered.

Another point of contention is that a screening process instituted by correctional officials in California (the state where most amenability research has been conducted) has limited the types of offenders who are considered for the CTP and other experimental programs. The result of the process is that only youths arrested for property offenses have been allowed entry to the CTP program. (In addition, studies of the California adult offender population do not consider individuals arrested for assaultive behavior or narcotic abuse.) The net effect of the restrictions appears to be that only offenders considered both "good risks" and "amenable" have been studied. More work such as that by Barkwell (1977), in which "poor risks" are incorporated into the research sample, is needed to produce confidence in research that purports to address the question of rehabilitating amenable offenders; data currently available may be biased because criteria other than amenability were used in selecting research populations.

Perhaps the greatest of the problems encountered in assessing research on amenability is definitional in nature. Although it is clear that the intent is to convey the idea that certain offenders can be more readily and effectively rehabilitated than can others, it is far from clear just who these "amenable" offenders are. For the most part, the term "amenable" has been attached to individuals on the basis of their performance on psychological measures or interviews (e.g., Grant and Grant 1959, Jesness 1965, Palmer 1974, Warren 1971); but research has also dealt with the issue of offenders who seem to take more advantage of rehabilitative programs: criteria that have been used in describing offenders who are least likely to recidivate range from prior offense records (including number and type of offenses), through various sociodemographic characteristics (e.g., Jew *et al.* 1975) and even extend to whether others were with an individual when the crime was committed (Knight 1970). Therefore, when discussion turns to the possibility of more success if only amenable offenders are included in rehabilitative programs, consideration should be given to what constitutes amenability. Such consideration would be greatly facilitated if more research comparing the various descriptive techniques were available.

The most researched and most extensively employed system of classifying juvenile offenders has been that used in the CTP, the interpersonal maturity or I-level system (see Warren 1969). Proponents of the system have contended that it is a dependable and useful way of classifying delinquents so as to permit differential treatment with improved efficacy. However, both the classification system and its purported effects have been called into serious question. In a thorough and penetrating review, Beker and Heyman (1972) have cast doubt on both the validity and the reliability of the I-level system. They point to definitional and logical problems in the description of I-levels that suggest that what it is measuring is very unclear. Moreover, the inter-rater agreement on which the notion of dependability must rest is still quite uncertain, and may well be lower than proponents, e.g., Palmer and Werner (1973), contend. Several writers have also questioned the efficacy of the I-level system on the grounds that the evidence now available does not establish any clear difference between experimental and control groups with respect to outcome measures, and even within experimental groups the results are inconsistent and often confusing (Beker and Heyman 1972, Gibbons 1970, Lerman 1975). Other systems of classification, such as that of Quay (1964), have not been tested for utility in increasing treatment effectiveness.

In addition to these obvious potentials for error in classification, the topic becomes even more important when one recognizes the growing trend in amenability research toward encompassing factors in addition to . the amenability of the offender. Research has begun to focus on the issue of matching the treater with the offender type (Palmer 1973) and on providing the appropriate environment in which to conduct the treatment (Wenk and Moos 1976). With the additional amount of error inherent in each of these added "matching" strategies, it becomes more difficult to assess treatments without a large number of subjects. Moreover, recognition should be given to the possibly limited usefulness of amenability findings as they increase in complexity. Even if it could be demonstrated that rehabilitation could work if *amenable* offenders were offered *appropriate* treatments by *matched* workers in environments *conducive* to producing maximal effects, is it likely that most correctional institutions or agencies would have the facilities to produce the desired results? The number of permutations could become so large and unwieldy that planning and control of rehabilitative efforts would prove virtually impossible.

On the other hand, the amenability issue remains a continuing hope (or excuse) in the face of failures to produce evidence of rehabilitation. A recent instance is provided by Sobel (1978), who commented on the long-term follow-up of the Cambridge-Somerville youth study (McCord 1978), which provided evidence indicative of negative effects on experimental subjects. Sobel suggested, without evidence, that perhaps some of the experimental subjects had been affected positively and some negatively. Certainly the amenability concept is intuitively appealing (Beker and Heyman 1972), and there are some hints in work to date that it may be worth pursuing. As of this time, however, the Panel does not believe that one could with any confidence classify offenders in any way with the expectation that treatment effects could be maximized by matching of treatments and offenders. More systematic and careful research than has yet been done is needed to determine whether amenability classification and differential treatment offer any hope of rehabilitation.

If the concept of amenability is to be pursued as a tool in rehabilitation, the Panel believes that theoretical issues will have to be developed and resolved. The I-level system appears to have a weak theoretical rationale at best (see Beker and Heyman 1972), and Quay's classification system is avowedly atheoretical (Quay 1964), as is Megargee's (1977).

The classification approach for juveniles of Quay and his colleagues was developed out of multivariate statistical research seeking to delineate subgroups of deviant children and adolescents in all settings (see Quay 1975, pp. 383–387). A modest initial effort to link the system to treatment was made by Ingram et al. (1970). Subsequently, it was used in a large-scale program in which an attempt was made to conceptualize different interventions for the four groups. The results, although flawed by the research design, did not indicate any real advantage for the experimental groups with regard to recidivism (Cavior and Schmidt 1978). A classification approach for adult offenders (Quay 1973) was developed expressly for use in institutions and has, to date, served primarily as a management tool (Smith and Fenton 1978).

WHITE-COLLAR CRIME

A major and costly area of illegality in our society is white-collar crime; there are few data, however, on the effects of criminal sanctions on white-collar criminals. Intuitively, the area raises unusual questions, particularly about the amenability of the white-collar criminal to traditional modes of rehabilitation. This section explores some of these questions.

Responsibility for the apprehension and prosecution of white-collar offenders varies markedly and is lodged both with disparate regulatory bodies (ranging from such federal agencies as the Securities and Exchange Commission to state insurance commissions) and with more traditional criminal justice agencies (the FBI and state and local police). The wide range of responsible agencies means that knowledge of the overall level or nature of white-collar crime is extremely difficult to determine. However, a recent U.S. Chamber of Commerce study (cited in Edelhertz 1977) estimated the financial cost of such offenses at $41 billion annually. This estimate did not take into account the cost to the public of price-fixing violations or industrial espionage.

Recently, attention has focused on the nonfinancial costs of those forms of white-collar crime that result in injury (Monahan *et al.* 1979). Corporate violence is defined by Monahan *et al.* as "behavior producing an unreasonable risk of physical harm to consumers, employees, or other persons as a result of deliberate decision-making by corporate executives or culpable negligence on their part." A similar definition could be developed for other organizations, e.g., government, and individuals, e.g., physicians, who by willful negligence or positive action cause harm to persons who are their employees or clients. While no reliable statistics exist concerning this severe form of white-collar crime, one investigation estimated that occupational health hazards result in 100,000 worker deaths each year and at least 390,000 new cases of job-related disease, many of them clearly foreseeable and preventable (Cooper and Steiger 1976).

(There is, of course, an additional broad category of civil offenses that, although not criminal in a legal sense, raise important questions concerning appropriate societal reaction and prospects for rehabilitation. It is possible, for example, to be a repeat offender of civil rights or of election laws in quite the same way as one may be a repeat burglar. This report does not address the many questions that are brought to the fore in considering civil offenses, but the issues may not be so much different from those that confront researchers studying rehabilitation of criminal behavior.)

Appropriate punishment for white-collar crime has been debated for a number of years, and innovative sanctions have often been suggested and occasionally tried. The continuing debate stems at least partly from the conflicting nature of the goals and beliefs of those concerned with white-collar crime. Of the seven major sanctions for the illegal acts—general deterrence, retribution, incapacitation, specific deterrence, moral education, prevention of personal vengeance, and rehabilitation—most writers dealing with white-collar crime have deemed general deterrence as the major justification for punishment (Chambliss 1967, Renfrew 1977, Baker and Reeves 1977). The belief in the effectiveness and importance of general deterrence stems at least in part from the idea that potential white-collar criminals are more aware and behave more rationally than other potential criminals; there is little or no empirical evidence bearing on the validity of this idea.

Attitudes toward retribution for white-collar crimes have been disparate. Many persons seem to believe that a prison sentence may be too severe a form of retribution because of the moral stigma attached to imprisonment in the social classes to which white-collar criminals generally belong. Others believe that imprisonment is necessary and desirable for equity as well as general deterrence purposes (e.g., Baker and Reeves 1977). Still others believe that only imprisonment can expiate the severe damage caused by some white-collar crime.

The need for specific deterrence and incapacitation has also been a controversial topic, some writers feeling that both are unnecessary (Renfrew 1977, Edelhertz 1970) and others thinking that there are benefits involved both in specific deterrence and in incapacitation of white-collar offenders (Geis 1973, Ogden 1973).

The sanction that is our major emphasis is rehabilitation. As in the case of specific deterrence and incapacitation, the potential benefits of programs to rehabilitate white-collar offenders depend upon the degree to which subsequent criminal behavior is likely. Effective rehabilitative programs for white-collar offenders who often need neither job training nor psychological counseling of the usual sort would have to be far different from the traditional in-prison programs. As an example, one of the two basic types of present rehabilitative programs seeks to change the personality or attitudes of offenders so they will not want to commit any future crime. In the case of the white-collar offender, it may indeed be appropriate to develop rehabilitation programs that focus on such things as attitude change, but standard psychological methods may not be appropriate for altering amoral attitudes toward white-collar offenses; other methods of enforcing awareness of relevant laws and the illegality of violating them may be more useful. As an illustration, forcing offenders to admit their guilt and to explain the nature of their offense publicly has been used and might be successful. As another possibility, white-collar offenders could be assigned the positive duty of documenting the costs resulting from their crime.

The second of the two basic types of rehabilitative programs seeks to change the opportunities facing an offender so that it will not seem beneficial for him or her to commit offenses. As in the case of changing personality or attitudes, efforts expended in altering the opportunity set facing white-collar offenders are likely to be effective only if the programs are of a nontraditional nature. In keeping with the view that white-collar offenders calculate courses of action and weigh risks against expected gains before deciding to commit a crime (Baker and Reeves 1977), programs should focus on either increasing the relative cost or decreasing the relative benefits of engaging in illegal rather than legal activity. For example, costs of illegal activity could be increased by greater publicity concerning offenders or by increasing fines or damage awards. The potential benefits of some illegal activity could be decreased by mechanisms designed to limit the amounts of money to which an employee might have access without monitoring.

Another potentially fruitful manner in which the problem of white-collar crime might be handled relies more on the incapacitation aspects of punishment than on actual rehabilitation. Since the commission of many white-collar crimes depends upon an individual's or firm's occupying a position of trust in a particular profession or industry, incapacitation could be achieved simply by barring activity in certain professions or industries. This prohibition might take the form of an injunction, a divestiture order, or suspension of the right to practice a particular profession. As is discussed below, this form of incapacitation is very similar to banishment in that an individual is removed from the area in which a crime had been committed and also faces the withdrawal of reinforcements that may have been associated with that place. Although they do not represent criminal penalties, the practice of disbarment in the legal area, withdrawal of privileges in medicine, and revocation of licenses in some other occupations also suggest that incapacitation might be an acceptable technique for dealing with some white-collar crimes. Innovative programs extending this concept to other classes of offenses and offenders may prove effective.

In summary, white-collar offenders are the group about which least is known at present. There is a great need to learn more about this population, for, as noted by Ogden (1973, p. 960): "in general, deterrence has not been realized, rehabilitation has been ignored, repeat offenders have not been removed from society, and victims have not been compensated." Our survey of the literature supports this view. We also believe that programs of a rehabilitative nature may prove effective, particularly if these programs are implemented in novel ways. Needless to say, caution will have to be exercised in adopting such programs: they may be opposed on equity as well as efficiency grounds, and they run the risk of appearing to treat white-collar offenders more leniently than other types of criminals.

MENTAL DISORDER AND CRIME

The Panel does not believe that the evidence supports the proposition that there is any particular relationship between mental disorder and crime (Guze 1976, Rabkin 1979). Mental disorder is a factor in some crimes, but, overall, it does not seem that persons suffering from mental disorders are any more likely than other persons to be involved in criminal activity. Criminals often have histories of alcoholism and drug abuse, and these problems may have a causal relationship to crime and indicate the need for special rehabilitative efforts. Some mentally disturbed persons do end up in prisons and others become disturbed while in prison, but there do not appear to be any special problems in rehabilitation of criminal offenders that relate to mental disorder.

ADULT VERSUS JUVENILE DISTINCTIONS

Offenders are almost everywhere classified as either adult or juvenile, with the point at which that distinction is made varying somewhat from 16 to 18 years of age. In every jurisdiction, however, it is possible for juveniles charged with heinous crimes to be tried as adults rather than as juveniles. The distinction between juveniles and adults is binary from a legal standpoint, but at least limited additional age distinctions may be made in practice, e.g., the practice in the Bureau of Prisons and in many state systems of distinguishing "youthful" adult offenders from older adult offenders.

At least some of the distinctions based on age seem premised on ideas about ease and appropriateness of treatment and rehabilitation. One rationale, for example, for the segregation of offenders according to age is that young offenders will thereby be spared the influence of older and more hardened offenders and will not so readily acquire criminal attitudes and skills. Newcomb (1978) has reported suggestive but inconclusive evidence that youths incarcerated in large institutions with many "veterans" have higher subsequent offense levels. The effect of incarceration was less both for large programs with few veterans and for small programs despite high proportions of veterans. Noting, however, that the veterans referred to by Newcomb were other youthful offenders, i.e., not adults, it appears that a classification based on characteristics beyond mere age may be called for. Another justification for age classification and segregation is that adult penal facilities are so hazardous to the welfare of youth that segregation is required on humane grounds.

It may be implicitly assumed by many that age is an important element in classification because it is, or should be, easier to rehabilitate youthful offenders. That seems a dubious prospect at best. By any measure currently available, rates of involvement in criminal activity subsequent to adjudication are at least as high for juveniles as for adults with similar offense histories. It could be argued that given the same circumstances it might be more difficult to rehabilitate juveniles than adults because their very youth is indicative that they have no prolonged periods of satisfactory behavior patterns to which they might be restored by proper treatment. In fact, however, very little is known about differential treatment or potential for rehabilitation of juveniles and adults. Certainly when the treatment methods that have been employed are examined, there do not appear to have been any startling differences between what has been tried with juveniles and adults. The one exception is temporary foster home placement of juveniles, but that tactic has never been subjected to a controlled test of its efficacy.

LIMITATIONS OF CLASSIFICATION SCHEMES

All classification for the purpose of maximizing response to treatment involves a predictive enterprise: the classification is a prediction that the person classified will respond better to one treatment than another. If classification is to be genuinely useful, the accuracy of the prediction must be high. Unfortunately, the history of prediction of human behavior by such means as are usually employed in classification—psychological tests, interviews, and biographical data—affords no grounds for optimism about the approach. The best predictions that have been made are in the area of academic performance, where, after a half century of effort, the correlations achieved are typically only around .50 (see Whitla 1968). The success of predictions involving nonintellectual aspects of personality functioning are invariably lower, and correlations of about .35 are considered evidence of success (Mischel 1968). While correlations of .35, or even lower, can be useful in situations in which a few persons have to be selected from a large population and when the costs of errors are large, this is not the situation that exists in most correctional institutions or organizations. There, decisions are being made on a case-by-case basis; the cost of errors may not be large, i.e., nothing much is invested and hence nothing much is lost if an offender is put in a less than optimal program; and errors may be largely reversible, i.e., if an offender is put into an unsatisfactory program, the decision can usually be changed. The cost of errors will be small if differences between programs are small, if the programs are themselves not inherently expensive, or if errors are likely to be evident at an early point in treatment. Errors will be reversible if, in case of a failure in one program, an offender can be assigned to another program.

The gains in accuracy of prediction for individual cases with a predictive coefficient of .35 are modest at best. With that correlation, a person scoring in the top half of the predictive scale has about a 61-percent chance of being in the top half of responders to the treatment in question, under the assumption that a binary decision is to be made (Peters and Van Voorhis 1940). Given that a chance level of accuracy would be 50 percent, the gain is obviously limited. Keeping in mind that those persons scoring in the lower half of the classification scale would have about a 40-percent chance of being in the top half of responders to treatment, one would have to be cautious in making distinctions between offenders on such a basis. If, for example, as is suggested by proponents of the I-level system, some offenders respond better to community programs and others to incarceration (e.g., Warren 1969), what level of error would be tolerable in deciding to leave some youths in the community and confine others? Or if a treatment involved some tangible good such as money, how good would one's prediction have to be to justify giving money to some prisoners and not others?

On the other hand, correlations of about .35 can be very useful for research purposes in providing a covariate by means of which error terms may be reduced in statistical tests. The consequence is that the sensitivity of experiments to program effects can be increased. It is also worth noting that for research purposes a predictor need not have face validity or apparent fairness, whereas for clinical use there may be distinct limits placed on variables that may be used in classification, e.g., race, religion, sibling position.

The Panel does not mean to deprecate work on offender types and classification, but it feels compelled to call attention to the potential limitations of such work in practical applications, limitations detailed clearly by others (e.g., Gibbons 1970, Gottfredson 1972, Hodd and Sparks 1970, Waldo and Dinitz 1967). Some of these limits are inherent in the nature of prediction, and, all predictions being in some degree in error, all distinctions made on the basis of those predictions are in some degree unfair. Some of the limits may, of course, lie in the treatments to which response is being predicted. Prediction may be limited because treatments are minimal and minimally different.

Even though the practical value of classification for day-to-day decision making about rehabilitation programs may be limited, there are other rationales for classification that justify continued research. One is that classification may facilitate development both of theory and of programs. That offenders differ among themselves in many ways and to marked degrees is evident, and it seems likely that at least some of those differences should be helpful in understanding offenders and their problems. Any improvement in that understanding should eventually be valuable in developing new programs to help offenders. Perhaps there are better approaches to classification than have characterized past efforts, which still locate the essential basis for classification within the offender, e.g., maturity level, personality type. Beginning instead with prisoners' problems and resources, for example, might be worth trying. Such a classification scheme would have the virtue of being a bit closer to the treatment planning process.

Improvement in classification will almost certainly have to go hand in hand with improvement in rehabilitative techniques. Classifications are summaries of knowledge and theory. The current impoverished state of the art in this area reflects the poverty of our theories and techniques. Although little in the current literature provides much hope for major advances in classification, progress in this area may presage progress in rehabilitative techniques.

4 Problems of Evaluation

Another set of problems in assessing the effectiveness of rehabilitative techniques concerns methodology. This chapter reviews the problems of evaluation and measurement, including a detailed consideration of evaluation methodology, an examination of the applicability of cost-benefit methodology to rehabilitation, and a brief discussion of the possible effects on crime rates of rehabilitation programs. It should be noted that there is little agreement with respect to what criteria will be employed as a standard for measuring success or failure in rehabilitation.

Those persons charged with responsibility for planning and delivering critical public services should be able to demonstrate and certify the effectiveness of the services with which they are involved. Otherwise there is the possibility that what is intended and proclaimed as a vital service will be at best a waste of resources and at worst harmful rather than helpful. Demonstrating effectiveness is as necessary for rehabilitative services offered to criminal offenders as it is for services designed to improve health or some other aspect of human welfare. In a June 1975 decision, the U.S. Supreme Court held that nondangerous mental patients may not be held against their will without being treated (*O'Connor* vs. *Donaldson*), and it seems quite possible that courts will eventually decide that the treatment provided must be of demonstrated effectiveness. A task force of the American Psychological Association (APA) has recently taken a strong position insisting that in the long run reimbursement provided under any national health insurance should be made only for services of demonstrated effectiveness (Task Force on Continuing Program Evaluation Under National Health Insurance 1978). The criminal justice system can demand no less from those efforts invested in rehabilitating criminal offenders. Another APA task force has insisted that those psychologists offering services to prisoners must be explicit about the empirical basis for their services and that they have an ethical obligation to cooperate in research to evaluate them (Task Force on the Role of Psychology in the Criminal Justice System 1978).

Insistence on careful, and even stringent, evaluation of rehabilitative programs is grounded in the legitimate concerns of several constituencies of the criminal justice system. First, there are the taxpayers, who ultimately pay for the system and the services it offers; they have a right to know that tax money is being well spent and with a fair return. In addition to paying for rehabilitative services, the public is implicitly promised that, through the provision of rehabilitative services, something is being done about the problem of crime. If there is no basis for that implicit promise, the public is being misled and would be justified in demanding that other measures be taken to reduce crime. Second, there is the constituency represented by the families of criminal offenders, for they almost certainly hope that the offender will return to them with brighter prospects for the future. It is unkind, to say the least, to lead families to believe that their errant member will be helped by the criminal justice system to make a new and more effective adjustment when, in fact, nothing at all helpful is being done. Third, those persons who are part of the criminal justice system—judges, caseworkers, wardens, and guards—also have a right to know that the things they do in the name of rehabilitation and in good faith are likely to be effective. It is demoralizing and leads to paralyzing cynicism for professionals to learn that what they do is a sham. Finally, the offenders have a right to have some confidence that their willing participation in some rehabilitative program is not a waste of effort and hope.

The problem, then, is how to determine whether rehabilitative programs are effective, whether they do, in balance, produce positive outcomes. The solution will only be found in careful evaluations of intervention programs and their elements. There is no substitute or short cut. Appeals to logic, assertions or promises of effectiveness, testimonials, and other alternatives to empirical verification have proven repeatedly wrong or, where not proven, such uncertain guides as to be worthless as a basis for decision making. Eisenberg (1977) has stated in a compelling way the social imperative for empirical evaluation of medical interventions, and the case would appear equally strong for rehabilitative interventions with criminal offenders.

Nearly 10 years ago, Donald T. Campbell (1969) set forth a proposal for an overall societal approach to its problems that has been termed "the experimenting society." Campbell's proposal would apply as well to subsystems within a society, such as the rehabilitation of criminal offenders. As applied to rehabilitation, Campbell's approach would call for systematic planning and testing of various interventions designed to achieve rehabilitation, the testing being accomplished by deliberate experiments. Programs would be proposed for testing rather than as solutions, and widespread implementation of programs would be delayed until there was evidence of effectiveness. Some delays in taking action would be inevitable, and some risks would be incurred, but a compensatory increase in program effectiveness should be realized.

There are, of course, objections to the concept of the experimenting society, even when it is limited to rehabilitation. One objection is that the process is slow and that it much underestimates what we already know or what we may come to know through methods other than experimentation. Unfortunately, it is all too clear that we know very little, at least with any certainty. The history of social intervention is replete with ideas that seemed good at the time, but that proved in the long run to be worthless or even harmful. Thus the slowness of experimentation must be weighed against the potentially slower process of simply learning from errors. It might be expected, for example, that an income subsidy would enable teenage girls to stay in school rather than drop out, but a 1969 experiment by G. D. Robin testing that idea revealed a higher rate of dropping out in the experimental group than in the control group (reported in Gilbert *et al.* 1975). For another example, intestinal bypass surgery was developed to alleviate conditions of extreme obesity, certainly a laudable goal. A recent study (Neill *et al.* 1978) has shown, however, that an apparently frequent but unanticipated outcome of the treatment for obesity is much marital discord, especially in relation to sexual problems.

Very recently there have been tests of a negative income tax, on the assumption that it would obviously be desirable to give poor families enough money to raise their incomes above the poverty level. One unexpected outcome was that additional family income apparently produces a degree of instability within the family that increases the likelihood of divorce, desertion, and other family break-up (Hannan *et al.* 1978).

Within the field of corrections there are similar examples of programs and interventions that resulted in counterintuitive negative outcomes. Putting street workers with juvenile gangs at one time seemed an eminently reasonable thing to do, but gangs blessed with such workers actually increased in delinquent activity (Klein 1971). Three kinds of volunteer programs employed with juvenile offenders in Michigan all resulted in temporary increases in police contact, with no long-term positive effects when compared to a control group (Berger *et al.* 1975). Intuition, logic, and theory are fallible guides to solving social problems. Even some of the results of the California community treatment project could be regarded as negative consequences, although they were anticipated, namely, that youths in the CTP spent more time incarcerated than did control youths, once the latter had completed their sentences (Lerman 1975).

Even the process of research itself may have unanticipated negative outcomes, for it must be recognized that research is usually an intervention. Any program or organization that is the focus of a research effort may have to adapt in numerous ways to the research and its demands; some of those adaptations may become distortions. Fry (1977) has shown how a research evaluation of a drug self-help program, by coopting leaders of the program with financial rewards for participation, alienating treatment staff, and fostering competition with other treatment units, essentially destroyed what had seemed an effective program. And no one had any but the best intentions.

For reasons detailed below, it does not seem likely that much reliance can be placed on methods of gaining knowledge other than experimentation. Case studies, demonstration projects, system analyses, surveys, and the like are simply untrustworthy as a basis on which to make policy and invest in programs. Although these methods, along with intuition and theory, may be a source of promising and testable hypotheses, they cannot substitute for experimentation as a means of gaining the degree of certainty of knowledge that justifies the risk of establishing an intervention or program as a policy (Gilbert *et al.* 1975, Rezmovic in this volume).

A second objection to experiments is that they are expensive (Adams 1975). Experimentation may indeed be expensive, but in the long run, and perhaps by a wide margin, unevaluated and ineffective programs are surely expensive since large sums of money may be spent on such programs year after year (Gilbert *et al.* 1975). As an example, consider the huge amounts of money that have been spent year after year on parole supervision. There is still so little clear evidence of its effectiveness that there are those who recommend doing away with parole altogether (Conrad 1975, von Hirsch and Hanrahan 1978). It is also true that weak methodology, whether by design or by carelessness, is expensive research, at least in terms of increments in certainty of knowledge and often on an absolute basis. Several years ago the Urban Institute (Nay 1973) reviewed 24 separate evaluation studies of federal manpower programs and concluded that the methodologies were all so weak that neither singly nor in the aggregate did the 24 studies provide any basis for federal policy with respect to manpower programs. Those 24 studies undoubtedly cost far more than would have two or three experiments, which probably would have provided reasonably definitive findings (Gilbert *et al.* 1975).

One's views about the cost of good research will depend somewhat on just what it is one thinks one is evaluating. It might be prohibitively expensive to evaluate a particular program in a particular location. The cost of a good experimental evaluation of a simple intervention can often exceed by a good bit the cost of the intervention itself. If one regards the focus of the evaluation as a prototype program, however, one that might be implemented on a widespread basis if it is proved worthwhile, the cost of the evaluation can be viewed from a more favorable perspective. Moreover, if it seems likely that some type of intervention will continue indefinitely if it is not properly evaluated, the costs are amortizable over a number of years (Sechrest 1977). A case in point is provided again by federal manpower programs, for which more than $12 billion was spent while 24 inconclusive evaluations were being carried out (*Manpower Report of the President 1974*, p. 358). Even a multimillion dollar price tag for a good evaluation study would not seem large in the context of a program costing billions of dollars and planned to continue indefinitely.

Another objection to experimentation is that the findings never have any impact on policy, because the findings are never timely: decisions must often be made within a very short time frame, while research findings become available only after an extended period of time (Adams 1975). Two responses can be made to this objection, one having to do with the nature of timeliness and the other with the nature of policy making. The reason that research results are not available when they are needed very often lies in the fact that the research was not conceived, planned, and funded until it was already too late for the results to be available when needed. If evaluation research is to be of maximal value, the research must be planned and funded so as to anticipate rather than react to information needs. For at least some problems, good and timely evaluation research is frustrated by the lack of more basic research, including development of methodology on interventions that are likely to produce change and on measurement of outcomes. Beyond the timeliness issue, however, there may also be a fundamental misunderstanding of the processes by which research findings become incorporated into policy. The researcher's model for relating research to policy may incorporate rather naive expectations of quantum changes in policy contingent upon research findings; i.e., if an evaluation shows that a program is good, it should be adopted, and if it is bad, it should be abandoned. That model is almost certainly wrong. Policy making is likely to be incremental in nature, with research findings, like other considerations, being gradually filtered into policy (Caplan *et al.* 1975, Patton 1978, Rein and White 1977). It may be possible to discern the impact of research on policy only in the long run and maybe then only with difficulty.

Finally, empirical, and especially experimental, program evaluations are often regarded as impractical, if not impossible, for logistical, administrative, moral, and legal reasons. Inability to control assignment of cases to treatments, problems in maintaining control over the treatments being administered, and difficulties in data control are among the practical objections to program evaluation that are frequently encountered. Robert Boruch (1974) has amassed a fairly extensive bibliography of true experiments carried out in the field, many of them evaluations of large-scale programs. That bibliography demonstrates conclusively that good-quality research in the field is quite possible; the bibliography does not, of course, suggest that such research is easy.

There is probably also a lack of understanding of the results likely to be achieved in most interventions, including those related to rehabilitation. What administrators and policy makers are looking for are large, clear-cut results of the type labelled "slam bang" effects (Gilbert *et al.* 1975). There are, unfortunately, few slam bang effects in any social interventions, and perhaps none will ever be achieved in rehabilitation. Science progresses incrementally in most cases, often in subtle ways, so that there are few discrete effects to which one can point with a firm recommendation for implementation. Progress may be discernible only in the long run and only to a viewer whose conceptual grasp of a field, its problems, its methods, and its findings, is extraordinary. When one considers that both the scientific and the policy-making processes are subtle, it is not all that remarkable that research findings, including those from program evaluations, are so difficult to translate into policy.

Knowledge about rehabilitation of criminal offenders will not come easily, but such knowledge as we are able to obtain will be most certain, most persuasive, and least costly if it develops out of good-quality research employing the strongest methods available. A critical area of human behavior, as offender rehabilitation clearly is, demands the strongest available methods and the greatest care in research.

CURRENT STATUS OF METHODOLOGY IN STUDYING OFFENDER REHABILITATION

Research on rehabilitative techniques for criminal offenders has until now been characterized by weak methodologies, with many projects and reports on rehabilitative effects being virtually devoid of considerations of research design. Case studies abound, comparison groups do not, and true experiments are conspicuous by their scarcity. The best evidence of the last point is that the same small set of studies gets repeatedly cited when instances of true experiments are to be adduced (e.g., Kassebaum *et al.* 1971, Waldo and Chiricos 1977).

Lipton *et al.* (1975) surveyed the literature from 1945 until 1968 seeking studies meeting even minimal criteria for methodological adequacy and managed to identify only 231 such studies, an average of only about one per month of the hundreds published each year. And as was noted above, Lipton *et al.* probably erred on the side of generosity in categorizing studies as methodologically adequate. Rezmovic (in this volume) notes that 8 percent of the studies included by Lipton *et al.* used no comparison groups and 29 percent were *ex post facto* studies. Even by liberal criteria, randomization was employed in no more than 35 percent of the 231 studies.

Table 2 presents illustrations of some of the common deficiencies in design and implementation of studies in corrections and the consequences of these deficiencies for interpreting the findings.

In general, the research to date on rehabilitation tends strongly to confirm the previous conclusion that weak methodology results in expensive research. The thousands of extant studies on rehabilitation scarcely add up to a single trustworthy conclusion. In short, we do not know whether rehabilitation is possible, we do not know a dependable way of effecting rehabilitation, and we also do not know that rehabilitation cannot be accomplished. A great deal of money has been spent on research on rehabilitation, and all we are left with is no conclusions, weak conclusions, and, all too frequently but unpredictably, wrong conclusions. What is now needed is research with the most rigorous design and of the highest quality.

THE CASE FOR RANDOMIZED EXPERIMENTS

At present we do not have any alternative methodology as powerful as the true experiment (Rezmovic in this volume), the defining characteristic of which is that subjects or cases are assigned randomly to treatment and comparison groups (Cook and Campbell 1966). Experiments must be favored because of the higher degree of certainty their results provide and because they provide that certainty in a shorter period of time and at lower total cost than is usually possible with other evaluative methods. Quasi-experimental and other methodologies leave so many unresolved problems that they usually require a longer time and more money in the aggregate to achieve what is even then likely to be a less certain conclusion (Gilbert *et al.* 1975). Therefore, the Panel recommends that randomized experiments should be the design of choice for evaluating every rehabilitation program or intervention and that the use of any alternative should require explicit justification subjected to rigorous and searching examination.

Arguments against randomization in social experiments are often based on the ethical imperative to deliver the most effective treatment or service available to every client. The precise reason for doing the research, however, is to determine what is the best treatment, and the ethical imperative begs the question. The ethical problem stems from early intuitions, logical derivations, or premature conclusions about the relative value of treatments, and these have proved time and again to be quite undependable foundations on which to base judgments about treatment effectiveness (Eisenberg 1977, Empey 1977). As Empey points out, the very treatments for delinquency that are today thought to be much in need of replacement, e.g., institutional treatment, were themselves once regarded as reforms replacing inadequate treatments. Even now, as evidence gradually accumulates on newer forms of treatment for criminal offenders (Greenberg 1977), it is becoming increasingly clear that there is little basis for ethical concern about which of alternative research treatments an offender receives. Absent the evidence that would make an evaluation of a treatment unnecessary, the ethical objection to randomization is unsustainable. Every proposal for research within a corrections system should, however, be guided and rigorously reviewed by guidelines for the conduct of research on prisoners such as those of the National Commission for the Protection of Human Subjects of Biomedical and Behavioral Research (1977). The selection and assignment of specific treatments must be ethically defensible in terms of the interests of the subject and the state of knowledge, but a comparison of the treatments so selected must be based on random assignment if the comparison is to be valid.

Randomized assignment of subjects to experimental or control treatments does not present an issue of treatment versus no treatment, nor does it necessarily preclude the ultimate delivery of the most effective treatment to every case. "Control" groups will almost always receive at worst the same treatment they would have received if the experiment were not being conducted, and often even control treatments are in some ways potential improvements over standard procedures. In many cases, when a baseline against which to judge an effect is not required, two experimental treatments can be tested against each other. Other research designs combined with appropriate delivery systems can make it possible for subjects in the least advantaged treatment group eventually to receive a treatment that proves the better, by using waiting-list control groups. Even if one treatment is strongly believed to be the preferable one, it is often impossible to deliver the treatment simultaneously to everyone, and in that case the fairest (Campbell 1969) and probably most acceptable (Wortman

TABLE 2 Common Deficiencies in Rehabilitation Designs and Subsequent Influence on Interpretations of Findings

Reference	Research Design	Intervention	Outcome	Design Flaw(s)	Criticism
Vera Institute (1972).	Experimental.	Postarrest disposition to counseling or educational or vocational assistance.	Reduction in rearrest rate of experimental group.	Selection bias in experimental group; possible occurrence of surveillance effect.	Reduction in recidivism was actually small or nonexistent (Greenberg 1977).
Moynahan (1975).	Experimental.	Probation (vs. fine vs. jail).	Probation group had fewer rearrests or reconvictions than jailed or fined groups.	Fined and jailed groups aggregated when compared with probation group; self-selection bias operating in probation group.	Rearrest rate and reconviction rate may not have been lower for probation group than jailed or fined group (Greenberg 1977).
Maiser (1969).	Experimental.	Intensive parole supervision and counseling.	No significant differences between experimental and control groups.	Background differences between experimental and control groups to the detriment of the experimental group.	Nonequivalence of groups may have contributed to lack of findings (Greenberg 1977).

Study	Design	Intervention	Findings	Problems	Comments
Sullivan and Mandell (1967).	Experimental.	Academic upgrading.	Recidivism rates for experimental group were significantly lower than rates for control group.	Breakdown of randomization procedure; selection bias in experimental group.	Differences in recidivism rates disappear when selection bias is corrected for (Martinson 1974).
Burkhart (1970).	Experimental.	Parole variations.	Reduction in reconviction rates for both experimental and control groups.	Hawthorne effect influencing control group.	Reduction in reconviction rates may be due to the "competition" between the two groups (Brody 1976).
Palmer (1972).	Quasi-experimental.	Placement in foster home.	Reduction in recidivism rate for experimental group.	Small sample size.	Results must be viewed with caution due to small sample size (Greenberg 1977).
Warren et al. (1966).	Experimental.	Multiservice probation, counseling, employment aid, academic aid based on I-Level classification (interpersonal maturity).	Subgroups of experimental group had fewer reconvictions or rearrests.	Lack of validity in classification system; more lenient handling of experimental group by administrators.	Success of I-Level typology should be qualified by two design flaws; experimental subgroup success may not be valid (Lerman 1975).
Jesness et al. (1972).	Experimental.	Residential treatment (transactional analysis vs. behavior modification).	Significantly less revocation of parole for experimental group.	Selection bias operating in experimental groups.	Lack of inclusion of experimental group "dropouts" may have affected detection of reduction in revocation rates (Sarri and Selo 1974).

TABLE 2 (continued)

Reference	Research Design	Intervention	Outcome	Design Flaw(s)	Criticism
Marvel and Sulka (1962).	Experimental.	Parole variations.	Smaller case loads produced an increase in parole success.	Lack of uniformity in administrators' implementing treatment; lack of construct validity.	Experimental effect was actually a result of certain administrators' use of severe sanctions, not only of smaller case loads (Martinson 1974).
Mueller (1964).	Nonexperimental.	Group counseling with vs. without a stable leader vs. no special prison services.	Groups with a stable leader had more favorable parole results.	Self-selection bias; experimental groups consisted of volunteers only.	Bias due to noncomparability of groups casts doubt on the results (Brody 1976).
Barbash (1962).	Matched samples for control and experimental groups.	Psychotherapy.	Treatment benefited experimental group.	Noncomparability of experimental and control groups.	Matching was on one variable only: release date. Differential success rates cannot be considered reliable (Brody 1976).
Murray et al. (1978).	Quasi-experimental.	Incarceration or sharply restrictive residential placement.	Reduction in number of postrelease offenses.	Subjects were selected because of high levels of criminal activity.	Reduction in number of offenses could have been a regression artifact (McCleary 1978).

and Rabinowitz 1979) way of distributing the treatment is through some form of lottery. There are a variety of research designs and statistical methods available when treatments can be delivered on an "as available" basis. Recently, the Vera Institute has reported (Baker and Rodriguez 1977) on a clever and potentially very useful variant on randomization that may make experimentation more palatable by obviating the need to deny treatment when it is actually available.

Once the decision to use a randomized treatment design has been made, it cannot be assumed that randomization will automatically take place. Greenberg's (1977) review of post-1968 research on rehabilitation points to a number of instances in which randomization was planned for and initiated, but in which the plan broke down over the course of the studies. Given the apparent difficulties in gaining assent to randomization that have characterized the history of research on rehabilitation, it is disappointing when there is a failure. Reasons for failure of randomization undoubtedly vary, and perhaps not all of them could have been avoided, but it is very clear that every study planned as a randomized experiment should include a formal mechanism for monitoring and maintaining randomization.

To as great an extent as possible, everyone involved in a randomized experiment should register assent to the experiment in writing before the experiment begins. Especially under current guidelines requiring informed consent from subjects participating in experiments, there is a risk of a Hawthorne effect, i.e., that the very knowledge of the fact that one is in an experiment might produce change. The Hawthorne effect achieved early and persistent notice as a threat to the interpretation of experiments, affecting as it did the construct validity of experiments (Cook and Campbell 1966). Some research indicates that the Hawthorne effect is not necessarily to be expected in many studies (Cook 1967) and therefore often needs little attention; however, there are some settings in which it may be maximized and in which it should be protected against if possible. One of these settings would exist with a design that used one or more informed experimental groups and either a baseline comparison or an uninformed control group as a comparison. In such a case, only those in the experimental groups or in the experimental phase would be aware that they were in an experiment, and to the extent that that knowledge had an effect in addition to that of the specific treatment, results would be biased. A Hawthorne effect might also occur in any study involving a particularly dramatic intervention, any abrupt and substantial change from usual conditions. When a Hawthorne effect seems likely, it may be necessary to establish additional experimental groups or procedures either to control for or to assess the effect. If a Hawthorne effect could dependably be produced, it would, itself, be a rehabilitative technique.

The Hawthorne effect is actually a generic term for a number of what have come to be known as nonspecific treatment effects that can jeopardize interpretations of experimental outcomes (Kazdin and Wilcoxin 1976). Some treatments are less believable than others, some arouse greater expectancies for change, some virtually demand a response (Orne 1962), and some may operate more on the basis of faith in the person giving treatment, e.g., a therapist, than by any features of the treatment per se. Work on nonspecific treatment effects has only barely penetrated some of the more advanced areas of research on treatment, and it may be some time before its potential importance is widely recognized in rehabilitation. However, it is likely that these effects will eventually have to be taken into account since they represent a distinct hazard to the interpretation of findings and to the derivation of appropriate policy recommendations.

Although a compelling case can be made for randomized experiments and although they are rarely impossible when otherwise appropriate (Boruch 1974), there are instances in which the obstacles may be insurmountable. *But the retreat from randomization should be as limited as possible.* There are too many instances in which it appears that the difficulties in mounting an experiment were responded to by abandoning all attempts at rigor instead of by using alternative research designs and methods that offer varying power to rule out plausible hypotheses rival to the one of interest. These alternative designs can greatly strengthen one's capacity to draw causal inferences, even if the designs do not provide quite the confidence that a true experiment would (Rezmovic in this volume). Not all designs are appropriate for every case, but the Panel believes that if a true experiment cannot be done, the *strongest* alternative design should be chosen. At a minimum, there should be some comparison set of data with which the outcomes from a treated group can be compared, and the comparison set should seriously weaken some hypothesis that might plausibly be suggested as an alternative explanation for any treatment effects.

It is the nature of many of the evaluations in the rehabilitation field that the intended result should be acceptance of the null hypothesis. Under the doctrine of the "least restrictive alternative" or when substitution of less expensive for more expensive treatment methods is at issue, it is not necessary that the less restrictive or the cheaper treatment be *better* than the alternative, only that it not be worse. That the null hypothesis cannot be proved and is improbably ever strictly true does not negate the necessity for accepting it as a practical necessity when it seems reasonable. However, because poor methodology is one of the major factors that can lead to the conclusion of "no difference," it is of critical importance that in those studies in which the acceptance of that conclusion would be desirable, the very strongest available methodology should be employed (Rezmovic in this volume). For example, Witte (1977) finds that work-release programs cost less than regular confinement; however, the evidence for any effect on recidivism was, at best, inconclusive. In order to make the case for work release it is necessary to conclude that work release does not produce worse outcomes than regular confinement, i.e., the null hypothesis must be accepted. Since small sample size, lax controls over the experimental treatment, and inadequate measurement procedures would all tend to increase the error term for statistical testing, the research would have to be done with great care to be persuasive.

Research on rehabilitation of criminal offenders seems to have taken little account of the importance of statistical issues involving the sizes of probable effects and the power to detect them (Rezmovic in this volume). Another of the major factors contributing to the conclusion that no difference exists between treatment groups is the size of the sample on which the conclusion is based. Sample sizes should be set on the basis of judgments about effects that might be produced and about the importance of detecting them (Cohen 1977). In rehabilitation research, it is rare, if not altogether absent, to find any rationale at all for the sample size chosen for study. There may be a tendency to underestimate the sample size needed to detect effects that are probable from the treatments being studied. A careful reader of Greenberg's review (1977) will often note a small consistent reported difference of about 5 percent to 10 percent less recidivism in various treatment groups when compared with control groups. Unfortunately, even with 100 subjects in each of two treatment groups, the probability of being able to detect a true difference of 10 percent in recidivism rates would be only about 0.40 (Chassan 1967). That is, if there is a true difference of 10 percent in the rate of recidivism between two populations, e.g., 55 percent and 45 percent, the actually observed difference would be likely to be significant at the 0.05 level only about 40 percent of the time if a series of samples of 100 cases were drawn from each group. (A 2×2 table with observed cell values of 55, 45, 55, 45 yields a χ^2 of 2.0, with 3.84 needed for significance at $p = 0.05$.) Treatment groups of 100 cases are rarely encountered in rehabilitation research. For groups of 25 subjects a true difference of 30 percent in recidivism rates would be detected only about 67 percent of the time (see also Gilbert *et al.* 1975).

One tempting "design" for rehabilitation research involves the "iron-bar" model of change (Campbell and Stanley 1966). Briefly, the iron-bar model suggests that since iron bars change so little in weight under natural storage conditions, if an iron bar weighing 100 g is stored overnight in a solution and is found in the morning to weigh only 95 g, the loss can be attributed to the solution, and the conclusion that the solution is corrosive is warranted. If it could be assumed that some human behavior were similarly immutable under normal conditions, then a change after treatment could be legitimately attributed to the treatment. One possibility might be to use "historical controls," data based on long experience with a phenomenon. Thus, if it were the case that detected repeated criminal activity regularly reaches 40 percent after 1 year, then an intervention that was followed by only 20-percent recidivism might be impressive. Unfortunately, criminal behavior rates seem scarcely likely to be so dependable, across either time or geography (Martinson 1976). Moreover, the iron-bar model is likely to be persuasive only if the change observed is fairly large. A loss of only 1 g from the 100-g iron bar might be suspected to be a reflection of an error in weighing. A change from 40-percent to 35-percent recidivism would not be a very persuasive datum. An additional problem with historical controls is that in few areas of human behavior can we be assured that conditions are going to remain so constant as would be required for correct inferences. Thus, for example, a relatively small change in patterns of parole supervision could result in a change in recidivism that would invalidate the concept of a dependable baseline.

The adequacy of baseline data as a control will depend on several factors (Glass et al. 1975). Stability of the baseline is an obvious one. It is difficult to detect a real change against the noisy background of a widely fluctuating baseline. It will also be difficult to detect change if a baseline is showing "deterministic drift," i.e., is changing regularly and persistently in the absence of any known intervention. An inability to introduce a treatment abruptly or a delayed treatment effect will also pose problems of detection in comparing data. Still another problem with baseline-experimental comparisons is the fact that observations within either period are not independent of each other, as is required by most statistical tests, but rather, are correlated. For example, any factor influencing criminal activity during the baseline period will tend to affect many cases or data points and, hence, represent a bias. One example of such a factor as noted above would be a change in patterns of parole supervision. Results from comparisons of experimental data with baseline data may be persuasive only if the difference is fairly dramatic. Many of the problems are the same as those for time-series designs (Glass et al. 1975).

It is often implicitly assumed that poor research methodology can only result in mistaken inferences that a program works. That assumption is completely wrong: poor research methodology can also result in the mistaken conclusion that a good program is worthless, sometimes with the unfortunate effect of terminating a promising line of work. In fact, there may be less risk from an unwarrantedly favorable impression of a program, since that favorable impression would probably be eventually corrected as experience with the program belied the initial evaluation. But a program that is erroneously dubbed ineffective may be abandoned altogether with no chance for the error to be corrected. Still, it is true that when a program is found to be effective, even if wrongly, it may be posed as a panacea and stifle research for several years while the truth is only gradually and painfully being discovered. It may be better under some circumstances not to evaluate a program or treatment if the evaluation cannot be done well (Campbell 1974). Any intervention should probably be evaluated eventually, but the evaluation might best be postponed until it can be done well.

Stuart Adams (1975) has taken a position with respect to experimental evaluations that is somewhat at odds with the one expressed here, and in view of the prominence of both Adams and his publication in the field, his arguments deserve a response. Adams has a rather pessimistic and otherwise unfavorable view of experimental research on rehabilitation, believing that it is difficult if not impossible to do and lacking in impact when it is done. Moreover, he believes that there are useful alternatives to experimentation, often rendering it unnecessary. Adams proposes the adoption of a general strategy of what he calls policy as opposed to evaluation research.

There is no question that there are research methods other than experiments; whether they are truly alternatives is another question. One example given prominence by Adams (1975, pp. 12–13) is of a survey concerning the need for a state subsidy to counties for probation departments that was followed by a decision to provide funds for the subsidy. There can be no objection to the proposition that surveys are useful in revealing perceived needs within communities, and when surveys show needs, funds may be appropriated to meet them. That, however, is not the same as saying that the intervention installed, i.e., the subsidy, actually does effectively meet the needs perceived, i.e., to improve probation supervision. Most of the alternatives to experimental research that are suggested by Adams are useful supplements or complements to experimental research and not substitutes for it. His conclusion that the payoff from evaluation has been more in the area of "system improvement" than rehabilitation (Adams 1975, p. 114) is revealing since it suggests that system improvement can be achieved and assessed independently of the outcomes that the system was designed to produce.

Adams's doubts about the usefulness of experimental research may often be justified and yet not constitute a genuine objection to such research. To consider one of his objections, it is not entirely clear to just what extent experimental research has been ignored by decision makers, as Adams claims. As was suggested earlier, there is no particular reason to expect an immediate and discrete impact on policy from an experimental finding. Probably no one of the several California studies on caseloads of parole supervisors has had any noticeable impact on policies about caseloads, but it seems quite likely that the cumulative effect has been toward keeping caseloads fairly high, since the results have been consistent in showing no substantial differences as a function of size of caseload. Had the results consistently favored smaller caseloads by substantial amounts, it is very likely that those results would have by now been detectable in policy changes, although no one study might have been directly linked to any change. As was noted by Campbell (Salasin 1973), there is probably not a large store of "red hot findings" currently being neglected.

On the other hand, the arguments made by von Hirsch (1976) in favor of "just deserts" sentencing are buttressed by his citation of such works as those of Kassebaum et al. (1971) and Martinson (1974) on the inefficacy of rehabilitation, and the equally pessimistic review by Greenberg (1977) was actually commissioned by von Hirsch. Clearly, research findings can be used to support recommendations for policy changes even if they do not in themselves command change.

Some of Adams's pessimism stems from his judgment that experimental research can rarely be done under the conditions and within the time frame required to have an impact on policy. The appropriate response to that problem is not necessarily to abandon our most dependable research tool. We might wish to persuade policy makers and others responsible for planning to try to anticipate their information needs so that research can be done before the results are needed. A research capacity better integrated into a decision-making administrative apparatus might well be able to provide useful experimental evidence at a time when it is most needed. Moreover, the very difficulty of doing action-oriented research instantaneously presents a strong argument for a more systematic program of basic research that would provide a foundation of knowledge from which recommendations about programs might be made as needed (Wolfgang 1977). Even a better capacity to review extant scientific research might benefit decision makers. For example, a review of outcome research on psychotherapy as tested on a wide variety of other populations (such as that of Bergin 1971) might suggest quite strongly that its utility in programs of offender rehabilitation would be very limited at best; there might not be a necessity to do any large-scale tests of counseling or psychotherapy with criminal offenders.

Finally, skepticism about the utility of experimental research in policy making may be warranted at present, but that lack of utility may stem in part from a remediable lack of understanding of research data on the part of policy makers. What may be needed is a systematic and continuing effort to upgrade the capacities of decision makers to comprehend and make use of research as appropriate. As Frederick Mosteller says: "The only alternative to experimenting with people is to fool around with people."

MEASUREMENT OF OUTCOMES

The commonly accepted goal of rehabilitation is a decrease in subsequent criminal activity, often referred to as a decrease in recidivism. Unfortunately, from the standpoint of its use as a scientific construct and as the critical index of effectiveness of rehabilitation, recidivism can be and has been defined in various ways (see Waldo and Griswold in this volume). In essence, however, recidivism means the commission of crimes by released offenders.

Rehabilitative interventions may be directed toward diverse goals. Such changes as improved adjustment to incarceration, improved reading skills, acquisition of vocational skills, enhanced self-concept, and increased earning capacity may all be legitimate outcomes for different treatment programs. Those who devise programs must do so with particular, and usually limited, goals in mind. Some goals will be proximate, achievable in the immediate future, and others will be achievable only in the long run, in the distant future. However, as important as immediate goals may be and as appealing as they may be in terms of the directness of the link they have with their corresponding treatments, it is the longer-run outcomes in terms of criminal activities that count in establishing policy. Therefore, we do not see any satisfactory alternative to decrease in criminal activity as a measure of the outcome of rehabilitative efforts. A more literate class of repeating offenders would not be a clear improvement, nor would more self-confident ones, nor ones with improved vocational alternatives if they continued in crime. Ultimately, rehabilitation programs must be evaluated according to their capacity to keep ex-offenders from committing offenses.

The use of recidivism as an outcome variable is replete with problems, one of which is that it is inherently limited in sensitivity by being assessed as a binary variable, as it usually is, for example, if reincarceration is the measure. A great deal of information is lost when something as complex as possible criminal activity that may or may not culminate in detection, arrest, and conviction is finally expressed as a simple dichotomy. Some persons engage in clear-cut criminal activity, some in borderline criminal activity, and some in no criminal activity; some persons are arrested without any hesitation, some are almost not arrested, some are almost arrested, and so on. Other repeat offenders end up with civil commitments and may not appear in criminal statistics at all. Situational factors, widely conceded to be powerful determinants of behavior (see e.g., Mischel 1968), are ignored in dichotomizing released prisoners into recidivists and nonrecidivists. Some offenders commit crimes with very little provocation, while others do so only with great provocation: such information is not conveyed in a binary variable. Account needs to be taken of such factors as whether a parolee is released into a high-crime or a low-crime area, levels of unemployment, probable opportunities for crime, and the general resemblance of the release environment to the environment of previous criminal activity.

Moreover, there are many ways in which a parolee can fail, and the ways have differential meaning with respect to understanding effects of rehabilitation. Any given offender may fail on parole for technical violations, for personal conflict with parole officer, because of vindictive acts by associates, and for many other reasons besides the commission of indictable offenses. Reasons for parole failure are infrequently considered in evaluating rehabilitation programs, particularly in advance of outcomes. At best there is merely the discovery after the data have all been collected that one or another group had a higher rate of parole failure for some reason, usually involving technical violations. More rigorous thinking and planning of outcome measurement would probably obviate some of the interpretive difficulties that are common in assessing recidivism outcome measures.

There have been, of course, attempts to assess criminal activity as a multicategory or continuous variable (see Waldo and Griswold in this volume). One approach has been to weight offenses by their seriousness, so that the scales become continuous, or nearly so (Sellin and Wolfgang 1964). Another approach is to count number of offenses, assuming that a meaningful scale of criminal activity is thereby created. Still another approach has been to treat extent of involvment in the criminal justice system as an ordinal scale, with, for example, a known offense being counted as 1, arrest as 2, indictment as 3, and so on (e.g., Witherspoon *et al.* 1973). Finally, Schmidt and Witte (in this volume), among others, have focused on total additional time sentenced as a variable, and it can be regarded as continuous; however, additional time sentenced has the considerable disadvantage of being in part a function of history and, therefore, of original crime and sentence. All of these approaches warrant study, but none is likely to be optimal as a measure of recidivism. More work is needed on measures of criminal activity that will capture the essence of the deeds involved while avoiding data and measurement requirements that will be beyond the capacity of the criminal justice system.

Waldo and Griswold (in this volume) have reviewed the varying definitions of recidivism, and there is not now a way of deciding from among them which should be preferred for evaluating rehabilitative programs. The best course for the immediate future would certainly be to follow their recommendation to employ multiple measures where possible and to compare them for the conceptual and measurement advantages that might eventually provide a basis for a recommendation about a standard measure of recidivism to be employed routinely.

At present, the timing, seriousness, and frequency of criminal activity appear to be the three measures that afford the most complete view of criminal activity. These three measures have the additional advantage of being compatible measures within any one study and of being very likely the most comparable across studies. The use and reporting of these three measures should be encouraged. The idea of working more rapidly and systematically toward a smaller set of standard measures is appealing, and it would be an attractive prospect if criminologists and journal editors could settle on some set of measures to be provided regularly in every instance possible.

An additional methodological embellishment might be the development of formulas that would make possible the conversion of various recidivism indices into other forms in much the same way that temperature in Fahrenheit may be transformed into Celsius. It does not, for example, seem impossible that recidivism measured in terms of rearrests might be multiplied by some fraction in order to get recidivism expressed in terms of convictions.

The Panel also believes that at the very least there could be agreement on a set of time periods at which recidivism measures should be reported. The problem of the time over which criminal behavior should be assessed has been a source of concern for a long time, since if the time period is too short, much criminal activity may be missed, and if the time period is too long, criminal activity may be observed that is unrelated in any way to earlier criminal behavior. Recent work (Maltz and McCleary 1977) implies that if criminal activity is assessed in terms of a failure *rate*, the follow-up period may not need to be as long as has often been assumed and feared. Follow-up periods of even a few months or a year may yield useful estimates of longer-term failure rates. Since the necessity for long-term criminal activity measures is both expensive and frustrating, the advantages of rate measures is clear. In order to calculate rate measures, however, it will be necessary to assess criminal activity at repeated and regular intervals rather than simply at one time. That requirement may not be easy to meet in all projects and circumstances. Information about an offender's status at the time parole supervision ends has the advantage of being more routinely collected at present.

As in all other areas of work pertaining to offender rehabilitation, it appears that outcome measurement, and specifically recidivism, could benefit from a clearer and more widely agreed upon conceptual framework. Thus, for example, there still appears to be no agreement, nor any basis for arriving at one, on the question of just what violations of criminal codes are to be counted as recidivism for what persons. Should trafficking in drugs, driving under the influence, or illegal gambling be counted as recidivist acts for a released burglar? What about a burglar who after release shifts to receiving stolen goods? One's view about such matters may depend on whether one accepts a more or less monolithic, continuous view of criminal activity or whether one views it as discontinuous. Is it merely out of expediency that recidivism is usually defined at an operational level by crimes known to authorities, or is there a sense that at a deeper conceptual level that definition is satisfactory because if crimes are not known then they are no different from those committed by other citizens that are unreported or unsolved? Until these and other conceptual issues are resolved, measurement of recidivism will surely lag. As Waldo and Griswold (in this volume) point out, the construct validity of recidivism measures, i.e., what they really measure, is an issue that cannot be ignored without jeopardy to the field of corrections.

METHODS NEEDED

If adequate evaluations of rehabilitative efforts are to be achieved, additions and improvements on our current stock of quasi-experimental research designs are needed. It is unrealistic to suppose that experiments will in the near future, if ever, be the only methodology used. There are simply too many factors operating in real life that make experiments difficult to plan and even more difficult to carry out. That being the case, the payoff from sound and systematic methodological developmental research might be substantial. In rehabilitation, as in so many other applied social science fields, methodological work is of critical importance; it should be accorded financial and political support by all those agencies and policy makers who support the work that is dependent upon sound methodology.

One innovation that is badly needed and that might yield at least in part to systematic study is a program evaluation method that permits continuing changes during the course of the evaluation. Great difficulty is often encountered in persuading administrators to submit a program to an evaluation because of the necessity to obtain a commitment to fix the nature and processes of that program for an extended period of time. Furthermore, that difficulty carries over into implementing an evaluation plan with any fidelity because there are almost inevitable changes (whether planned, inadvertent, or forced by circumstances) when an intervention is studied over any period of time. Therefore, it appears that, for at least some types of interventions, explorations into variants on time-series analysis might be of value in building into the analyses some corrections for changes in programs.

A possible evaluation model is provided by Tharp and Gallimore (1979) in what they refer to as "evaluation succession." Using the analogy of a biotic community progressing toward a climax condition, Tharp and Gallimore present an eight-step model for program design and development that incorporates a variety of evaluation procedures or "ways of knowing," ranging from qualitative/personal through experimentation to full-fledged program evaluation. An important aspect of their approach is that programs must be carefully designed and developed in an evolutionary way before it makes sense to evaluate them. Although the strategy offered by Tharp and Gallimore is as yet rudimentary, it is promising, especially since it seems highly applicable to programs in the process of change and development.

A second methodological innovation worth exploring is the development of what might be termed "fall-back" designs, featuring built-in alternatives to be employed should the implementation of the preferred and planned design prove impossible. For example, when randomization fails, an experimenter is often left with, at best, a partially interpretable nonequivalent control group design. However, that fall-back position might be much strengthened if such problems as randomization failure could be anticipated and planned for in the original design.

If consideration were given to the inclusion of alternatives in original designs, even those projects that "go bad" might be salvaged in part. A first step in developing a fall-back design should probably be an analysis of common sources of difficulty in various types of designs. A compilation of instances in which designs actually did break down might also be useful in order to determine what alternatives might be possible. At the very least, some sort of patched-up design (Rezmovic in this volume) should usually be possible. It should be emphasized, however, that fall-back designs can never be as conclusive as the original experiment, and there is a risk that the very existence of a fall-back position might lessen commitment to the original design. Any fall-back design should be regarded as a last resort, to be avoided if at all possible.

Reference may also be made to work comparing true experiments and quasi-experiments (Deniston and Rosenstock 1972, Boruch 1975) that provides some indications of ways in which quasi-experiments may be embedded in true experiments and, hence, suggests possibilities for the development of fall-back designs. Opportunities to embed quasi-experiments within true experiments should be exploited in rehabilitation research in order to provide a better empirical basis for estimating the imprecision involved in quasi-experimental designs.

Sherwood *et al.* (1975) have developed and tested a method for improving on the nonequivalent control group design by a system of extensive *ex post facto* multivariate matching of cases in a treated group with cases available but not selected for treatment. They contend that by matching on a large number of variables, equivalence on the pretreatment dependent variable is virtually assured, and, indeed, their empirical data suggest that pretreatment differences might be smaller than would be produced even by random selection. The case matching method obviously needs more developmental work before it can be recommended as a dependable alternative to randomization, especially in rehabilitation, where it has not yet been tried. Still, the method would appear to be quite adaptable to rehabilitation research, where, often, only a relatively few persons can be selected for treatment but not on a random basis and where there is available a large pool of additional cases from which matching might be done.

The above three kinds of research do not begin to exhaust the possibilities for advantageous methodological research in rehabilitation. They are meant only to be illustrative. The papers by Schmidt and Witte and by Waldo and Griswold in this volume are specific examples of methodological work that can facilitate evaluation: in one case by providing a way of constructing what are, in effect, historical controls that improve estimates of effects and in the other making evident the relationships between different measures of recidivism. It is important that our capabilities for generating programs to be evaluated not be allowed to outstrip our capabilities for evaluating them. If that is not to happen, good methodological developmental work will be needed on a continuing basis.

THE PROBLEM OF FUGITIVE LITERATURE

A frequent and serious obstacle to the determination of the state of knowledge about rehabilitation is the prevalence in the field of what is often called "fugitive" literature, i.e., technical reports, unpublished papers, or articles published in out-of-the-way places. There are two different issues concerning fugitive literature: accessibility and quality.

Fugitive literature is difficult to locate and even more difficult to retrieve. Unpublished works may not get into the information network for considerable periods of time, if, indeed, they get into the network at all, and articles published in peripheral journals or books may be similarly troublesome to locate. Even when one knows about unpublished materials, they may be difficult or even impossible to retrieve. Panel members have had the experiences of receiving no reply from authors or institutions from whom unpublished materials were requested, of being told that the materials are no longer available, of being sent substitute materials of uncertain substitutability, and of being sent materials apparently quite unlike those originally cited (see, for example, Fienberg and Grambsch Appendix in this volume).

The second issue associated with fugitive literature concerns the lack of controls for quality that characterize the literature. Technical reports and other unpublished papers vary enormously in quality, but all too often the quality is dismal. Many reports are sketchy at best, are often preliminary, contain little in the way of program description, involve faulty or incomplete statistical analyses, or cannot even be deciphered. Perhaps it would not matter if such papers were simply ignored, but they do get cited—and probably secondarily cited—so that they become part of the folklore and information base about rehabilitation, along with impeccable literature.

Some measures need to be taken to improve both the accessibility and quality of fugitive literature. The problem of accessibility could be alleviated, if not resolved, by requiring authors who do cite such literature to give sufficiently complete information to enable others to retrieve it. The required citation might even include a mailing address of the person or institution from which copies should be available. In extreme circumstances, authors might even be required to commit themselves to providing copies of works not likely to be available otherwise. Funding agencies might well increase the pressure on researchers to publish their materials through regular channels, e.g., by making prior publications a more important criterion in evaluating requests for funding. Certainly if an agency has funded research of good quality that produced clear findings, the agency cannot be disinterested in the proper publication and dissemination of the research.

The second issue is, in almost every respect, the more important one, for if quality is lacking in a research report, that cannot be compensated for by wider dissemination. The often dismal quality of research reports should be of great concern to funding agencies. To some extent the quality problem may stem from the way in which much research gets funded by federal and other agencies, with funding decisions being too often based on considerations unrelated or even negatively related to the probable quality of the final product (e.g., see Bernstein and Freeman 1975). Even after research is funded, however, agencies probably do less than they should to monitor progress and to facilitate quality in the final product. When research is submitted for publication, it almost always undergoes a rather rigorous and searching review by readers who are experts in the field in question. On the other hand, technical reports, final reports, and in-house documents almost never undergo any such review, and many are probably not reviewed at all. One obvious and not adminstratively difficult measure that funding agencies could take would be to require outside review of all technical and final reports before their acceptance and certainly before their entry into information systems. If reports cannot withstand the scrutiny involved, that is probably a good indication that they should not be cited.

The National Criminal Justice Reference Service (NCJRS) is useful, and, at the very least, cited papers should all be available through that service. Still, inclusion in that service is no mark of quality. Papers definitely should not be cited on the basis of abstracts alone, and some thought should be given to screening of NCJRS papers or to grading them for adequacy.

THE BENEFITS AND COSTS OF REHABILITATION

BENEFIT-COST METHODOLOGY

Benefit-cost analysis evolved from welfare economics and, like its parent, is mainly concerned with questions of efficiency rather than of equity. Welfare economics defines a system as efficient if, given the productive resources and technology available, no reallocation of resources (inputs or outputs) can improve the welfare of some persons (or other units of analysis) without worsening the welfare of others. Benefit-cost analysis judges a particular project as efficient if the sum of the values of the direct monetary benefits of the project and the indirect benefits valued in monetary terms exceed the value of the sums of the direct monetary costs and the indirect costs valued in monetary terms.[1] If the benefits so calculated exceed the costs, it would be possible to make someone better off without making anyone else worse off by fully compensating those experiencing net costs from the larger benefit pool. For example, a new highway might result in overall higher productivity in the long run by an amount exceeding the costs of the road, but with some persons being worse off by having their neighborhoods destroyed. It would be possible for those

[1]Mishan (1976) provides a good exposition of the current state of benefit-cost analysis, and Aldine annually publishes a compilation of current cost-benefit studies under the title *Benefit-Cost and Policy Analysis*.

who benefit to compensate those who lose and still be better off after the compensation was paid than before the highway was built. In general, economists do not require that any potential redistribution actually be made (see Harberger 1971), but benefit-cost analyses will often be supplemented by a section that accounts for any income redistribution that occurs as a result of the project.

The actual process of benefit-cost analysis is not by any means so simple as implied in the preceding paragraph. For one thing, both benefits and costs must be appropriately discounted when they are not incurred immediately, for a deferred benefit is not as valuable as one obtained immediately, nor is a deferred cost as great. But discounting is not straightforward and can involve many assumptions. Currently, for example, deferred costs are difficult to project in the light of inflationary trends. Moreover, putting a monetary value on what economists refer to as externalities, the benefits and costs to those not involved as direct program targets, is almost always very difficult and can be virtually impossible. (Externalities nearly always reflect changes in status that are not easily expressed in dollar amounts.) One of the benefits of improved employment prospects might be an increase in family stability, but how could one put a monetary value on such a benefit? Or on such a cost of education as reduced time for leisure activities? Economists do put values on such things as family stability and leisure time but, obviously, only by making many assumptions to which others, especially noneconomists, often object.

Another complication in many cost-benefit analyses is the need to account for what economists call opportunity costs, i.e., the opportunities sacrificed in accomplishing an economic gain. For example, if a prison system makes an investment in industrial training facilities, it may have to forgo gains that might have been achieved by an alternative investment in a counseling program. All valuation rests on the concept of opportunity costs: all resources used should be valued at their opportunity cost. Thus, the labor used in a rehabilitative program should be valued at its next best alternative use, which may be in the private sector. The opportunity cost of labor is usually assumed to be equal to the wage rate: one difficulty in cost-benefit analysis of a prison program is "what is the opportunity cost of inmate labor?"

As will be shown below, benefit-cost analysis is an interesting prospect for evaluating offender rehabilitation programs, but it is one whose advantages are difficult to realize, as it represents a step beyond traditional rehabilitative evaluation and requires a strong evaluative design. However, benefit-cost analysis does provide a number of useful insights for evaluations of rehabilitative programs, even if the full technique is not used.

THE STATE OF THE ART FOR REHABILITATION

Benefit-cost analysis was originally developed for the evaluation of prospective water projects, and the use of benefit-cost analysis even in that area is still subject to many debates. The use of the technique for evaluating rehabilitative programs is still in its infancy.

Most applications of benefit-cost analysis to rehabilitative programs have sought to evaluate an ongoing program. Perhaps the earliest application was W. D. Cooper's (1968) benefit-cost analysis of the North Carolina prisoner work-release program. Cooper details the historic costs and benefits of the work-release program and compares them to an alternative program, prison industries. He finds that the work-release program increases efficiency—that benefits exceed costs. Specifically, he estimates that, considering only benefits and costs accruing while an individual is imprisoned, transferring one man from prison industries to work release results in a $2,056 yearly net gain to society, assuming that no other workers lost employment possibilities by being displaced by the prisoners.

Benefit-cost analysis has not been used extensively to evaluate rehabilitation programs since Cooper's work, although the number of applications has increased somewhat (see the literature survey in Weimar and Friedman in this volume). One of the best uses of the technique to evaluate a rehabilitative program and an excellent indication of the state of the art is a recent paper by Friedman (1977). In this paper, Friedman conducts an unusually careful and thorough benefit-cost analysis of a supported work program conducted by the Vera Institute of Justice in New York City. Although his follow-up period is short (an average of 4 months), Friedman, in contrast to Cooper, attempts to quantify effects that occur after the program is completed as well as during its operation. He carefully estimates both the change in output that occurred as a result of the program and the change in the level of externalities (e.g., reduction in the number of known criminal offenses). Both estimates are based on comparing the activities of a control and experimental group, a classic experimental design. Friedman's estimate of the change in output as a result of the program compares the average value added, to the offender, while participating in the program and of postprogram earnings to the opportunity cost to program participants as estimated by control group earnings during the period.

Friedman's study diverges somewhat from classic benefit-cost analysis as it mixes employment and earnings effects; i.e., the effect of increased probability of employment is added to the effect of increased wages in determining total economic benefit. Since lowered unemployment rates are likely to be a substantial benefit of any successful work-oriented rehabilitative program, it is extremely important to take such effects into account. The generally accepted and probably most informative way of doing so is to provide a supplemental analysis that details such effects. A separation of the earnings and employment effect is important since one would expect employment effects to vary directly with business cycles and with geographic area, thus limiting the generalizability of findings related to employment. For example, since the rate of unemployment is currently much greater in New York than in Houston, any employment effect would be expected to be greater in New York.

Consideration of the earnings or production effects of a rehabilitative program brings up an important factor in using benefit-cost analysis to evaluate rehabilitative programs. Benefit-cost analysis is most easily used and, generally, most accurate in situations in which benefits and costs are valued in the market, as they usually are in the case of earnings or production effects. When there is no market to establish a price or value, it is difficult to estimate the magnitude of a benefit or cost. Thus, a psychological or psychiatric program that had as a major benefit making people happier would be difficult if not impossible to evaluate using benefit-cost analysis, whereas an employment-oriented program, such as those discussed above, would be a more appropriate candidate for such an analysis.

Changes in the level of externalities, i.e., effects on those not the direct recipients of the treatment or intervention, are generally much more difficult to value in dollar terms than direct earnings or production effects. Friedman's (1977) article provides an extremely careful attempt to value such things as improved health and decreased crime.

Valuation of decreased crime is extremely difficult but is of major importance in benefit-cost analyses of rehabilitative programs. The first problem, as discussed above, is that one observes arrests, convictions, etc., when one wants to observe actual crimes. Victimization surveys provide some understanding of the relationship between actual and reported crime; they can be used to estimate actual crime if one makes some heroic assumptions.

The second problem stems more directly from valuation. What is the value of a crime that has not occurred? Using mainly insights from the evaluation of medical programs (see Acton 1976 and other articles in the autumn 1976 issue of *Law and Contemporary Problems*), one might arrive at a dollar value for assaultive crimes prevented by considering earnings and criminal justice systems costs forgone and medical costs incurred. The valuation of property offenses avoided is much more difficult. One cannot, in general, value such an offense by the value of goods stolen, since the goods have, in general, only been transferred and not destroyed. As noted previously, benefit-cost analysis deals with efficiency and not equity and thus transfers, even forced ones, are not directly considered. Although property offenses undoubtedly have both production effects, e.g., decreased work incentive, and externality effects, e.g., fear and anxiety, such effects are extremely difficult to value. The current state of the art is either to disregard property offenses or to value them at the average amount, or some multiple thereof, actually spent by society in apprehending, prosecuting, and punishing them (see Friedman 1977 for an example). Theoretically, a more satisfying measure would include the extra (marginal) costs (rather than average costs) involved in apprehending, prosecuting, and punishing an additional offender, the value of resources destroyed, and the extra private crime prevention costs incurred as a result of an extra offense.

If the valuation of property offenses avoided is difficult, the valuation of offenses against social mores, e.g., drug, sex, and gambling offenses, is extremely difficult. Undoubtedly, there are both some production effects, e.g., physical debilitation due to excessive drug use, and some externality effects, e.g., an increase in other crime, but such effects are extremely difficult to measure. The current state of the art is, as with property crime, either to ignore such offenses or to value the prevention of such crime as worth the average amount we as a society spend to apprehend, prosecute, and imprison those who commit such offenses.

LIMITATIONS OF THE TECHNIQUE OF BENEFIT-COST ANALYSIS

Some of the more obvious limitations of benefit-cost analysis for evaluating rehabilitative programs, e.g., the concentration on efficiency and valuation, have been discussed above. The technique has a number of additional limitations, however, some of which are unique to its application to rehabilitation and some of which are inherent in the technique.

First, as detailed above, existing evaluations of the effect of rehabilitative programs have, in general, used weak research designs. With such designs, it is very difficult to determine what changes are due to the program being evaluated. Since benefit-cost analysis requires placing a monetary value on all changes due to a program, a necessary prerequisite to its use is relatively firm evidence of the nature of the changes caused by the program. If such evidence is not available, the use of benefit-cost analysis is not justified. Benefit-cost analysis is, thus, probably most justified when experimental evaluation designs are possible, although it may be feasible when strong quasi-experimental designs are used.

Second, benefit-cost analysis is useful only if a program has been shown to have benefits. As discussed previously, the benefits of many rehabilitative programs are unknown. Such programs are not potential candidates for a benefit-cost analysis unless, as in the case of work release, there are substantial in-program earnings or production effects.

As discussed in some detail by Weimer and Friedman (in this volume), one of the greatest strengths of benefit-cost analysis is also one of its greatest weaknesses: it provides a final dollar figure that indicates whether a program is socially beneficial. This fact often makes program directors shy away from such analysis. Dollars and cents are the language of many legislators and administrators, and programs that are shown to have net costs are highly vulnerable to being terminated.

In addition, the size of many of the costs and benefits and their valuation will not be exact, but rather best guesses. The uncertainty inherent in such estimates would be more accurately represented if a range of likely benefit-cost ratios were provided or if the probability that the benefit-cost ratio exceeded some figure (e.g., 1) were given.[2] A recently reported benefit-cost study of a Baltimore program of transitional financial aid to released prisoners (Mallar and Thornton 1978) reported upper- and lower-bound benefit-cost ratios derived from making different assumptions about probable benefits and costs. Even more interesting, however, is the fact that Mallar and Thornton actually did four benefit-cost estimates by looking at the problem from different perspectives. Thus, for participants in the program, increased tax payments was a cost, while for nonparticipants (taxpayers) increased tax payments by the participants was a benefit. The lower-bound benefit-cost ratios were as follows:

Social benefit = 4.02, meaning that society in general received 4 times as much benefit as the program cost to administer, there being no need from a societal perspective to consider benefits merely redistributed.

Budgetary benefit = 0.49, meaning that the program cost twice as much in money as it produced in monetary benefits.

Nonparticipant benefit = 0.78, meaning that taxpayers got about $3 in benefit for every $4 in cost, the major difference between this perspective and the budgetary one being that averted losses from theft are counted as a benefit and reduced earnings from displacement are counted as a cost.

Participant benefit = 1.94, meaning that participants got about twice as much out of being in the program as it cost them to be in it.

The point should be reiterated that the estimates given above are the

---

[2]In the field of transportation, it has been suggested (Duhs and Beggs 1977) that an ogive of benefit-cost ratios be presented.

lower bounds and may minimize program worth. Upper-bound estimates ranged up to 53.73 for overall social benefit. The variability in the estimates makes very clear the fact that estimating benefit-cost ratios is no simple matter and that the perspective from which one starts is of great importance.

Friedman (1977) provides an example of how benefit-cost analysis might be conducted from the following points of view: (1) the taxpayer, (2) the administering departments, and (3) the program participant. Such limited benefit-cost analyses are often more policy relevant than are the more global analyses advocated by most economists.

Another problem with classical benefit-cost analysis is that it assumes that the primary objective is efficiency. As anyone who has studied organizational behavior will recognize, efficiency is not always the goal, and hence benefit-cost analysis may seem, if not irrelevant, at least not particularly interesting.

In order to do a benefit-cost analysis, one must specify the time span over which benefits may be expected and assessed. Evaluations of manpower programs have often assumed beneficial earnings effects for 10 years or more (Goldstein 1973). If one views rehabilitative programs as experiments, it may well be the case that one should only realistically expect benefits in the relatively distant future.[3] The appropriate rate of discount to use in a benefit-cost analysis has been vigorously debated in the literature (see Weimar and Friedman in this volume). Whatever discount rate is used, an important insight of benefit-cost analysis is that benefits that occur in the future are not as valuable as those that occur today. This fact is, of course, not considered in traditional evaluations.

Finally, in conducting benefit-cost analyses (or indeed traditional evaluations) of rehabilitative programs, the researcher must be careful to evaluate any effect that the program under consideration may have on the other goals of the criminal justice system, e.g., specific and general deterrence, retribution, and incapacitation. For example, in conducting a benefit-cost analysis of a work-release program, one should consider the lowered level of incapacitation and perhaps specific and general deterrence that may occur as a result of the program.

Economists, like most other scientists, have to make a lot of assumptions in doing their work; sometimes those assumptions make noneconomists quite uncomfortable. For example, assuming that there is no loss involved in transfer of property by theft may make good sense from the

---

[3]The classic example of this is, of course, Griliches's (1958) study of hybrid corn research. He documents the fact that while the experimental programs may have costs that exceed benefits for many years, their long-term overall effect may be highly beneficial.

perspective of a theoretical economist, but it is not an assumption most citizens would like to see built into analyses of the benefits and costs of rehabilitative programs. Compounding economists' problems is the fact that the quality and dependability of the data with which they must work are often distressingly poor, so that the values that are estimated may be well off the mark. Police departments and the judicial system do not have accounting procedures that make it simple to determine how much money might be saved if a burglary were averted, and any estimates made might not even be in the figurative ballpark.

COST REDUCTION AS A CRITERION

In addition to benefit-cost analysis, economics offers a number of other techniques such as cost and cost-effectiveness analysis that could be valuable adjuncts to more traditional evaluative techniques. All too often, when one has finished reading an evaluation report, one will have no information on the price at which any benefits achieved have been bought. Costs are important and must be considered. Unfortunately, the state of cost accounting in agencies responsible for running rehabilitative programs is not good. A recent survey (Witte *et al.* 1977) of eight states and the federal prison system found that only the federal system included depreciation of buildings and equipment in its cost data. Many state systems have no data available at the prison unit or program level, and much of the data that are potentially available are difficult to obtain and use. Correctional systems and other agencies administering rehabilitative programs should be encouraged to do better. While resources are scarce and should be effectively utilized, even simple reporting of total program cost would be a valuable step forward.

Once cost information is generally available, it will be possible to compare the relative costs of alternative programs through cost-effectiveness studies with much greater ease and on a continuing basis. Cost-effectiveness analysis involves selecting a program that will achieve a targeted level of output at the lowest possible cost. The cost effectiveness of different programs can only be compared if they are very similar. In particular, for rehabilitative programs where number of individuals "rehabilitated" is the goal, the levels of incapacitation, deterrence, and retribution must be similar. Costs should reflect the opportunity cost of all resources utilized and should not be merely expenditure figures. The general availability of such information should make program directors more cost conscious and will provide valuable information for analyses requiring cost data, such as cost-effectiveness studies and studies of the determinants of average costs.[4]

We believe that a number of insights of benefit-cost analysis, e.g., the importance of discounting, should be reflected in evaluations of correctional programs. We believe, however, that the utilization of the full technique is only appropriate in certain types of evaluations. First, as was stated earlier, we recommend that intensive benefit-cost analysis be utilized only when experimental or strong quasi-experimental designs show that substantial postrelease benefits exist or when substantial in-program production or externality effects are present. Second, we believe that benefit-cost analysis is most appropriate when at least some program effects are explicitly valued by the market. For example, programs explicitly designed to affect the labor market performance of participants are better candidates for benefit-cost analyses than are programs designed to improve psychological or social adjustment. Finally, we recommend that evaluators carefully consider the appropriate point of view to assume in conducting benefit-cost analysis. The results of analyses that assume a social viewpoint are very valuable, but may be less policy relevant than analyses that take the viewpoint of the organizations funding or administering the program.

IMPLICATIONS OF REHABILITATION FOR CRIME RATES

In a response to a critique by Palmer (1975), Martinson (1976) urges that we would do well to adopt the economists' viewpoint, since they have the scope to enter the epoch of social planning research with the crime rate as their dependent variable. He then comments (p. 190):

> The *addition* of isolated "treatment" elements to a system (probation, imprisonment, parole) in which a given flow of offenders has generated a gross rate of recidivism has very little effect (and, in most cases no effect) in making this rate of recidivism.

Since such a focus on crime rates has both public appeal and public policy implications we feel compelled to address this issue here, if only briefly.

There is a sense in which looking at the effects of rehabilitative efforts on crime rates in specific jurisdictions, such as states, is an eminently sensible activity. At the outset, we would need a portfolio of proven rehabilitative techniques to deal with a wide variety of offenders in many different

[4]The potential fruitfulness of the latter type of analysis is illustrated by a recent study (McGuire and Witte 1978), which found that rehabilitative expenditures in the federal prison system actually reduced average costs, as a result of improved morale and lessened guard costs.

settings. Then we would examine the implications of various levels of "success" on the flows of offenders through the criminal justice system for the state in question and then how these changes would ultimately be reflected in actual crime rates. Since most offenders are not caught, and of those caught only a small proportion are actually tried and convicted, even powerful rehabilitative techniques, when implemented in the context of a state prison system, may have little impact on crime rates, at least in the short term. The question is in part a moot one, since, as we have noted elsewhere, we have found little evidence of proven rehabilitative techniques of widespread applicability.

Unfortunately, we believe that Martinson has in mind a different form of analysis than the one just mentioned. His reference to the economists' approach and the use of crime rates as dependent variables is suggestive of the regression-like approach used by Ehrlich (1973, 1975) and others to assess the deterrent effect of criminal sanctions on crime rates. That literature has been recently examined by another panel. Its report (Blumstein *et al.* 1978) points out the many errors and biases inherent in the work on this topic to date and the difficulties associated with crude and often inaccurate aggregate data on crime being used. It notes (p. 7) that "none of the evidence available thus far provides very useful guidance" on "the magnitude of the effects of different sanctions on various crime types." Our Panel sees little hope that this form of analysis will provide any usable information on the effects of rehabilitative efforts, and we strongly discourage efforts in this direction.

The preceding comments relate primarily to the short-term implications of rehabilitation for crime rates. The long-term implications are another matter and are extremely difficult to assess. If we distinguish between adult and juvenile offenders, and if we consider the possibility of differing degrees of successful programs for rehabilitation, we might well discover that the cumulative long-term effects on specific categories of crime within restricted jurisdictions may be substantial. How one models such effects is not clear to the Panel, and we believe that workable rehabilitative programs need to be developed and tested before one can sensibly go about the task of assessing their impact on crime rates.

5 The Prospects for Rehabilitation

Before concluding definitively that rehabilitation does not work, or even that its effects are limited, one should consider whether there may be techniques or even programs that have not been tried, but that offer promise. The more restrictive form of the question is whether there are things that have not been tried and tested, for there have clearly been many more strategies and tactics tried at some point or other than have been empirically tested. Enthusiasm for these untested interventions can often run high.

ONGOING PROGRAMS

In addition to considering innovative possibilities, some current efforts on which evidence is still coming in should be noted, along with trends in the criminal justice system that might have implications for what has been and is being done.

One ongoing program that shows promise, alluded to above, involves providing economic subsidies to released offenders who committed crimes against property, enabling them to survive without having to turn to criminal activities while seeking legitimate employment. Early results from a test of the program in Baltimore were encouraging. Involvement in crimes of theft was lower for ex-offenders receiving both the subsidy and vocational counseling than for those receiving either subsidy or counseling alone or neither (Lenihan 1977). Moreover, the subsidy program was judged to be cost-beneficial within a rather wide range of benefit estimates

(Mallar and Thornton 1978). Mallar and Thornton also reported that there seemed to be little fading of results over a 2-year period; in fact, the control groups seemed to be diverging from the experimental group as reflected in increased frequency of subsequent incarceration.[1] The subsidy program is now being tested on a much larger scale in Texas and Georgia, and the results are anticipated with great interest. The Panel is aware, however, that recently presented data (Rossi 1978) indicate that the findings reported by Mallar and Thornton may not be very robust.

Another study of interventions designed to increase employment rates of released felons is being carried out in Chicago. With support from LEAA, the SAFER Foundation (1977) is carrying out a randomized experimental test of three interventions evaluated against a control group. All three interventions are aimed at increasing the employment prospects and community stability of released adult felons. Essentially, the three interventions involve provision of services, such as counseling and support, by three types of service providers: volunteers from the community, including ex-offenders; VISTA volunteers; and trained paraprofessionals who are ex-offenders. No data are yet available from the project.

A movement that now seems to be gaining momentum in the United States is toward fixed or determinate sentencing for felons, greatly reducing the discretion of judges in sentencing. The idea of fixed sentencing is associated closely with the philosophy of just deserts, that a prisoner should receive a punishment deserved for the crime committed. Under this philosophy, the role of prisons is seen as retribution, pure and simple. On other grounds, however, most adherents to a just-deserts philosophy believe that rehabilitation and ameliorative services should be available in prisons, but not even implicitly required by conditions of confinement. Under the assumptions of just-deserts sentencing, a prisoner would have no external or inappropriate instrumental motive for participating in a therapeutic or rehabilitative program since participation would have no bearing on release date. Just what impact that philosophy would have on rehabilitation is difficult to say with certainty, but Morris (1974) has suggested that we would not be worse off by adhering to such a philosophy. The effects of fixed sentencing certainly should be studied carefully as opportunities to do so become available.

What appeared to be an excellent opportunity to study fixed sentencing

[1]This finding could be considered an example of London's (1977) concept of cumulative convergence in that an initially small push toward normalization of the experimental group grows over time. Of course, that depends on whether the experimental group is considered to be converging on normal or the control group is diverging even further, for there is a counterpart concept of cumulative divergence. An example of the latter might be the consequences of labeling juveniles as delinquent.

occurred with the opening of the federal correctional facility at Butner, North Carolina. Although not planned to test the effects of fixed sentences, changes in philosophy represented in the prison administration turned the plans in that direction. The research provided for random assignment of a group of federal prisoners to the Butner facility, where they would serve a sentence with a known date for discharge. Unfortunately, crowded conditions in the federal prison system when combined with knowledge of empty beds at Butner and a rather slow rate of selection of prisoners for the study led to seemingly inexorable pressure to permit transfer of prisoners to Butner without regard to needs of the study. Thus a potentially important and informative study was aborted.

The Panel met at the University of North Carolina with Dr. Lee Bounds and several research staff members associated with the Butner facility. Plans to maintain Butner as a research facility within the Bureau of Prisons have not been abandoned, but when asked what the really distinctive feature of Butner is that might make it of research interest, the research staff replied "its architecture." Apparently, however, there is a renewed effort at Butner to evaluate the effects of fixed parole dates on prisoner behavior and future criminal activity (Bounds 1977). If that study is successful, it could be of great value.

Implementation of just-deserts sentencing would presumably result in the intertwining of volition and rehabilitation, i.e., prisoners would be involved in rehabilitation only on their own volition. Whether that might make rehabilitation more effective remains to be seen. Given that they participate voluntarily, prisoners in rehabilitation programs should be more motivated to take advantage of program activities, and so rehabilitation might be more effective. On the other hand, if all participants are highly motivated, and there is a large gap between what a program offers and what it delivers, there might be an adverse reaction. Very careful experimentation will be required to determine the consequences of offering completely voluntary rehabilitative services to imprisoned felons.

Much about the relationship of rehabilitative efforts to just-deserts sentencing will depend on specific schedules of sanctions developed: there might eventually be fewer or more persons in prison for longer or shorter times. In the context of the corrections system, fixed sentences may have far-ranging effects for rehabilitative programs. The characteristics of people in prisons and those on parole may shift gradually, but over a relatively brief period of time, with prison populations consisting more and more of hard-core offenders while parole and probation caseloads include fewer and fewer of such offenders. Just how this change may affect rehabilitative programs and their effectiveness probably cannot be foreseen, but must be anticipated in a general sort of way so that early findings are not totally misleading.

INNOVATIVE POSSIBILITIES

It is clear that no ideal combination of treatments, no really massive intervention, has ever been empirically tested for its capacity to produce rehabilitation. Consider, for example, even a limited prescription such as might be derived from research reviewed by Glaser (1975) concerning juveniles with a commitment to criminal careers: they appear to respond better to incarceration in a traditional institution (Palmer 1974); with typical institutional programs rather than psychotherapy (Carney 1969); with release on a graduated basis from a halfway house (Hall *et al.* 1966); and with exposure to intensive programmed education within the correctional program (Odell 1974, Cohen and Filipczak 1971). Aside from the dubious methodological adequacy of the studies cited to support the conclusions, the fact that each conclusion is supported by a separate study demonstrates the fragmented nature of efforts to test rehabilitative programs. There is no assurance that the combination of techniques would be cumulatively efficacious, but if that is the prescription, then that is what should be tested initially, not the separate treatment elements. Once a treatment effect is established, subsequent research can decompose the treatment into its elements to determine which are essential and why.

Even the combination of treatment elements just described barely begin to exhaust the logical possibilities for interventions that might be imagined for youthful offenders with serious criminal tendencies. For example, extensive family interventions[2] might be desirable in some cases, e.g., to alleviate poverty, reduce drunkenness, improve social surroundings, and cope with runaways. Although family interventions have been attempted experimentally and show some promise (Alexander and Parsons 1973), they have not been attempted in the context of a whole program of rehabilitation in which one can have confidence. The Community Justice Project in Kinnebec County, Maine (Blazek 1977), was to be an attempt at providing comprehensive services (in a community context) to criminal offenders and their families, but the program was never fully implemented, and the evaluation never took place. The older Cambridge-Somerville Youth Study (McCord 1978, Powers and Witmer 1951) is another

[2]Family therapy is supposed to have been a component of some Community Treatment Program interventions (Warren 1967), but it is not clear how much family treatment occurred nor how appropriate it may have been.

example of a comprehensive plan that was never implemented as intended (Gonzalez 1975).

Another innovative program that should be explored is truly early intervention. Glaser (1975), on the basis of evidence presented by England (1957), states that with adult first offenders, probation success rates are very high, a conclusion partially supported by recent evidence of small positive correlations between age at first arrest, age at release, limited prior criminal involvement, and favorable parole outcome (Gottfredson et al. 1977). However, England's data are now more than 20 years old, and there have been many changes in the criminal justice system in that time. There have been assertions in recent years that probation is failing, that few first offenders are ever apprehended, and that nothing much happens to offenders until they are finally incarcerated (e.g., Fishman 1977). It does seem likely that many offenders, perhaps especially juveniles, can develop impressive criminal credentials before they are ever exposed to any real sanctions from the criminal justice system. One reason may be that the alternatives available to the system are so limited, often requiring fairly drastic first steps. Expanding those alternatives through systematic experimental tests may provide a basis for better interventions and decision making.

One intervention that has been suggested sporadically and that is now apparently being systematically tested (Friday and Peterson 1973), is the "quick dip" sanction in which offenders apprehended for the first time are given a brief exposure to a maximum security penal environment. The intervention is based on the idea that if first offenders get a good idea of what is in store for them, they will be deterred from further criminal activity. There has already been a report on a "shock parole" program in Ohio in which adult felons are given early and unanticipated release from prison on the theory that any deterrent effects will be achieved quickly (Vaughan et al. 1976). In the Ohio program, however, the time served prior to release ranges from a very few months to 2 years: to the extent that what is provided is more in the way of information than punishment, the quick dip intervention could be regarded as rehabilitative rather than as specific deterrence.

Most current rehabilitative efforts do not begin—and perhaps do not even have a chance to begin—until a person's case is fully adjudicated and often not until the person is incarcerated. But by the time of incarceration, most of the targets for rehabilitative interventions will either have committed such serious crimes that they will be facing long sentences, or they will have such well-developed criminal careers that the concept of rehabilitation may be scarcely applicable to them. While ways may have to be sought to avoid the potentially bad effects of labeling and of its detrimental effects on self-image, interventions that can be applied on the occasion of the first apprehension of either juvenile or adult offenders may have a high payoff.

Restitution is a concept that has been more talked about than implemented in dealing with criminal offenders, and it has not been the subject of much research to date. The rehabilitative rationale for restitution would, presumably, include such propositions as avoidance of incarceration and disrupting of family and community ties, necessity of admitting guilt, enhancing of self-respect, and continuing reinforcement of socially responsible behavior. A current project to implement restitution as a sanction in Minnesota may produce useful information and a basis for more systematic tests (Minnesota Department of Corrections 1976). There is, of course, a rationale for restitution other than rehabilitation, but it would seem that rehabilitation would have to be one goal of a restitution program: it would not do to have a burglar continuing his or her criminal activity and making restitution occasionally when caught.

Most of the interventions that have been empirically tested have been designed to be carried out within institutions. The vast majority of interventions tested to date on non-inmate samples have been probation and parole and variants on them. The most salient exception is the financial subsidy program tested in Baltimore (Lenihan 1977, Mallar and Thornton 1978). Certainly there are many other possibilities for interventions that might take place outside prisons and other correctional facilities. One source of hypotheses for developing innovative programs might be the variables related to success on probation and parole. As an example, one of the variables seemingly associated with such success is strength of family ties. A potential element in an intervention program, then, would be some way of maintaining or even strengthening family ties. One of the services of the Kinnebec County project (Blazek 1975) was transportation of family members of incarcerated inmates to facilitate visitation.

Prison furloughs may be another way of maintaining family ties. There is no evidence on their rehabilitative effect, but the concept is a reasonable one to test. Recent evidence suggests that furloughs are highly successful in the sense that few of the inmates selected fail to return and few commit known crimes while on furlough (Ostrow 1978). Interestingly, Norman A. Carlson (quoted by Ostrow 1978, p. 38), director of the federal Bureau of Prisons, suggests that one of the reasons for the success of the furlough program is that there is "tremendous amount of peer pressure inside institutions. Inmates exert pressure on their peers to respond to things they want to preserve." The idea of mobilizing prisoners' interests in support of rehabilitation is of more than passing interest.

The Baltimore study of financial subsidy of released offenders suggests that more thought should be given to the possibility of providing more substantial supportive services and treatments to released offenders than typical parole programs now provide. For example, the best time to provide counseling and psychotherapy to offenders may be after they are released rather than while they are in prison. Substance abuse programs might also be more effective when provided after release rather than during imprisonment. Even job training might better be given in the community than within the prison walls, e.g., with prisoners being released for job training (as they are for work) or with job training being a condition of parole and subsidized. Naturally, such job programs would have maximum chance for success if they prepared persons for good jobs for which workers are needed. Quality job placement efforts beyond those typically available to parole agencies (such as through the U.S. Employment Service) may also be worth experimental testing. The Panel really has no idea whether such programs would be effective in reducing criminal behavior; they merely illustrate some of the interventions that perhaps ought to be tested empirically since they seem more reasonable than many of the interventions that have been tested and found wanting.

Alternative and innovative sentencing and confinement possibilities have also not been explored to any extent, and no actual evaluation of innovative sentencing or confinement has been carried out. As an instance of innovative confinement, it is worth considering the fairly radical suggestion of David Clement (1977, also Horn 1978) that he calls "in-and-out jail therapy." It is said to be based on the well-established behavioral principles of making punishment for undesirable acts as specific and inevitable as possible and of offering immediate rewards for good behavior. Under Clement's scheme, offenders would be given sentences proportional to the seriousness of their offense, and the proportion of the sentence served would depend on their behavior during the sentence. But Clement would require an offender to serve a relatively brief period of continuous confinement, followed by a period in the community, followed by an even briefer period of confinement, followed by another release into the community. Over time, the confinements would be briefer and less frequent and the release periods would be longer. If, however, the offender did anything wrong, he would be returned to jail immediately for a brief period of confinement, and the confinement schedule would be stretched out in response to bad behavior. Since jail sentences could be highly flexible, relatively small offenses such as loitering or public drunkenness could be responded to at an appropriate level without the necessity for revoking parole and returning the offender to serve the remainder of a long sentence. The in-and-out confinement would also facilitate the maintaining of family relationships and even employment and education in some cases.

Moreover, the relatively brief periods of continuous confinement would remove some of the pressures to make jail a less unpleasant experience so that time actually spent in jail would be a meaningful punishment.

Clement's idea of in-and-out jail therapy is clearly intended to have a rehabilitative rather than simply a deterrent effect since the intent is to reward good behavior as well as punishing bad. The Panel does not wish to endorse Clement's idea, but merely to call attention to it as one of many types of innovations that perhaps should be considered for empirical trial. It might not be as radical as it would appear to some. In the Community Treatment Project (CTP) in California, youths released into the community were frequently placed in detention for brief periods for minor offenses on the sole authority of their probation officer. In fact, the community youths experienced more detention than the youths who originally had been confined once the latter had been released (Lerman 1975). Interestingly, the proponents of the CTP claim that the community placement group has a better subsequent outcome than the group continuously confined. The treatment of the former group was not unlike that proposed by Clement except for the fact that they never experienced an initial short imprisonment.

One suspects that the choice of interventions to be tested and the conditions of their test have been dictated more by practicalities than by logic. Similarly, simply because an inmate population is captive, it is probably easier to administer a program within the prison walls, and it is simpler to put together a group counseling program than a program of work release, and it may be cheaper to study parole supervision than to study financial subsidies. But rehabilitation research is going to have to attempt some of the more difficult things if it is to achieve any real progress. Probably the easy interventions do not work very well.

Some might argue that the kinds of interventions mentioned for testing could be impossibly expensive, akin to a $1 million treatment for cancer, impossible for any system to afford. Such an argument can be answered in two ways. First, the criminal justice system as it now operates could be regarded as both almost impossibly expensive and not working well. The costs involved in keeping prisoners in the style to which we have become accustomed—and which the courts demand—amount to thousands of dollars per prisoner per year. An intervention that costs, say, $10,000 per prisoner might well be cost effective if it resulted in 1 year's less imprisonment and no increase in crime rates.

The second answer to the $1 million treatment argument is that it would be worth a great deal of money to show that, in principle, rehabilitation can work. If we as a society knew that it is possible to achieve rehabilitation, even at great cost, we could make a rational decision about what to attempt and with what expectations. Moreover, if we knew of a treatment that worked dependably, we could initiate research to decompose the treatment into its elements to determine the essential, and presumably cheaper, ones, and we could try to find ways of delivering the treatment at lower cost. To return to a medical example: in the early days of kidney dialysis the treatment was extremely expensive, $50,000 per year or so, but it was important to have discovered, even at that cost, a way of cleansing the blood through artificial kidneys. Subsequent research and engineering technology have produced kidney dialysis machines that make home treatment possible, in many cases at a cost of $6,000 per year or so, quite a dramatic decrease, especially given the enormous cost increases associated with other aspects of medical care. The Panel believes that even near-heroic measures to achieve rehabilitation dependably would be worthwhile at this time, especially in view of the growing belief among many observers that it may not be possible at all.

LEGAL LIMITATIONS

There are legal constraints on what may be done with prisoners, with respect to both the treatments they may be exposed to and the conditions under which they may become research subjects. Deliberate account must be taken of legal and constitutional constraints in planning interventions and in evaluating those interventions. There is no point in recommending a course of action that will be impermissible, and it may even be desirable to try to anticipate what is likely to produce controversy.

Two recent papers set forth many of the legal issues and provide a sound basis for further work when that becomes possible. Specifically, Wexler (1973), in the general context of work on behavior modification, has reviewed a sizable body of law bearing on many of the issues surrounding treatments to which prisoners may be exposed, and Singer (1977) has written a paper raising many of the issues concerning what conditions of research may be imposed upon prisoners. Of great importance also is the report of the National Commission for the Protection of Human Subjects of Biomedical Research (1977), *Research Involving Prisoners*. The Commission suggests that standards for research designed to *benefit* prisoners may be less rigorous than for research *about*, or merely *on*, prisoners.

The Panel is not able at present to do a great deal more than describe some of the issues and point to some unresolved problems. Careful work on legal issues in the treatment of and experimentation with prisoners is much needed.

LEGAL LIMITATIONS OF TREATMENTS

We note first that in the eyes of the law, treatments may not be justified by their effects. For example, a rehabilitative effort could be efficacious in every respect and be prohibited by the constitutional provision against cruel and unusual punishment. A more subtle and complex legal problem stems from the proposition that prisoners share in certain human rights that may call into question the legitimacy of some forms of treatment involved in behaviorally oriented programs, such as token economies. Wexler (1973) cites a number of cases in which it has been ruled that persons confined by the state are entitled to a nutritious diet, a regular bed, reasonable privacy, sufficient and acceptable clothing, and other things or aspects that are thought to be minimal requirements for human comfort. Some judges have even ruled that confined persons have a right not to be bored, on the grounds that prolonged boredom and lack of stimulation may result in actual deterioration rather than maintenance of desirable behavior. Recently, two prisoners in Florida have sued the state over their claimed right to have access to television. But for certain types of rehabilitative programs, good food, desirable clothing, a soft bed, and access to television are employed as rewards for desired behavior and, hence, are temporarily withheld from prisoners, perhaps for relatively long periods for inept or recalcitrant inmates. Wexler notes that one study (Glicksman *et al.* 1971) found that narcotics offenders treated by a token economy program actually spent less time in confinement than those treated by usual standards; yet the withholding of the "rewards" needed to operate the token economy might be ruled unconstitutional. Thus, presumably, if we do not have any other ways of reducing the period of confinement, prisoners will experience longer confinement in greater comfort to meet constitutional requirements. Is there a way out of this dilemma? The Panel does not know. But careful legal thought needs to be given to the situation in which desirable outcomes must be traded off against each other, e.g., greater comfort versus early release.

Many writers, e.g., Hirschi (1969), Morris (1974), and von Hirsch (1976), have questioned whether the state has any right to force rehabilitation on criminal offenders, which, it is contended, is what the state does when it plans prison programs with the aim of producing rehabilitation and then arranges prison conditions in such a way that participation in rehabilitative programs is all but mandatory. When the only prison programs available are for rehabilitation and when prison life is otherwise excruciatingly boring, when release dates are contingent upon participation in programs, or when prisoners are simply assigned to activities that have a rehabilitative intent, then treatment is being imposed upon prisoners, and many would contend that the imposition is unjust and perhaps even unconstitutional. In principle, it is argued that people have a right to behave badly and to suffer the consequences of their actions if that is their desire; the state has no right to attempt to enforce behavior change. Although some who object to enforced treatment by the state have in mind a *Clockwork Orange* type of inhuman reprograming of prisoners, and perhaps of political as well as criminal prisoners, other writers (e.g., Morris 1974, von Hirsch 1976) discern a principle that applies in absolute form, under which prisoners may not be seduced, let alone coerced, into even the most benign therapies.

Obviously, though, the matter is by no means so simple, since the question of when a prisoner is exercising free choice is a difficult one, and there is a continuum rather than a dichotomy between voluntary and coerced behavior. Treatments can be made so attractive that prisoners desire to be in them for reasons beyond their inherent purposes, a prison administration can allow to exist a prevailing belief that program participation will facilitate early release or promote better prison conditions, and therapies may be oversold to prisoners desperate to straighten out their lives. The Panel believes that careful legal scholarship and thinking need to be applied to the question of conditions under which treatment programs may be offered to prison inmates.

Nor do the problems of coerced or enforced treatment end at the prison boundaries. There are many similar problems facing those who deal with offenders outside prisons. To what extent may the state require treatment, e.g., therapy or treatment for alcoholism, as a condition of probation and parole? If offenders perceive that a promise to seek treatment may affect their chances to remain outside prison, then the constitutional problem becomes the same as for inmates. And if the state has no right to coerce a change in behavior, does it have a right to rehabilitate by enticement, e.g., by offering released offenders special economic benefits that are for the sole purpose of enticing them into a law-abiding way of life?

Similar issues also may arise from the special interest the state has in children and the consequent interest of the state in intervening when children are poorly reared. Under what circumstances may the state intervene to remove children from the influence of their families? Is persistent delinquent behavior a sufficient justification for placement of a youth in a foster home? May the state intervene with a family known to have criminal propensities to protect younger children not yet delinquent, or must any intervention await actual delinquent behavior? Would it be constitutional for the state to require treatment of family members, e.g., for alcoholism or child abuse, as a condition for keeping children in the home? Again, careful legal scholarship needs to be applied to these and similar questions.

LEGAL LIMITATIONS ON EXPERIMENTATION

Not only are there legal constraints on the treatments to which prisoners may be exposed, but there are also legal and constitutional constraints on the ways in which the evaluations of treatments may be carried out. These constraints seem to involve four major issues: due process, equal treatment under the law, voluntary participation, and informed consent. For none of these issues does there seem to have been a complete and satisfactory resolution of legal and constitutional questions.

Due process may become involved in the conduct of research when the research design calls for assignment of subjects to experimental or other treatment conditions on any automatic basis that precludes an offender's presentation of his or her case before a court for disposition according to its merits. For example, assignment of juveniles to treatment conditions without adjudication would be open to question on due process grounds. Thus, the desire to avoid the stigma associated with labeling of a youth as delinquent could run afoul of the requirement that a youth not be punished or otherwise treated without court hearings to determine culpability.

A closely related issue is the principle that persons of equal standing should be treated equally under the law. Under this principle, two offenders carefully matched by offense and other characteristics could not be randomly assigned to different treatments, e.g., probation versus institutionalization. The Provo experiment (reported in Empey and Rabow 1961) had to be terminated because of this issue, since it was declared unacceptable that two boys equally culpable should receive treatments so disparate as probation with counseling and confinement in the state reformatory (Glaser 1965). Morris (1969) has suggested that constitutional requirements might be met if a "not worse off" doctrine were adhered to, that doctrine being that no offender should be worse off because of an experiment than he or she would be were no experiment being conducted. It is not known whether this doctrine would actually be held constitutional.

Whether there is any way in which it might be constitutional to assign equivalent offenders to different treatments needs to be explored. It would seem that if penal sanctions are imposed without rehabilitative aims and if participation in programs intended to be rehabilitative were voluntary, it should be possible to effect random assignment for research purposes. Since the reason for doing the research would lie in the uncertainty about the advantages of any of the treatments in question, there would be no obvious ethical or legal restriction on allocating treatments.

An additional question relates to the standing of those who turn out to have been in the least favorable treatment, especially when the treatment may have been severe and protracted in time. It is not possible to undo treatments that have resulted in unnecessary time in confinement—or in an increased propensity to criminal activity resulting in an increase in the probability of confinement. It has been proposed in connection with biomedical research that the state might be obliged to recompense those persons actually damaged by participation in an experiment.

The third major legal issue has to do with whether prisoners, or even those threatened with imprisonment, can ever be free to decide whether or not to participate in an experiment. Singer (1977) has addressed this question at some length and concludes that the argument that prisoners can never be considered voluntary participants in research is unjustified. Nonetheless, the proponents of the other side are many and vociferous. Perhaps voluntary participation is a question for empirical research, since it would seem quite possible to do experiments in which the independent variable was represented by different levels of pressure to participate in research and the dependent variable was degree of participation. As an example of the type of work that might be done, Rosen (1977) developed the hypothesis that applicants for mental health services in a public clinic were coerced into signing a form permitting release of personal information to other state agencies by the implicit belief that if they did not sign the form, they would not receive services. In a quasi-experimental study, some applicants were given the usual instructions used in the clinic and others were told that they would receive services whether they signed the release form or not. With the usual instructions, virtually 100 percent of applicants signed the form; with the special instructions, the percentage was as low as 20 percent in one group and no larger than 60 percent in any group. Research of this type, in which special experimental procedures are compared to standard or usual procedures, is not difficult to justify even though the "rights" of some participants may appear to have been slighted. The importance of the knowledge gained is great. Obviously, mechanisms for the review of such research that will prevent abuse but not drastically impede the research should be developed. Although some of the questions involved in voluntary participation might be resolved by empirical research, there are likely to be other questions that will require legal study.

The final major issue to be mentioned here is informed consent, a difficult and controversial issue in every area of treatment and research. Informed consent, like voluntary participation, is in part an empirical as well as a legal issue. One extremely difficult question to resolve is whether, or at least under what circumstances, it is possible to get truly informed consent. Given, for example, the generally low educational and literacy levels that obtain in offender populations and the often complex nature of social science research, it is open to serious question whether most prisoners could completely understand the explanations that would be necessary in order for them to be informed about the nature of the experimental treatment and the balance of risks and benefits they might face. Obviously, "informed consent" does not constitute one alternative in a dichotomy, but rather is one end of a continuum: at what point on that continuum "partially informed" becomes "sufficiently informed" is most difficult to say. Perhaps an applicable legal standard might reflect general community consensus about sufficiency, in which case the issue would become in part empirical.

A second problem with the principle of informed consent surrounds the question how that consent is to be documented. Merely to obtain a signed form may not be sufficient, either ethically or legally, for people may be coerced or cajoled into signing things they do not want to sign or things they do not understand. Moreover, the experience of the large-scale clinical trial of mastectomy surgery shows that even when people have seemingly been well instructed and have signed an informed consent form, there is no guarantee that the consent is truly informed. Some of the women in the mastectomy study were exposed to lengthy and detailed explanations by their surgeons of the nature of the experiment and the treatment options to which they might be exposed, explanations that could be documented by tape recordings. Yet, apparently because of the shock and stress of learning they were at high risk for cancer, many women could remember nothing of those explanations and could scarcely be regarded as having given informed consent. Very likely, similar conditions of stress could prevail in a criminal justice setting and make it quite difficult to deliver information effectively and to obtain, in return, a truly informed consent to be assigned to a treatment condition in an experiment. The problem involved has both empirical and legal ramifications, empirical research being needed on ways of delivering information effectively and legal scholarship being needed on the question of just when informed consent may be considered to be effective.

A final problem related to informed consent to be considered here, but one that does not exhaust the possibilities, is the problem of getting informed consent on behalf of persons who, themselves, are legally or otherwise unable to give it. In criminal justice, this problem applies most often to consent for juveniles, but it may also arise in relation to mentally limited or incompetent offenders. Courts have already ruled that parents may not consent to medical experimentation on their children if that experimentation has no direct therapeutic intent with respect to the child: e.g., parents may not consent to have tissue biopsies taken from their children if the tissue is to be used solely for research purposes (Shirkey 1968). Under what circumstances, then, can parents agree to their children's becoming subjects of research on offender rehabilitation? The basis for limiting medical experimentation presumably is the risk, however small, to the child from being a participant in any medical research study. Is there a comparable risk in rehabilitation studies that might also be a basis for limiting participation of children even if their parents consent? It is clearly possible to envision distinctly risky interventions to which some desperate or uncaring parents of juvenile offenders would be willing to give consent for participation. Clear legal and scientific thinking on this problem is needed.

The Panel recommends strongly that high-level legal scholarship be brought to bear on these legal and constitutional issues and that such study be supported appropriately and expeditiously by funding agencies with an interest in offender rehabilitation.[3]

RECOMMENDATIONS

The research literature currently provides no basis for positive recommendations about techniques to rehabilitate criminal offenders. The literature does afford occasional hints of interventions that may have promise, but to recommend widespread implementation of those measures would be irresponsible. Many of them would probably be wasteful, and some might do more harm than good in the long run. The strongest recommendation that can be made at the present time is that research on ways of rehabilitating offenders be pursued more vigorously, more systematically, more imaginatively, and certainly more rigorously.

Paradoxically, there is a basis for a recommendation of a negative sort: given our current state of knowledge about rehabilitation of criminal offenders, no recommendations for drastic or even substantial changes in rehabilitative efforts can be justified on empirical grounds. At the present time, no recommendations about ways of rehabilitating offenders could be made with any warranted confidence, and, therefore, no new major rehabilitative programs should be initiated on a widespread basis. At the same time, neither could one say with justified confidence that rehabilita-

[3]The Federal Judicial Center took a strong step in this direction in 1978 with the establishment of the Advisory Committee on Experimentation in the Law. This committee, which includes legal scholars, social scientists, and judges, was created to evaluate ethical and legal issues arising from research involving innovations in the justice system.

tion cannot be achieved, and, therefore, no drastic cutbacks in rehabilitative effort should be based on that proposition.

As a prerequisite for more extensive change, a major and continuing research and development effort is called for. That effort must begin with more careful and systematic formulation of treatments based on the best current thinking about the nature of crime and the ways in which criminals may be changed, without harm to them and for society's benefit. The theories within which treatment plans are formulated must be explicated so that it can be determined that there is an *a priori* reason to believe that a given treatment or program might work.

An example of a broad framework that encompasses both treatment planning and evaluation methodology is provided by Tharp and Gallimore (1979). Their strategy of beginning with a fairly standard and reasonable treatment and then iteratively changing it toward accomplishment of desired goals is appealing. It is important to note, however, that the program by Tharp and Gallimore, which was designed simply to teach reading, required implementation of an extensive intervention into the school-day lives of the children who were involved. It seems improbable that criminality will yield to intervention more easily than poor reading, and future efforts to develop and test rehabilitation methods should move toward total programs rather than the testing of isolated, and often weak, techniques.

Every proposed intervention or program to be tested should be accompanied by a research protocol reflecting the strongest possible design to permit causal inferences. Of equal importance is the requirement that every proposed intervention be accompanied by a protocol indicating in detail the ways in which the strength of the treatment will be assessed and the ways in which the integrity of the treatment will be monitored and maintained. We note that the successful program reported by Tharp and Gallimore (1979) required constant monitoring of the behavior of teachers to determine that they were meeting the requirements of the intervention and also required planned interventions to improve teacher performance when it began to lag. Treatments should not be evaluated, nor their success reported upon, when there can be no assurance that the treatment is reasonably strong and delivered according to plan.

It is also essential that every intervention tested be fully documented so that it can be implemented and fully replicated in any setting comparable to the one in which the development and testing took place. The literature on rehabilitation is characterized by descriptions of treatments that range from sketchy to nonexistent, so that it would be virtually impossible for any other administrators or researchers to replicate the treatment. Funding agencies should require that one of the products of every intervention study should be a manual detailing the treatment involved. (Recently, Klerman [1978], the head of the Administration on Drug Abuse, Mental Health, and Alcoholism, indicated that such a manual will be required as a condition of funding of research on psychotherapy.) Information provided should include descriptions of the following: (1) personnel and their training, with careful description of any special training given; (2) samples exposed to the intervention with special note of populations for which the treatment is deemed optimal; (3) protocols followed in conducting treatment sessions or in providing services; (4) the nature of outcome measures and the exact schedule for obtaining them; (5) extent and sources of attrition to be expected in treatment groups. It would even be desirable to have at least estimates of staff attitudes toward the intervention and their judgments of its chances for success. Such information is now only infrequently available.

Boruch and Gomez (1977) have shown that it is almost inevitable that when a treatment is taken from the site of its development and initial testing to be implemented elsewhere, it will be weakened. Staff attitudes are likely to be less favorable, seemingly inconsequential but important aspects of the treatment will be deleted, staff training will be neglected, protocols will not be followed exactly, different outcome measures may be used, and the intervention may be applied to samples of populations different from those originally studied. The net result is almost certain to be a disappointing failure of the intervention to meet expectations. There is probably no way of avoiding some degree of degradation of treatment, but a carefully developed treatment manual should at least help, and it could greatly facilitate the interpretation of failures of replication, even when only partial.

Careful documentation of the costs associated with a treatment program should also be required by funding agencies. The documentation should include both the procedures by which costs were established and explicit statements of the cost factors considered and how they were allocated. Lerman (1975) has shown how easy it is to reach seriously wrong conclusions about the costs of interventions, and those who would implement seemingly successful interventions at new sites need to know quite precisely how to estimate probable costs. Consideration should be given to the development of standard cost-accounting methodology for use in rehabilitation research so that interpretation across studies might be facilitated.

As discussed above, a serious obstacle to determining the state of knowledge about rehabilitation is the prevalence of fugitive literature, i.e., technical reports, unpublished papers and articles published in little-known or not widely circulated journals. Such literature is difficult to locate and retrieve and of widely varying, but frequently abysmal, quality. Both the accessibility and the quality of this material need to be improved.

Much more attention needs to be paid to the needs and opportunities for rehabilitative programs outside prisons. As was noted earlier, a prison may be an inappropriate place for many interventions such as job training and counseling. These interventions might better be implemented when a prisoner is nearly ready for release or has actually been released. More emphasis should be put on job counseling and other programs for probationers rather than for incarcerated felons. A variety of supportive services could easily be imagined and planned for implementation outside institutions. Moreover, these supportive services might well need to continue for varying, but in some cases protracted, time periods for postrelease or postprobation criminal activity to be reduced. While the time limits on the legitimate intervention of the state in the lives of convicted offenders will probably be determined by sentence length, which may pose an obstacle to effective treatment, no such limits would apply to purely voluntary participation in treatment, and development of appropriate safeguards to ensure the voluntary nature of postsentence rehabilitation services should be pursued as energetically as the development of the services themselves.

There are still serious gaps in our knowledge about how to evaluate specific treatments and, especially, complex programs. Our ability to measure phenomena of vital interest, e.g., criminality or degree of rehabilitation, is still very limited at best. Although in eagerness to get on with the task of solving critical social problems, work on methodology often seems mundane and is given low priority, such a reaction is shortsighted. Methodologies are the critical tools of the scientist, and just as no one, save for in an emergency, would try to build a house with only a brick for a hammer, so should scientists not be asked to contribute important knowledge without the opportunity to develop their methodologies. Researchers should be bolder in their requests for funds to develop and improve their methods, and funding agencies should both insist on the best methods available and give priority to support the development of better ones. The impatience for answers that leads to short-circuiting the research and evaluation process also leads to disappointment with the results.

Agencies concerned with the rehabilitation of criminal offenders should set aside funds for research on rehabilitation. Given the amount of money spent on the corrections system, let alone the criminal justice system as a whole, the amounts of money that have been spent on research are minuscule in almost all areas. It seems unlikely that the corrections field now has the wisdom, the administrative capabilities, or the research methodologies to be able to absorb and spend well any really massive increases in funding. But it is also clear that if progress in understanding the processes of rehabilitation is to be made, steady and dependable but gradually increasing levels of funding for research will be required (see Tharp and Gallimore 1979). Moreover, it is of greatest importance that those who provide funds for research insist on the highest standards of the design and execution of that research.

Responsibility for the unimpressive and inconclusive body of work on offender rehabilitation that now exists belongs as much to the agencies that funded it as to the investigators who carried it out. Funding agencies have accepted proposals with weak designs, have paid little attention to theoretical premises, and have not insisted on provisions for monitoring the integrity of either the treatments or the research. Also responsible, however, are practitioners who administer corrections programs and who are so confident of their professional judgment that they will not tolerate the penetrating questions of a researcher or who are so cautious that they will not permit the interventions necessary for meaningful study. To indict the research process, as many have done, for its failure to deliver clear-cut evidence on important questions is to single out a set of participants who have often been powerless to do the very things that need to be done to obtain that clear-cut evidence. At best, the development of scientifically sound evidence bearing on the effectiveness of interventions into human problems is never easy. The task should not be made more difficult than necessary. The research enterprise only occasionally bears fruit in the best of circumstances; it withers and is barren when neglected or abused.

Practical problems have strewn boulders in the path of research on rehabilitation. Considerations of justice, equity, and legal tradition have provided extraordinary constraints on the conduct of research. Any effort to evaluate long-term treatment programs, for example, will face limits based on sentence lengths. Random assignment to correctional alternatives routinely runs afoul of efforts to avoid the appearance of capriciousness. Furthermore, research takes place within a criminal justice system that is riddled with discretionary decisions that are difficult to trace and in which much of the relevant information is simply hidden. To make research even more difficult, research designs are continually corrupted by events, including administrative or budgeting changes that make orderly program implementation, monitoring, and evaluation exceedingly difficult. Added to these difficulties are constraints on research with human subjects, especially with vulnerable populations of subjects such as incarcerated offenders, and the general poor morale inherent in a poorly funded system attempting to cope with difficult problems. Under these circumstances, the ambiguous state of the literature is understandable and perhaps unavoidable. Under these circumstances, methodological and theoretical critiques are easy. Good research will be difficult, perhaps requiring Herculean effort. Better resources and renewed effort, rather than resignation, will be required to make progress in developing knowledge about the rehabilitation of criminal offenders.

References

Acton, J. P. (1976) Measuring the monetary value of life saving programs. *Law and Contemporary Problems* 40(4):46–72.

Adams, S. (1975) *Evaluative Research in Corrections: A Practical Guide.* Washington, D.C.: U.S. Department of Justice.

Adams, S. (1976) Evaluating Correctional Treatments: After Martinson, What? Unpublished paper presented at the annual meeting of the American Psychological Association.

Alexander, J. F., and Parsons, B. V. (1973) Short term behavioral intervention with delinquent families: impact on family process recidivism. *Journal of Abnormal Psychology* 81:219–225.

Allen, F. (1959) Criminal justice, legal values and the rehabilitative ideal. *Journal of Criminal Law, Criminology, and Police Science* 50:226–232.

Bailey, W. C. (1966) Correctional outcome: an evaluation of 100 reports. *Journal of Criminal Law, Criminology and Police Science* 57:153–160.

Baker, D. I., and Reeves, B. A. (1977) The paper label sentences: critiques. *Yale Law Journal* 86:619–625.

Baker, S. M., and Rodriguez, O. (1977) Court Employment Project Evaluation, Research Design and Implementation: A Preliminary Report. Vera Institute of Justice, New York.

Bandura, A., and Walters, R. H. (1963) *Social Learning and Personality.* New York: Holt, Rinehart & Winston.

Barbash, J. T. (1962) A study of psychological therapy on post-release adjustment. *American Journal of Correction* 25:26.

Barkwell, L. J. (1977) Differential treatment of juveniles on probation: an evaluative study. *Canadian Journal of Criminology and Corrections* 18:363–378.

Beker, J., and Heyman, D. S. (1972) A critical appraisal of the California differential treatment typology of adolescent offenders. *Criminology* May 1972:1–59.

Bennett, C. A., and Lumsdaine, A. A. (1975) *Evaluation and Experiment: Some Critical Issues in Assessing Social Programs.* New York: Academic Press.

108

Berecochoa, J. E., Jaman, D., and Jones, W. (1973) Time Served in Prison and Parole Outcome: An Experimental Study. Research Report no. 49. California Department of Corrections, Research Division, Sacramento.

Berger, R. J., Crowley, J. E., Gold, M., Gray, J., and Arnold, M. S. (1975) *Experiment in a Juvenile Court—A Study of a Program of Volunteers Working with Juvenile Probationers.* Ann Arbor, Mich.: Institute for Social Research.

Bergin, A. E. (1971) An evaluation of therapeutic outcomes. Pages 217–270 in A. E. Bergin and G. L. Garfield, eds., *Handbook of Psychotherapy and Behavior Change.* New York: John Wiley.

Bernstein, I., and Freeman, H. E. (1975) *Academic and Entrepreneurial Research: Consequences of Diversity in Federal Evaluation Studies.* New York: Russell Sage.

Blazek, H. D. (1977) The Community Justice Project: A Study in Change. NIMH Evaluation Report #ADM-42-74-49-(OP). Department of Mental Health and Corrections, Kenebec County, Me.

Blumstein, A., Cohen, J., and Nagin, D., eds. (1978) *Deterrence and Incapacitation: Estimating the Effects of Criminal Sanctions on Crime Rates.* Panel on Research on Law Enforcement and Incapacitative Effects, Committee on Research on Law Enforcement and Criminal Justice, Assembly of Behavioral and Social Sciences, National Research Council. Washington, D.C.: National Academy of Sciences.

Boruch, R. F. (1974) Illustrative controlled experiments for planning and evaluating social programs. Pages 279–324 in H. W. Ricken and R. F. Boruch, eds., *Social Experimentation: A Method for Planning and Evaluating Social Intervention.* New York: Academic Press.

Boruch, R. F. (1975) Coupling randomized experiments and approximations to experiments in social program evaluation. *Sociological Methods and Research* 4:31–53.

Boruch, R., and Gomez, H. (1977) Sensitivity, bias, and theory in impact evaluations. *Professional Psychology* 8:411–434.

Bounds, V. L. (1977) Evaluation Study of the Butner Correctional Experiment: Preliminary Report II. Institute for Research in Social Science, Chapel Hill, N.C.

Brenner, H. (1976) *Estimating the Social Costs of National Economic Policy: Implications for Mental and Physical Health, and Criminal Aggression.* Paper #5 prepared for the use of the Joint Economic Committee, U.S. Congress. Washington, D.C.: U.S. Government Printing Office.

Brody, S. R. (1976) *The Effectiveness of Sentencing—A Review of the Literature.* Home Office Research Report #35. London: Her Majesty's Stationery Office.

Burkhart, W. P. (1970) The Parole Work Unit Program: an evaluation report. *British Journal of Criminology* 9:125.

Campbell, D. T. (1969) Reforms as experiments. *American Psychologist* 24:97–103.

Campbell, D. T. (1974) Qualitative Knowing in Action Research. Unpublished paper presented as Kurt Lewin Award Address, Society for the Psychological Study of Social Issues, meeting with the American Psychological Association.

Campbell, D. T., and Stanley, J. L. (1966) *Experimental and Quasiexperimental Designs for Research.* Chicago, Ill.: Rand McNally.

Caplan, N., Morrison, A., and Stambaugh, R. J. (1975) The Use of Social Science Knowledge in Policy Decisions at the National Level. Center for Research on Utilization of Scientific Knowledge, Institute for Social Research, University of Michigan, Ann Arbor.

Carney, F. J. (1969) Correctional research and correctional decision-making: some problems and prospects. *Journal of Research in Crime and Delinquency* 6:110–112.

Cavior, H. E., and Schmidt, A. (1978) A test of the effectiveness of a differential treatment strategy at the Robert F. Kennedy Center. *Criminal Justice and Behavior* 5(2):131–139.

Chambliss, W. J. (1967) Types of deviance and the effectiveness of legal sanctions. *Wisconsin Law Review* 167:703–719.

Chassan, J. B. (1967) *Research Design in Clinical Psychology and Psychiatry.* New York: Appleton-Century-Crofts.

Clement, D. E. (1977) In and Out Jail Therapy: A Proposal for Nontraditional Confinement. Paper presented at the American Society of Criminology, Atlanta, Ga.

Cloward, R. A., and Ohlin, L. E. (1961) *Delinquency and Opportunity.* London: Routledge and Kegan Paul.

Cohen, H. L., and Filipczak, J. (1971) A New Learning Environment. San Francisco, Calif.: Jossey Bass.

Cohen, J. (1977) Statistical Power Analysis for the Behavioral Sciences. Revised ed. New York: Academic Press.

Conrad, J. P. (1975) The Lessons of a Little Knowledge. Unpublished paper presented at the conference, "The Criminal and Society: Should We Treat or Punish?", Academy for Contemporary Problems, Columbus, Oh.

Cook, D. (1967) *The Impact of the Hawthorne Effect in Experimental Design in Educational Research.* Office of Education, Washington, D.C.: U.S. Department of Health, Education, and Welfare.

Cook, T. D., and Campbell, D. T. (1966) The design and conduct of quasi-experiments and true experiments in field settings. Pages 223–235 in M. D. Dunnete and J. P. Campbell, eds., *Handbook of Industrial and Organizational Research.* Chicago, Ill.: Rand McNally.

Cooper, W. D. (1968) An Economic Analysis of the Work-Release Program in North Carolina. Unpublished Ph.D. dissertation. North Carolina State University, Raleigh.

Cooper, R., and Steiger, P. (1976) How one big firm fought health perils. *Los Angeles Times*, June 27, p. 1.

Cronin, R. C. (no date) A Report on the Experience of the Probation Employment and Guidance Program: September 1973–May 1975. University of Rochester, Graduate School of Management, Rochester, N.Y.

Deniston, O. L., and Rosenstock, I. M. (1972) The Validity of Designs for Evaluating Health Services. Research report. University of Michigan School of Public Health.

Dershowitz, A. (1976) Background paper. In Twentieth Century Fund, ed., *Fair and Certain Punishment.* New York: McGraw-Hill.

Duhs, L. A., and Beggs, J. J. (1977) The urban transportation study. Pages 228–251 in D. A. Hensher, ed., *Urban Transport Economics.* Cambridge, England: Cambridge University Press.

Edelhertz, H. (1970) *The Nature, Impact and Prosecution of White-Collar Crime.* National Institute of Law Enforcement and Criminal Justice, Law Enforcement Assistance Administration. Washington, D.C.: U.S. Department of Justice.

Edelhertz, H. (1977) *Investigation of White Collar Crime: A Manual for Law Enforcement Agencies.* Office of Regional Operations, Law Enforcement Assistance Association. Washington, D.C.: U.S. Department of Justice.

Eisenberg, L. (1977) The social imperatives of medical research. Science 198:1105–1110.

Ehrlich, I. (1973) Participation in illegitimate activities: a theoretical and empirical investigation. *Journal of Political Economy* 81:521–65.

Ehrlich, I. (1975) The deterrent effects of capital punishment: a question of life and death. *American Economic Review* 63:397–417.

Empey, L. T. (1977) *A Model for the Evaluation of Programs in Juvenile Justice.* Report prepared for the National Institute for Juvenile Justice and Delinquency Prevention, Office of Juvenile Justice and Delinquency Prevention, Law Enforcement Assistance Administration. (STR #027-000-00482-2.) Washington, D.C.: U.S. Department of Justice.

Empey, L. T., and Rabow, J. (1961) Experiment in delinquency rehabilitation. American Sociological Review 26:679–696.

England, R. (1957) What is responsible for satisfactory probation and post-probation outcome? *Journal of Criminal Law, Criminology and Police Science* 47:667–674.

Fishman, R. (1977) *Criminal Recidivism in New York City: An Evaluation of the Impact of Rehabilitation and Diversion Services.* New York: Praeger Publishers.

Fowler, R. D. (1977) Classification as a Means of Rehabilitating a Correctional System: The Alabama Experience. Invited paper presented at the Woods Hole Conference of the Panel on Research on Rehabilitative Techniques, National Research Council. Woods Hole, Mass.

Friday, P. L., and Peterson, D. M. (1973) Shock of imprisonment: short-term incarceration as a treatment technique. *Probation and Parole* 5:33–41.

Friedman, L. S. (1977) An interim evaluation of the supported experiment. *Policy Analysis* 3:147–170.

Fry, L. J. (1977) Research grants and drug self-help programs: what price knowledge? *Journal of Health and Social Behavior* 18:405–417.

Geis, G. (1966) *The East Los Angeles Halfway House for Narcotics Addicts.* Los Angeles Calif.: Institute for Crime and Delinquency.

Geis, G. (1973) Deterring corporate crime. Pages 182–197 in Ralph Nader and M. J. Green, eds., *Corporate Power in America.* New York: Grossman Publishers.

Gibbons, D. C. (1970) Differential treatment of delinquents and interpersonal maturity levels theory: a critique. *Social Service Review* 44:22–33.

Gilbert, J. P., Light, R. J., and Mosteller, F. (1975) Assessing social innovations: an empirical base for policy. Pages 39–194 in C. A. Bennett and A. A. Lumsdaine, eds., *Evaluation and Experiment.* New York: Academic Press.

Gilbert, J. P., McPeek, B., and Mosteller, F. (1977) Statistics and ethics in surgery and anesthesia. *Science* 198:684–689.

Glaser, D. (1965) Correctional research: an elusive paradise. *Journal of Research in Crime and Delinquency* 2:1–11.

Glaser, D. (1969) *The Effectiveness of a Prison and Parole System.* Abridged edition. Indianapolis, Ind.: Bobbs-Merrill.

Glaser, D. (1975) Achieving better questions: a half century's program in correctional research. *Federal Probation* 39:3–9.

Glass, G. V., Willson, V. L., and Gottman, J. M. (1975) *Design and Analysis of Time Series Experiments.* Boulder, Colo.: Colorado Associated University Press.

Glicksman, M., Ottomanelli, G., and Cutler, R. (1971) The earn-your-way credit system: use of a token economy in narcotic rehabilitation. *International Journal of the Addictions* 6:525–532.

Goldstein, J. H. (1973) The effectiveness of manpower training programs: a review of research on the impact on the poor. Pages 338–393 in W. A. Niskanen *et al.,* eds., *Benefit-Cost and Policy Analysis.* Chicago, Ill.: Aldine.

Gonzalez, J. L. (1975) Research in Psychotherapy of Offenders: A Critical Review. Unpublished manuscript, Department of Psychology, Florida State University, Tallahassee.

Gottfredson, D. M. (1972) Five challenges. *Journal of Research in Crime and Delinquency* 9:68–86.

Gottfredson, S. D., Gottfredson, D. M., and Wilkins, L. T. (1977) A comparison of prediction methods. Unpublished manuscript, School of Criminal Justice, Rutgers University, Newark, N.J.

Grant, J. D., and Grant, M. Q. (1959) A group dynamics approach to the treatment of non-conformists in the Navy. *Annals of the American Academy of Political and Social Sciences* 322:126–135.

Greenberg, P. F. (1977) The correctional effects of corrections: a survey of evaluations. Pages 111–148 in D. F. Greenberg, ed., *Corrections and Punishment*. Beverly Hills, Calif.: Sage Publications.

Greenwood, P. W., Petersilia, J., and Lavin, M. (1977) *Criminal Careers of Habitual Felons*. Santa Monica, Calif.: RAND Corporation.

Griliches, Z. (1958) Research costs and social returns: hybrid corn and related innovations. *Journal of Political Economy* 66:419–431.

Guze, S. B. (1976) *Criminality and Psychiatric Disorders*. New York: Oxford University Press.

Hall, R. H., Milazzo, M., and Posner, J. (1966) *A Descriptive and Comparative Study of Recidivism in Pre-Release Guidance Center Releasees*. Washington, D.C.: Bureau of Prisons, U.S. Department of Justice.

Halleck, S. L. (1967) *Psychiatry and the Dilemmas of Crime*. New York: Harper and Row.

Halleck, S., and Witte, A. (1977) Is rehabilitation dead? *Crime and Delinquency* 23:372–380.

Hannan, M., Tuma, N. B., and Groenevelt, L. P. (1978) Income and independent effects on marital dissolution: results from the Seattle and Denver income maintenance experiments. *American Journal of Sociology* 84:611–633.

Harberger, A. C. (1971) Three basic postulates for applied welfare economics. *Journal of Economic Literature* 9:785–797.

Hirschi, T. (1969) *Causes of Delinquency*. Berkeley, Calif.: University of California Press.

Hogan, R. (1973) Moral conduct and moral character: a psychological perspective. *Psychological Bulletin* 79:217–232.

Hood, R., and Sparks, R. (1970) *Key Issues in Criminology*. New York: McGraw-Hill.

Horn, J. C. (1978) Prisons—we pay too much for too little. *Psychology Today* 11:14–18.

Ingram, G. L., Gerard, R. E., Quay, H. C., and Levinson, R. B. (1970) Looking in the correctional wastebasket: an experimental program for psychopathic delinquents. *Journal of Research in Crime and Delinquency* 7:24–30.

Jeffrey, R., and Woolpert, S. (1974) Work furlough as an alternative to incarceration: an assessment of its effects on recidivism and social cost. *Journal of Criminal Law and Criminology* 65:405–415.

Jesness, C. F. (1965) The Fricot Ranch Study. Research report no. 47. California Department of the Youth Authority. Sacramento, Calif.

Jesness, C. F., deRisi, W. J., McCormick, P. M., and Wedge, R. F. (1972) *The Youth Center Research Project*. Sacramento, Calif.: American Justice Institute in cooperation with California Youth Authority.

Jesness, C., Allison, T., McCormick, P., Wedge, R., and Young, M. (1975) *Cooperative Behavior Demonstration Project*. Sacramento, Calif.: California Youth Authority.

Jew, C. C., Kim, L. I. C., and Mattocks, A. L. (1975) Effectiveness of Group Therapy with Character Disordered Prisoners. Research report no. 56. California Department of Corrections, Research Division, Sacramento, Calif.

Kassebaum, G., Ward, D. A., and Wilner, D. M. (1971) *Prison Treatment and Parole Survival*. New York: John Wiley.

Kazdin, A. E., and Wilcoxin, L. A. (1976) Systematic desensitization and nonspecific treatment effects: a methodological evaluation. *Psychological Bulletin* 83:729–758.

Klein, M. (1971) *Street Gangs and Street Workers*. Englewood Cliffs, N.J.: Prentice-Hall.

Klerman, G. L. (1978) Psychotherapy Research and Public Health Policy. Paper presented at the Society for Psychotherapy Research, Toronto, Ontario.

Knight, D. (1970) The Marshall Program: Assessment of a Short-Term Institutional Treatment Program. Part II: Amenability to Confrontive Peer-Group Treatment. Research report no. 59. California Department of the Youth Authority, Sacramento, Calif.

Kohlberg, L. (1964) Development of moral character and moral ideology. Pages 383–431 in M. S. Hoffman and L. W. Hoffman, eds., *Review of Child Development Research.* Vol. I. New York: Russell Sage Foundation.

Lebra, T. S. (1976) *Japanese Patterns of Behavior.* Honolulu, Hi: University Press of Hawaii.

LeClair, D. P. (1973) An Evaluation of the Impact of the MIC Concord Day Work Program. Unpublished paper, Department of Corrections, Commonwealth of Massachusetts.

Lemert, E. (1967) *Human Deviance, Social Problems and Social Control.* New York: Prentice-Hall.

Lenihan, K. J. (1977) *Unlocking the Second Gate: The Role of Financial Assistance in Reducing Recidivism Among Ex-prisoners.* R&D Monograph 45. Employment and Training Administration. Washington, D.C.: U.S. Department of Labor.

Lerman, P. (1975) *Community Treatment and Social Control: A Critical Analysis of Juvenile Correctional Policy.* Chicago, Ill.: University of Chicago Press.

Lipton, D., Martinson, R., and Wilks, J. (1975) *The Effectiveness of Correctional Treatment: A Survey of Treatment Evaluation Studies.* New York: Praeger Publishers.

London, I. D. (1977) Convergent and divergent amplification and its meaning for social science. *Psychological Reports* 41:111–123.

Maiser, T. (1969) *Resocialization of the Paroled Non-Aggressive Predatory Offender.* Washington, D.C.: U.S. Department of Justice.

Mallar, C. D., and Thornton, C. V. D. (1978) Transitional aid for released prisoners: evidence from the life experiment. *Journal of Human Resources* 8:209–236.

Maltz, M. D., and McCleary, R. (1977) The mathematics of behavioral change: recidivism and construct validity. *Evaluation Quarterly* 1:421–438.

Mandell, W., *et al.* (1967) Surgical and Social Rehabilitation of Adult Offenders, Final Report. Montefiore Hospital and Medical Center with Staten Island Mental Health Society, New York City Department of Corrections.

Manpower Report of the President: 1974 (1974) Washington, D.C.: U.S. Government Printing Office.

Martinson, R. (1974) What works? questions and answers about prison reform. *Public Interest* 10:22–54.

Martinson, R. (1976) California research at the crossroads. *Crime and Delinquency* 22:180–191.

Martinson, R., and Wilks, J. (1977) Recidivism and Research Design: Limitations of Experimental Control Research. Paper presented at the National Conference on Criminal Justice Evaluation, Washington, D.C.

Marvel, J., and Sulka, E. (1962) Special Intensive Parole Unit: Phase III. Research Report no. 3. California Department of Corrections, Sacramento.

Matlin, M., ed. (1976) *Rehabilitation, Recidivism and Research.* Hackensack, N.J.: National Council on Crime and Delinquency.

McCleary, R., Gordon, A. C., McDowall, D., and Maltz, M. D. (1978) A Reanalysis of UDIS. Center for Research in Criminal Justice, University of Illinois, Chicago.

McCleary, R., Gordon, A. C., McDowall D., and Maltz, M. D. (1979) How a regression artifact can make any delinquency intervention program look effective. In L. Sechrest, M. Phillips, R. Redner, S. West, and W. Yeaton, eds., *Evaluation Studies Review Annual*, Vol. 4. Beverly Hills, Calif.: Sage Publications.

McCord, J. (1978) A thirty-year follow-up of treatment effects. *American Psychologist* 33:284–289.

McGuire, W. J. (1977) Cost-Output and Cost-Environmental Relations Characterizing Criminal Correctional Institutions. Paper presented at the annual meeting of the Southern Economics Association.

McGuire, W. J., and Witte, A. D. (1978) An Estimate of an Average Cost Curve for Large Scale Correctional Institutions. Working paper. Department of Economics, University of North Carolina, Chapel Hill.

Mead, G. H. (1934) *Mind, Self and Society*. Chicago, Ill.: University of Chicago Press.

Megargee, E. I. (1977) A new classification system for criminal offenders. *Criminal Justice and Behavior* 4:107–114.

Merton, R. K. (1937) Social structure and anomie. *American Sociological Review* 3:672–682.

Merton, R. K. (1968) *Social Theory and Social Structure*. New York: Free Press.

Minnesota Department of Corrections (1976) Interim Evaluation Results. Minnesota Restitution Center, Office of Restitution Unit One, Metropolitan Training Center, Circle Pines, Minn.

Mischel, W. (1968) *Personality and Assessment*. New York: John Wiley.

Mishan, E. J. (1976) Cost Benefit Analysis. New York: Praeger Publishers.

Monahan, J. (1977) Prisons: retreat from rehabilitation. *Los Angeles Times*, June 3, Part 2, p. 5.

Monahan, J., Novaco, R., and Geis, G. (1979) Corporate violence: research strategies for community psychology. In T. Sarbin, ed., *Challenges to the Criminal Justice System*. New York: Human Sciences Press.

Morris, N. (1969) Impediments to penal reform. *University of Chicago Law Review* 627:646–653.

Morris, N. (1974) *The Future of Imprisonment*. Chicago, Ill.: University of Chicago Press.

Morris, N., and Zimring, F. (1969) Deterrence and corrections. *Annals of the American Academy of Political and Social Science* 381:137–146.

Mowrer, O. H. (1960) *Learning Theory and Personality Dynamics*. New York: Ronald Press Co.

Moynahan, M. J. (1975) *Volunteer Probation Counselors in Spokane County, Washington*. Spokane, Wash.: District Court Probation Office.

Mueller, P. F. (1964) Summary of Parole Outcome Findings in Stable Group Counseling. California Department of Corrections, Research Division.

Mullen, J. (1974) Pre-Trial Services: An Evaluation of Policy Related Research. Abt Associates, Cambridge, Mass.

Murray, C. A., and Cox, C. A. (1979) Juvenile corrections and the suppression effects. In L. Sechrest, M. Phillips, R. Redner, S. West, and W. Yeaton, eds., *Evaluation Studies Review Annual*, Vol. 4. Beverly Hills, Calif.: Sage Publications.

Murray, C. A., Thompson, D., and Israel, C. B. (1978) UDIS: Deinstitutionalizing the Chronic Juvenile Offender. Prepared for the Illinois Law Enforcement Commission. American Institutes of Research in the Behavioral Sciences, Washington, D.C.

National Commission for the Protection of Human Subjects of Biomedical and Behavioral Research (1977) Research involving prisoners. *Federal Register* 42:3075–3091 (Doc. GS4.107).

Nay, J. N. (1973) *Benefits and Costs of Manpower Training Programs: A Synthesis of Previous Studies*. Washington, D.C.: Urban Institute.

Neill, J. R., Marshall, J. R., and Yale, C. E. (1978) Marital changes after intestinal bypass surgery. *Journal of the American Medical Association* 240:447–450.

Newcomb, T. M. (1978) Youth in colleges and in corrections: institutional influences. *American Psychologist* 33:114–124.

New York Governor's Special Committee on Criminal Offenders (1972) The penal system: treatment as prevention. In R. Gerber and P. McAnany, eds., *Contemporary Punishment.* Notre Dame, Ind.: University of Notre Dame Press.

Odell, B. N. (1974) Accelerating entry into the opportunity structure. *Sociology and Social Research* 58:312–317.

Ogden, R. W. (1973) The ineffectiveness of the criminal sanction in fraud and corruption cases: losing the battle against white-collar crime. *American Criminal Law Review* 11:959–988.

Orne, M. T. (1962) On the social psychology of the psychological experiment. *American Psychologist* 17:776–783.

Ostrow, R. (1978) The success of prison furloughs. Page 38 in the *Chronicle World*, S.F. *Sunday Examiner*, April 23.

Packer, H. (1968) *The Limits of the Criminal Sanction.* Palo Alto, Calif.: Stanford University Press.

Palmer, T. (1973) Matching worker and client in corrections. *Social Work* 18:95–103.

Palmer, T. (1974) The youth authority's community treatment project. *Federal Probation* 38:3–14.

Palmer, T. (1975) Martinson revisited. *Journal of Research in Crime and Delinquency* 12:133–152.

Palmer, T. B. (1972) Differential Placement of Delinquents in Group Homes: Final Report, Group Home Project, California Youth Authority, Sacramento.

Palmer, T. B., and Werner, E. (1973) California's Community Treatment Project. The Phase III experiment: progress to date. Research report no. 13, California Youth Authority. Sacramento, Calif.

Patton, M. Q. (1978) *Utilization-Focused Evaluation.* Beverly Hills, Calif.: Sage Publications.

Peters, C. C., and Van Voorhis, W. R. (1940) *Statistical Procedures and Their Mathematical Bases.* New York: McGraw-Hill.

Powers, E., and Witmer, H. (1951) *An Experiment in the Prevention of Delinquency.* New York: Columbia University Press.

President's Commission on Law Enforcement and Administration of Justice (1967) *Task Force Report: Crime and Its Impact—An Assessment.* Washington, D.C.: U.S. Government Printing Office.

Quay, H. C. (1964) Personality dimensions in delinquent males as inferred from factor analysis of behavior ratings. *Journal of Research in Crime and Delinquency* 1:33–37.

Quay, H. C. (1973) What corrections can correct and how. *Federal Probation* 27(7):3–5.

Quay, H. C. (1975) Classification in the treatment of delinquency and antisocial behavior. Pages 377–392 in N. Hobbs, ed., *Issues in the Classification of Children.* Vol. I. San Francisco, Calif.: Jossey-Bass.

Quay, H. C. (1977) The three faces of evaluation: what can be expected to work. *Criminal Justice and Behavior* 4:341–354.

Quay, H. C., and Love, C. T. (1977) The effects of a juvenile diversion program on rearrests. *Criminal Justice and Behavior* 4(4):377–396.

Rabkin, J. G. (1979) Criminal behavior of discharged mental patients: a critical appraisal of the research. *Psychological Bulletin* 86(1):1–27.

Rein, M., and White, S. H. (1977) Can policy research help policy? *Public Interest* 49:119–136.

Reinarman, C., and Muller, D. (1975) Direct Financial Assistance to Parolees: A Promising Alternative in Correctional Planning. Research Report no. 55, California Department of Corrections, Sacramento.

Renfrew, C. B. (1977) The paper label sentences: an evaluation. *Yale Law Journal* 86:590–618.

Ricker, L. H., and Walker, F. C. (1976) Effectiveness of a therapeutic camping program for delinquent adolescents. *JSAS Catalog of Selected Documents in Psychology* 6(1):43.

Robinson, J. O., Wilkins, L. T., Carter, R. M., and Wahl, A. (1969) The San Francisco Project: A Study of Federal Probation and Parole: Final Report. Unpublished paper. San Francisco Project.

Rosen, C. (1977) Why clients relinquish their rights to privacy under sign-away pressures. *Professional Psychology* 8:17–24.

Rossi, P. (1978) Money, Work, Time. Paper presented at the Second National Workshop on Criminal Justice Evaluation. Washington, D.C.

Rudoff, A., and Esselstyn, T. C. (1973) Evaluating work furlough: a followup. *Federal Probation* 27:48–53.

Sarri, R. C., and Selo, E. (1974) Evaluation process and outcome in juvenile corrections: musings on a grim tale. Pages 253–302 in P. O. Davidson, F. W. Clark, and L. A. Hamerlyak, eds., *Evaluation of Behavioral Programs in Community Residential and School Settings.* Champaign, Ill.: Research Press.

SAFER Foundation (1977) *Challenge Experimental Evaluation Proposal.* Chicago, Ill.: SAFER.

Salasin, S. (1973) Experimentation revisited: a conversation with Donald T. Campbell. *Evaluation Magazine* 1:7–13.

Scriven, M. (1967) The methodology of evaluation. *American Educational Research Association Monograph Series on Curriculum Evaluation* 1:39–83.

Sechrest, L. (1977) Evaluation results and decision-making: the need for program evaluation. Pages 16–23 in L. Sechrest, ed., *Emergency Medical Services: Research Methodology.* National Center for Health Services Research, Research Proceedings Series, DHEW publication no. (PHS) 78-3195. Washington, D.C.: U.S. Department of Health, Education, and Welfare.

Sechrest, L., and Redner, R. (1979) Strength and integrity of treatments in evaluation studies. In *Review of Criminal Evaluation Results 1978.* National Criminal Justice Reference Service. Washington, D.C.: U.S. Department of Justice.

Sellin, J., and Wolfgang, M. E. (1964) *Measurement of Delinquency.* New York: John Wiley.

Shah, S., and Roth, L. H. (1974) Biological and psychophysical factors in criminality. Pages 101–174 in D. Glaser, ed., *Handbook of Criminology.* Chicago, Ill.: Rand-McNally.

Sherwood, C. D., Morris, J. N., and Sherwood, S. (1975) A mulitvariate, non-randomized matching technique for studying the impact of social interventions. Pages 183–224 in E. L. Struening and M. Guttentag, eds., *Handbook of Evaluation Research,* Vol. 1. Beverly Hills, Calif.: Sage Publications.

Shirkey, H. (1968) Therapeutic orphans. *Journal of Pediatrics* 72:119.

Singer, R. (1977) Consent of the unfree: medical experimentation and behavior modification in the closed institution, part I. *Law and Human Behavior* 1:1–43.

Sloane, H. N., and Ralph, J. L. (1973) A behavior modification program in Nevada. *International Journal of Offender Therapy and Comparative Criminology* 17:290–296.

Smith, W. A., and Fenton, C. E. (1978) Unit management in a penitentiary. *Federal Probation* (September):40–46.

Sobel, S. B. (1978) Throwing the baby out with the bathwater: the hazards of follow-up research. *American Psychologist* 33:290–291.

Sommer, R. (1976) *The End of Imprisonment.* New York: Oxford University Press.

Sullivan, C. E., and Mandell, W. (1967) *Restoration of Youth through Training: A Final Report.* Staten Island, N.Y.: Wakoff Research Center.

Sutherland, E. H., and Cressey, D. R. (1970) *Principles of Criminology.* New York: Lippincott.

Task Force on Continuing Program Evaluation under National Health Insurance (1978) Continuing evaluation and accountability controls for a national health insurance program. *American Psychologist* 33:305–313.

Task Force on the Role of Psychology in the Criminal Justice System. (1978) *Report. Board of Social and Ethical Responsibility for Psychology.* American Psychological Association.

Tharp, R. G., and Gallimore, R. (1979) The ecology of program research and development: a model of evaluation succession. In L. Sechrest, M. Philips, R. Redner, S. West, and W. Yeaton, eds., *Evaluation Studies Review Annual,* Vol. 4. Beverly Hills, Calif.: Sage Publications.

U.S. Congress, Senate. (1976) *Examination of the Treatment of Breast Cancer, What Treatment Is Best, Where Physicians Differ, and the Risks and Costs Involved.* Hearing before the Subcommittee on Health of the Committee on Labor and Public Welfare. 4(LI1/2):B74/1976. U.S. Senate 94th Congress 2nd Session. Washington, D.C.: U.S. Government Printing Office.

van den Haag, E. (1975) *Punishing Criminals: Concerning a Very Old and Painful Question.* New York: Basic Books.

Vaughan, D., Scott, J. E., Bonde, R. H., and Kramer, B. C. (1976) Shock parole: a preliminary evaluation. *International Journal of Criminology and Penology* 4:271–284.

Vera Institute (1972) *The Manhattan Court Employment Project of the Vera Institute.* New York: Vera Institute.

von Hirsch, A. (1976) *Doing Justice: The Choice of Punishments.* New York: Hill and Wang.

von Hirsch, A., and Hanrahan, K. J. (1978) *Abolish Parole? Criminal Justice Perspectives.* National Institute of Law Enforcement and Criminal Justice, Law Enforcement Assistance Administration. Washington, D.C.: U.S. Department of Justice.

Waldo, G. P., and Chiricos, T. G. (1977) Work release and recidivism: an empirical evaluation of a social policy. *Evaluation Quarterly* 1(1):87–108.

Waldo, G. P., and Dinitz, S. (1967) Personality attributes of the criminal: an analysis of research studies (1950–1965). *Journal of Research in Crime and Delinquency* 4:185–202.

Warren, M. Q. (1969) The case for differential treatment of delinquents. *Annals of the American Academy of Political and Social Science* 38:47–59.

Warren, M. Q. (1971) Classification of offenders as an aid to efficient management and effective treatment. *Journal of Criminal Law, Criminology and Political Science* 62:239–258.

Warren, M. Q., Palmer, T. B., Neto, V. V., and Turner, J. K. (1966) Community Treatment Project: An Evaluation of Community Treatment for Delinquents. Fifth Progress Report. CIP Research Report no. 7. California Youth Authority, Sacramento.

Wenk, E. A., and Moos, R. H. (1976) Social climates in prison: an attempt to conceptualize and measure environmental factors in total institutions. Pages 187–204 in J. Monahan, ed., *Community Mental Health and the Criminal Justice System.* New York: Pergamon Press.

Wexler, D. B. (1973) Token and taboo: behavior modification, token economies, and the law. *California Law Review* 61:81–109.

Whitla, D. (1968) Evaluation of decision making: a study of college admissions. Pages 456–490 in D. Whitla, ed., *Handbook of Measurement and Assessment in Behavioral Sciences.* Reading, Mass.: Addison-Wesley Publishing Co.

Wilkins, L. (1965) *Social Deviance: Social Policy, Action and Research.* Englewood Cliffs, N.J.: Prentice-Hall.

Wilkins, L. (1969) *Evaluation of Penal Measures.* New York: Random House.

Witherspoon, A. D., deValera, E. K., and Jenkins, W. O. (1973) The Law Encounter Severity Scale (LESS): A Criterion for Criminal Behavior and Recidivism. Experimental Manpower Laboratory for Corrections, Rehabilitation Research Foundation, Montgomery, Ala.

Witte, A. D. (1977) Work release in North Carolina: a program that works! *Law and Contemporary Problems* 41:230–251.

Witte, A. D., McGuire, W. J., and Hoffler, R. A. (1977) An Empirical Investigation of the Short and Long Run Cost Functions Characterizing Criminal Correctional Institutions: Conventional and Frontier Analysis. Department of Economics, University of North Carolina, Chapel Hill.

Wolfgang, M. (1977) *Testimony on Federal Role in Criminal Justice and Crime Research.* Pages 4–26 in the Joint Hearings before the Subcommittee on Crime of the Committee on the Judiciary and the Subcommittee on Domestic and International Scientific Planning, Analysis, and Cooperation of the Committee on Science and Technology. U.S. House of Representatives, 95th Congress. Serial No. 15. Washington, D.C.: U.S. Government Printing Office.

Wortman, C. B., and Rabinowitz, V. C. (1979) Random assignment: the fairest of them all. In L. Sechrest, M. Philips, R. Redner, S. West, and W. Yeaton, eds., *Evaluation Studies Review Annual*, Vol. 4. Beverly Hills, Calif.: Sage Publications.

Yochelson, S., and Samenow, S. E. (1976) *The Criminal Personality.* Vol. I: *A Profile for Change.* New York: Aronson.

Appendix: An Assessment of the Accuracy of *The Effectiveness of Correctional Treatment*

STEPHEN FIENBERG *and*
PATRICIA GRAMBSCH

This appendix gives the details of an assessment of the accuracy of the evaluation of studies on the effectiveness of rehabilitation by Lipton, Martinson, and Wilks (1975)—hereafter referred to as LMW. Chapter 3 of the report details the methodological criteria used by the authors in selecting studies for inclusion in their evaluation. This assessment is based only on those studies. The LMW evaluation covers 231 studies, while the LMW bibliography lists 174 entries. There is overlap in both directions; i.e., some bibliographic entries cover more than one study, and some studies have more than one bibliographic entry.

METHODOLOGY

For this assessment, we chose from the LMW bibliography two simple random samples of 17 works (each approximately 10 percent of the whole) using a table of random numbers. A detailed listing of the sample items is given below.

Of the 17 works in the first sample, 11 were available from the University of Minnesota library or directly from the authors. Consultation with the author of two others (Ericson 1965, 1966) revealed that they no longer existed in his files, but he made available what he said was a suitable substitute. Of the 5 studies that we could not locate, 4 are unpublished dissertations, and 1 is a mimeographed report. In the second sample, 9 of the 17 works were available from the University of Minnesota library or from the authors. Of the 8 studies that we could not locate, 1 is an unpublished dissertation, and 7 are unpublished or mimeographed reports.

To avoid potential bias, each study was read before examining its summaries and annotations in LMW. (The exception to this was the long book by Glaser, for which the annotations were consulted to discover which portions of the book were relevant.) For each study, a written summary was prepared in the format of a LMW annotation. The research design was described by an extensive commentary in addition to the alphanumerical rating scheme employed in LMW. Further, reanalyses of the data were done wherever possible, and all pertinent critical comments were recorded.

The LMW annotations and summaries pertaining to each reference were then read, and a brief summary on the accuracy of each was written. Further data analysis or critical commentary was often carried out at this point, especially in those cases where sufficiently detailed data were reported. Also, if any annotation or summary appeared to involve more than the reference or study selected for inclusion in this assessment, the additional studies listed in the LMW bibliography were traced and reviewed.

Finally, a brief discussion was written for each bibliographic entry, summarizing the important problems with each study and describing how well the LMW summaries and annotations handled that study. (Six summaries were prepared for the Glaser book, one for each LMW summary, since different, although occasionally interrelated, projects were involved.) Although Lipton, Martinson, and Wilks claim to rely on the annotations for the preparation of their summaries, results reported in the summaries were often not mentioned in the annotations, and vice versa. As the assessment progressed, it became apparent that the LMW summaries were often more accurate and more readable than the annotations. Therefore, the summaries are emphasized in the discussions.

We do not attempt to point out every single error made by LMW or by the original authors, but rather to concentrate on major problems in experimental design and statistical analysis.

Because we were unable to locate several source documents, our conclusions are somewhat weaker than we had hoped they would be. On the basis of the works we examined, we find that LMW gives reasonably accurate summaries and annotations of the cited documents.

At least two studies they have chosen to include do not, in our opinion, meet their own criteria and thus should probably have been excluded. These studies claim to show positive or partially positive results.

The summaries and annotations in LMW often contain minor errors and omissions, and they occasionally either report inappropriate statistical tests or overinterpret reported data. These infelicities, however, only detract a small amount from the overall assessment provided in LMW. In only one instance did we feel that LMW did not give enough attention to a well-designed and properly implemented study.

We discovered several instances where statistical analyses in the original works were incorrect or inappropriate, and LMW almost always reported on these analyses without correction. The net effect of these occasionally serious analysis and reporting problems is to make rehabilitative treatment appear more successful in special circumstances than we believe to be warranted.

The LMW summaries of studies are often difficult to read, and comparative conclusions involving multiple studies are not as clear as we would like. Yet our overall impression is that, despite the errors, omissions, and infelicities noted above, LMW gives a reasonably accurate portrayal of the source documents we have examined. Moreover, the errors and omissions do not provide evidence of a systematic attempt to distort the assessment of the efficacy of correctional treatment, in either a positive or a negative direction.

The studies that we have been unable to obtain, according to LMW, rarely involved the use of rigorous methodologies. Given the unpublished and elusive nature of those studies, we doubt that, had we been able to review them, we would have changed our view regarding LMW's assessment.

The next section of the Appendix lists the items in the random samples; the final section presents our discussions of those items we located and our comments on the LMW annotations and summaries.

THE TWO 10-PERCENT SAMPLES OF SOURCE WORKS

This section lists the references that were part of our 10-percent samples of all references in LMW. All information in each reference is taken from LMW. Those references preceded by an asterisk (*) are additions to the two original lists of 17 that were required because annotations involved multiple works or were ambiguous. Those references preceded by a dagger (†) were not obtained and examined.

SAMPLE 1

1. Stuart Adams. Effectiveness of the Youth Authority Special Treatment Program: First Interim Report. Research Report No. 5. Mimeographed, California Youth Authority, March 1959.

2. Sir George Benson. Prediction methods and young prisoners. *British Journal of Delinquency* 9(3)(1959):192–199.

3. Cambridge University, Department of Criminal Science. *Detention in Remand Homes*. London: Macmillan, 1952.

4. Richard C. Ericson and David O. Moberg. The Rehabilitation of Parolees: The Application of Comprehensive Psychosocial Vocational Services in the Rehabilitation of Parolees. Minneapolis Rehabilitation Center, 1967.[1]

*†5. Richard C. Ericson *et al.* The Application of Comprehensive Psycho-social and Vocational Services in the Rehabilitation of Parolees. Period covered by report: October 1, 1964, through February 28, 1965. Mimeographed, Minneapolis Rehabilitation Center, March 1965.

†6. Richard C. Ericson *et al.* The Application of Comprehensive Psycho-social Vocational Services in the Rehabilitation of Parolees. Period covered by report: January 1, 1965, through December 31, 1965. Mimeographed, Minneapolis Rehabilitation Center, January 1966.

†7. D. M. Friedland. Group Counseling as a Factor in Reducing Runaway Behavior from an Open Treatment Institution for Delinquent and Pre-Delinquent Boys. Unpublished Ph.D. dissertation, New York University, 1960.

†8. A. Froelich. The Contribution of Probation Supervision toward the Modification of Certain Attitudes toward Authority Figures. Unpublished Ph.D. dissertation, New York University, 1957.

9. Daniel Glaser. *The Effectiveness of a Prison and Parole System*. New York: Bobbs-Merrill, 1964.

†10. Frank Jacobson and Eugene McGee. Englewood Project: Re-education: A Radical Correction of Incarcerated Delinquents. Mimeographed, Englewood, Colo., July 1965.

†11. Marvin E. Ketterling. Rehabilitation of Women in the Milwaukee County Jail: An Exploratory Experiment. Unpublished master's thesis, Colorado State College, 1965.

*12. Jerome Laulicht *et al.* Recidivism and its correlates: the problems of statistical research. *Berkshire Farm Monographs* 1(1)(1962):23–36.

13. Jerome Laulicht *et al.* Selection policies, recidivism, and types of rehabilitation programs in a training school. *Berkshire Farm Monographs* 1(1)(1962):37–48.

*14. Jerome Laulicht *et al.* A study of recidivism in one training school:

---

[1]Item 4 was substituted for items 5 and 6; see below.

implications for rehabilitation programs. *Berkshire Farm Monographs* 1(1)(1962):11–22.

15. Joseph L. Massimo and Milton F. Shore. The effectiveness of a comprehensive vocationally oriented psychotherapeutic program for adolescent delinquent boys. *American Journal of Orthopsychiatry* 33(4)(1963):634–642.

16. Martin J. Molof. Forestry Camp Study, Comparison of Recidivism Rates of Camp-Eligible Boys Randomly Assigned to Camp and to Institutional Programs. Research Report No. 53. California Youth Authority, October 1967 (Processed).

†17. Howard Martin Newburger. The Effect of Group Therapy upon Certain Aspects of the Behavior and Attitudes of Institutionalized Delinquents. Unpublished Ph.D. dissertation, New York University, 1952.

18. Ernest L. V. Shelley and Walter F. Johnson, Jr. Evaluating an organized counseling service for youthful offenders. *Journal of Counseling Psychology* 8(4)(1961):351–354.

19. Shlomo Shoham and Moshe Sandberg. Suspended sentences in Israel: an evaluation of the preventive efficacy of prospective imprisonment. *Crime and Delinquency* 10(1)(1964):74–83.

20. Marguerite Warren. The Community Treatment Project After Five Years. California Youth Authority, 1966a (Processed).

21. Marguerite Warren *et al.* Community Treatment Project, an Evaluation of Community Treatment for Delinquents: Fifth Progress Report. CTP Research Report No. 7. California Youth Authority, August 1966b (Processed).

*22. Marguerite Warren *et al.* Community Treatment Project, an Evaluation of Community Treatment for Delinquents: Sixth Progress Report, Part 2: The San Francisco Experiment. CTP Research Report No. 8, Part 2. California Youth Authority, September 1967 (Processed).[2]

SAMPLE 2

23. Stuart Adams. Development of a Program Research Service in Probation. Research Report No. 27. (Final Report, NIMH Project MH009718) Los Angeles County Probation Department, January 1966 (Processed).

[2]Item 22 was added initially but then not evaluated; see below.

24. LaMay Adamson and H Warren Dunham. Clinical treatment of male delinquents: a case study in effort and result. *American Sociological Review* 21(3)(1956):312–320.

25. Harry Brick, W. H. Doub, Jr., and W. C. Perdue. A further study of the effect of meprobamate on anxiety reactions in penitentiary inmates. *Journal of Social Therapy* 5(1–3)(1959):190–198.

†26. California Department of Corrections. Intensive Treatment Program: Second Annual Report. Prepared by Harold B. Bradley and Jack D. Williams. Mimeographed, Sacramento, Calif., December 1958.

†27. California Department of Corrections. Parole Work Unit Program: An Evaluation Report. A memorandum to the California Joint Legislative Budget Committee. Mimeographed, December 1966.

28. Charles Gersten. Group therapy with institutionalized juvenile delinquents. *Journal of Genetic Psychology* 80(1)(1952):35–64.

29. Charles Gerstenlauer. Group therapy with institutionalized male juvenile delinquents. *American Psychologist* 5(1950):325.

30. J. Douglas Grant and Marguerite Q. Grant. A group dynamics approach to the treatment of nonconformists in the Navy. *Annals of the American Academy of Political and Social Science* 322(2)(1959):126–135.

31. Charles L. Hulin and Brendan A. Maher. Changes in attitude toward law concomitant with imprisonment. *Journal of Criminal Law, Criminology and Police Science* 50(3)(1959):245–248.

†32. Bertram Johnson. An Analysis of Predictions of Parole Performance and of Judgments of Supervision in the Parole Research Project. Research Report No. 32. Mimeographed, California Youth Authority, December 1962.

†33. Newton McCravy, Jr., and Dolores S. Delehanty. Community Rehabilitation of the Younger Delinquent Boy, Parkland Nonresidental Group Center. Final report, Kentucky Child Welfare Research Foundation, Inc. Mimeographed. September 1967.

34. H. S. McWalter. A preliminary comparative study of E.C.T. and chloropromazine in the treatment of certain prison neuroses. *British Journal of Criminology* 2(4)(1962):381–385.

†35. Robert Martinson and W. J. O'Brien. Staff Training and Correctional Change: A Study of Professional Training in Correctional Settings. Mimeographed, School of Criminology, University of California, 1966.

†36. New York State Department of Corrections. Educational Achievement Research Report on Male Adolescent Offenders, June 1957–May 1958. Mimeographed. April 1961.

†37. Ruth Ochroch. An Evaluation of Comparative Changes in Personality in Adolescent Delinquent Boys and Girls in a Residential Treatment Setting. Unpublished Ph.D. dissertation, New York University, 1957.

38. Roy W. Persons. Psychotherapy with sociopathic offenders: an empirical evaluation. *Journal of Clinical Psychology* 21(2)(1965):205–207.

†39. John M. Stanton. An empirical study of the results of the special narcotics project. Part II of An Experiment in the Supervision of Paroled Offenders Addicted to Narcotic Drugs. Final report of the Special Narcotics Project, L. Stanely Clevenger, Administrative Director. New York State Division of Parole, 1956.

DISCUSSIONS OF THE LMW SUMMARIES AND ANNOTATIONS

1. Adams 1959 (summary, pp. 211–212, 281; annotation, pp. 214–215, 291).

Adams studied the effect of a psychiatric treatment program on the recidivism of disturbed juvenile delinquents at Los Giulicos School for girls.

The LMW summary and annotation are insufficiently critical of this study, failing to mention even the problems Adams himself discusses. The experimental group was poorly defined: 14 of its 47 members had received their psychiatric treatment independently of the treatment program whose effectiveness the study was to assess. The control group was even more poorly defined: from among those released the previous year, prior to the inception of the program, the investigators chose a group of girls whose clinical records revealed a severe or very severe need for treatment. The inter-rater reliability for judging the need for treatment was low; the highest κ coefficient for any pair of raters was 0.76, and for some pairs of raters it failed to differ significantly from zero. When the members of the treated group were themselves rated on their severity of treatment need, only 76.6 percent fell into the categories of "severe" or "very severe." Therefore, it is apparent that the makeup of the control group was rather arbitrary and that the control and experimental groups were not really comparable. The LMW summary does not mention these problems, and the annotation's rating suggests a high-quality design.

The LMW annotation and summary accurately report the findings of the study, but uncritically accept Adams's statistical analyses. In addition to the main finding of no difference in parole suspension rate between the treated and the untreated girls, Adams reports a number of ancillary conclusions restricted to the treatment group itself. He examines the relationship between parole success and such variables as length of treatment, type of therapy, type of therapist, estimated progress in therapy, use of tranquilizers, age, and race by means of two-dimensional contingency tables. Therefore, he is examining only the marginal distributions of a multidimensional relationship and not allowing for interactions. Although he frequently reports mean severity of need for treatment score for each cell of the tables, he does not include this important risk variable as a third category in the analyses themselves. Therefore, the influence of need for treatment is difficult to assess. Neither the LMW annotation nor the summary mentions these problems.

2. Benson 1959 (summary, p. 85; annotation, p. 89).

Sir George Benson compared Borstal training with imprisonment to determine their effects on recidivism for male youths in Great Britain. The study is *ex post facto*. Its major problem is the lack of comparability between the two samples: those sentenced to imprisonment were 2 years older on the average than the Borstal group, and their records were considerably worse. The two samples were obtained by different individuals for different time periods (1951–1952 for the prisoners and 1946–1947 for the Borstal trainees). Neither the LMW summary nor the annotation mentions this problem.

Benson controlled for risk level using five categories from the Mannheim-Wilkins Borstal formula, which is based on such factors as the kind and number of previous sentences, the longest period on one job, and whether or not the boy was living with his parents. Despite these controlling factors, no differences in recidivism were found between the imprisoned group and the Borstal group. Unlike the LMW annotation, the LMW summary fails to mention the control for risk level.

Both the LMW summary and the annotation emphasize that the imprisoned group served shorter terms than the Borstal group. There was, however, much overlap in the distributions of time served for the two groups, and Benson's comparison of the Borstal group with those prisoners whose terms were of similar length failed to reveal any difference in recidivism. The LMW summary and the annotation are misleading in their failure to report this finding. This failure is a minor matter considering the fact that Benson presented no statistical analyses and LMW reports none.

3. Cambridge University 1952 (summary, p. 84; annotation, p. 92).

The Cambridge University Department of Criminal Science studied the effect of detention in remand homes on recidivism for male youths. The book summarizes data on all male youths committed to remand homes in four cities (Birmingham, London, Liverpool, and Manchester) in Great Britain in 1945–1946. There is no control group of boys treated differently, and no before-after treatment comparisons are given. All comparisons are internal to the one group, i.e., younger versus older youths, first offenders versus recidivists, etc. Therefore, the study does not meet LMW's criterion 3, and we question its inclusion.

There is great variability in the role played by remand homes in the correctional system among the four cities; the LMW summary and annotation ignore this variability (see Cambridge University, Part II, pp. 29–40). The cities differ in the relative emphases placed on training and punishment, in their view as to which offenders are best served by remand homes, and in the relationship between detention in the remand home and subsequent probation when both are necessary. We carried out a log-linear-model analysis of the data in Table 45 (p. 38) of the source document (a four-dimensional contingency table involving recidivism, city, age of offender, and previous record), and we found that the age distribution of offenders, the distribution of number of previous offenses, and, most importantly, the success record differ from city to city. The significant three-way interaction—success by city by previous offenses—reveals that the cities have differential strengths in dealing with the various categories of offenders.

The great city-to-city variability suggests that meaningful (although confounded and hard-to-interpret) comparisons could have been made among the cities. This variability also means that the presentation in the LMW summaries and the annotations is not the best possible: LMW neglects city-to-city differences and gives only overall percentages.

The LMW summary and the annotation are accurate in relation to that part of the source-document information they present.

4. Ericson and Moberg 1967.
5 and 6. Ericson *et al.* 1967 (summary, pp. 176–179, 336, 427; annotation, pp. 181, 338–339, 430).

In the Ericson *et al.* study, the population was male parolees from a state prison. The treatment was a comprehensive flexible program providing social services, vocational counseling and placement, and psychological services. The dependent variables were recidivism, employment adjustment, and personality change. It was impossible to locate the two articles dealing with this project listed in the LMW bibliography, and after consultation with Ericson, another paper (item 4) was substituted.

Because of the three dependent variables, the study is summarized in LMW three times. The project was well designed. It used random allocation of subjects to treatment or control (standard parole supervision) conditions and was fairly large, involving 82 experimental (E) and 82 control (C) subjects.

The dependent variables had some weaknesses that the LMW summaries and the annotations do not discuss. Ericson and Moberg felt that the recidivism measure based on official data was potentially contaminated by the fact that the E's were under greater supervision than the C's during the period of treatment and were, therefore, more likely to be caught if they engaged in any illegal activity. The employment measure was based on self-report information obtained in an interview with the experimenters. The authors worried that the more favorable orientation of the E's toward the project could have affected their interviews. The information obtained in the interview was used by two panels of raters to score each man's vocational adjustment in terms of his personal potential as measured by IQ, previous training, employment record, etc. The LMW summary emphasizes the fact that these ratings were blind, but it neglects to mention that they were based on potentially biased self-report data gathered in a far from blind manner. Personality adjustment was measured by pretreatment and posttreatment MMPI scores. The article does not mention whether either administration or scoring of this instrument was blind.

The LMW summary on recidivism was fairly accurate. It pointed out the lack of significant difference between E's and C's. The information it presented on elapsed time to reimprisonment was not available in the paper reviewed here. The LMW summary fails to mention the high quality of the basic design.

The LMW summary on employment outcome is somewhat misleading. It does not mention the lack of statistical significance of the slight difference between E's and C's. This LMW summary discussed at some length a set of minor ancillary findings on the influence of some prerelease factors on recidivism and employment. In the paper reviewed here, the findings are merely stated and no data are given to support them. Since these findings refer to the E's and C's considered as one group, they are not relevant to the variables manipulated in the study, and it is not clear why they are allotted so much space. The LMW discussion of anxiety and of elapsed time to recidivism is not available in the paper reviewed here.

The LMW summary on personality adjustment is very good. Unlike the other two LMW summaries, it emphasizes the strength of the study and points out the lack of difference between E's and C's. It has one minor flaw: it implies that two institutions were involved, Minnesota State Prison and Minnesota State Reformatory for Men, whereas only one was used, the Minnesota State Reformatory for Men.

The LMW annotations all appear to err in the time of treatment and time of follow-up. They stated that the time in treatment was "up to one year." In fact, it was 1 year with the exception (not noted by LMW) of a small group of 18 E's, who, owing to special circumstances, received a minimal amount of treatment. The time in follow-up was not 1 year, as stated by LMW, but varied, depending on the time of randomization, and was as long as 19 months in some cases.

9a. Glaser 1964—Study pp. 302–330 (summary, p. 83; annotation, pp. 95–96).

To study the effect of time served on recidivism, Glaser used a 10-percent systematic sample of all men released from federal prisons in 1956, obtaining data on recidivism rates for several sentence lengths and for various categories of offenders.

As the LMW summary points out, the *ex post facto* nature of the study means that sentence length is hopelessly confounded with other variables, such as risk level. In reporting, Glaser controls separately for prior commitment, for age at release among those with no prior commitment, and for prison adjustment among those with some prior commitments. This collapsed form of the data makes a proper analysis impossible to carry out, although analyses of one three-way marginal table and two internal three-way tables are possible.

Glaser reports no formal analyses, and his discussion of these data is limited to observations such as "older inmates without previous incarceration were good risks regardless of how long they were confined, while those young inmates without previous incarceration who were released late were worse risks than those released early." This implied second-order interaction is not supported adequately by the data, as our own statistical analysis showed. The LMW summary and annotations repeat the misinterpretations and overinterpretations of the Glaser study and so are in a limited sense accurate. They do suggest a further misinterpretation of the data (not borne out by a more careful statistical analysis that we performed) to the effect that the curvilinear relationship between length of sentence and recidivism is more pronounced for those without than for those with prior commitments.

9b. Glaser 1964—Study pp. 162–163, population described pp. 19–20 (summary, p. 86; annotation, pp. 94–95).

In this study, Glaser considered the effect of custody grading on recidivism for young and adult U.S. federal prisoners.

The adult prisoners were a 10-percent systematic sample of all federal prisoners released in 1956. The young prisoners consisted of the first 322 cases completing full sentences under the Federal Youth Correction Act of 1954. The study is *ex post facto*. The effect of custody grading is confounded with risk level, since the lowest risk prisoners would be selected for the lowest level of custody.

The LMW summary reports these problems and accurately summarizes the findings. For both youths and adults, the level of custody is inversely related to success on parole.

The LMW summary and the annotation fail to report the special nature of the youth sample.

9c. Glaser 1964—Study pp. 277–279, sample described pp. 22–23 (summary, p. 188; annotation, pp. 200–201).

Glaser studied the effect of prison academic education on recidivism for a sample consisting of the first 322 juvenile males sentenced under the Federal Youth Correction Act of 1954. The study was *ex post facto*. The LMW summary points out the *ex post facto* nature of the study, but not the special nature of the sample. The data are presented in the form of two interrelated three-dimensional contingency tables. One shows how duration of prison school attendance relates to recidivism, controlling for time served. The other shows how achievement in prison education relates to recidivism, again controlling for time served. These tables are the two three-dimensional margins of a four-dimensional table.

Neither Glaser nor LMW reports any careful statistical analyses of the data. To fully understand the effects of attendance and education on recidivism, controlling for time served, one should analyze the full four-dimensional table. Since this was unavailable, we carried out separate log-linear-model analyses on the two three-dimensional marginal tables to explore the two effects of interest. The first table (Table 12.3 in Glaser) shows a significant (at the 0.05 level) effect linking time confined and recidivism and a marginally significant effect (p is just slightly greater than 0.05) linking prison school attendance and time served. The chances of success on parole are greater the less the time confined. The relationship between the duration of prison school attendance and success on parole is not significant, however. The discussion of this table in the LMW summary and annotation is confusing, and it is difficult to determine if the statements there are even consistent with the relatively simple findings of our analyses.

The second table (Table 12.4 in Glaser) shows the same relationship between time served and recidivism as the first, but, unlike the first, this table shows a significant effect linking the education variable, academic achievement or failure, and recidivism. Those youths improving academically were less apt to recidivate than those who did not improve. We note that the LMW summary devotes less space to the second table, which shows a significant effect, than to the first, which does not.

The analyses carried out by Glaser on these two tables are not really appropriate because they involve collapsing over the intervening variable, time confined. One fact that neither Glaser nor LMW points out directly is that the data involve youths from five different federal institutions, and any serious analysis must control for institution. This fact is alluded to in Glaser and in the LMW summary, but detailed data were not reported by Glaser and thus we could not carry out a proper analysis controlling for institution.

The LMW summary and annotation are reasonably accurate in relation to the information reported in the source.

9d. Glaser 1964—Studies p. 256, sample described Appendix D and p. 257, sample described pp. 19–20 (summary, pp. 190–191; annotation, p. 199).

Glaser studied the relationship between recidivism and work and training experiences in prison in two separate studies on two very different populations. The LMW summary and the annotation give the impression that only one study was involved. They are both *ex post facto* studies.

The first study was intended to compare a sample of returned violators released from federal prisons with a matched sample of successful releasees. Difficulties were encountered in matching, and the final group of successful releasees differed from the returned violators in several respects. They were older (median age 29.8 versus 26.4 for the returned violators), had much longer sentences (103 months versus 42 months), and had served longer time on those sentences (33 months versus 25 months). Many more of them were auto thieves (46 percent versus 27 percent). The two groups were similar in marital status, racial composition, and previous criminal record. (A full comparison is given in Table D.1, p. 546, in Glaser.)

This first study involved an interview in which the subjects were asked about their prison work and training experiences and their postrelease jobs to find out which prison experiences were useful later. The LMW summary accurately reports the findings from Glaser's Table 11.5 (p. 256), which shows the percentage of each group using various categories of prison experience on postrelease jobs. It fails to point out that the two groups differ in other ways than the success-failure dimension, as discussed above. It neglects to include the first three lines of Glaser's table, which show that, compared to the failures, relatively more of the successes had postrelease jobs that required training and relatively fewer were unemployed. The first three lines put the rest of the table in perspective. Unfortunately, none of Glaser's statistical tests can be repeated because of the form in which the data are reported. The LMW annotation is equally remiss in its failure to point out other differences in the two groups and in its neglect of the first three lines of the table.

The LMW summary then describes the second study. It involved a 10-percent systematic sample of all federal prison releasees in 1956. This is the sample that the LMW annotation improperly describes as common to both studies. Table 11.6 (p. 257) in Glaser shows the failure rates of these releasees for each of seven categories of the final prison work assignment. If one treats these data as a two-way contingency table, recidivism by work assignment, one finds no reason to assume any relationship between work assignment and failure rate. Glaser's contention that the lowest failure rates were associated with semiskilled work assignments and the highest failure rates were associated with influential jobs is not justified. (The statement is based on only one out of a set of multiple comparisons that need to be carried out with the data. Unless one treats this comparison in the context of the set of possible comparisons, one will mistakenly think it is justified.) The LMW summary and annotation repeat the Glaser contention and so in that limited sense are "accurate."

9e. Glaser 1964—Study pp. 275–279 (summary, p. 192; annotation, p. 200).

Glaser studied the relationship between enrollment in a prison academic education program and recidivism, using a 10-percent systematic sample of all men released from federal prisons in 1956. As with the other Glaser studies, this one is *ex post facto*. A major weakness here is that one does not know what factors may have been confounded with enrollment in prison education. Neither the LMW summary nor the annotation mentions this problem.

Glaser presented his findings in two tables (Table 12.1, p. 276, and Table 12.2, p. 277) that related recidivism and enrollment controlling for various factors. He performed a separate analysis for each level of each factor and the LMW summary concurred with his analysis. The data could better have been analyzed as five different three-dimensional contingency tables. We carried out such analyses, and we note that, since each of the tables contains the same data, the five analyses are not independent. In three of the five tables, the relationship between enrollment and recidivism is not significant at the 0.05 level. In the two tables in which the relationship is significant, recidivism by previous commitment by enrollment and recidivism by type of institution by enrollment, enrollment is found to have a small negative effect on success. (Strictly speaking, the significance of the effect of enrollment on recidivism can be evaluated only in the first of these tables, since in the second table the second-order interaction term involving the joint effect of enrollment and type of institution was significant at the 0.05 level.) The most reasonable conclusion to be drawn from these data (ignoring the *ex post facto* caveat) is that the effect of prison education on recidivism is either nonexistent or slightly negative.

The LMW summary and annotation err in emphasizing specific comparisons from Glaser's tables. With the exception of the data on institution type, there is no second-order interaction and, therefore, no reason to single out specific comparisons as important. This is again a reasonably accurate job of reporting the statements and analyses in Glaser. The one exception to this reporting accuracy in the LMW annotation is the test on the marginal negative relationship between enrollment and recidivism and the emphasis on this in the summary.

9f. Glaser 1964—Study pp. 250–252, sample described Appendix C, pp. 534 ff. (summary, p. 342; annotation, pp. 344–345).

By interviewing a panel of men recently released from U.S. federal prisons, Glaser's research team studied the relationship between prison work experience and postrelease work experience. The interviews dealt with the influence of prison work on postrelease employment: the researchers tried to determine to what extent and in what manner prison work experience was helpful after release.

This study does not fit the LMW definition of a study: the data summarized come from only one group, those men who had both prison work experience and postrelease jobs, and so the study is not a comparison of several groups treated differently. It is also not a before-after comparison within a group because there is no dependent variable that is measured both before and after the treatment, which is work experience in prison. The LMW summary and annotation ignore this problem, but are otherwise accurate.

12, 13, and 14. Laulicht *et al.* 1962 (summary, p. 248; annotation, p. 261).

Laulicht and his coauthors compared the recidivism rate at Berkshire Farm, an institution for male juvenile delinquents, at two different time periods with two different treatment regimes. Initially the institution had a child-care program stressing rehabilitation and education services. In 1954, it adopted a milieu therapy program emphasizing group therapy and individual counseling. This study was, therefore, *ex post facto*, and treatment effects are confounded with time trends and with the differences in the subject populations.

The LMW summary and annotation are slightly misleading regarding both the quality of the study and the advantages of milieu therapy. Neither mentions the finding that the child-care program success rate (60 percent) was significantly lower than the milieu therapy success rate (75 percent). Of course, this comparison of overall success rates is difficult to interpret because the length of the follow-up period tends to be shorter for the milieu therapy group. The findings that are reported in the summary and annotation are the success rates given in the published articles for comparable follow-up periods.

The LMW summary and the annotation neglect to mention the many differences the authors found between the two populations at the two time periods. Although the statistical problem of multiple comparison makes the differences between the two populations difficult to evaluate, it is probably safe to conclude, as did Laulicht *et al.*, that the milieu therapy delinquents were at greater risk for recidivism. They tended to be older at admission, to have received treatment for shorter periods of time, and to be released at a younger age. These last two factors were associated with higher risk of recidivism. The milieu therapy program also treated more youths with prior records or more severe offenses. The lack of difference between the two treatment periods should be seen in this context, as Laulicht *et al.* point out. The *ex post facto* nature of this study is ameliorated by the fact that the authors examined many risk factors in their two populations to see which ones might be confounded with the treatment differences.

With the exceptions noted above, the LMW summary and annotation of this study are substantially accurate, although they do not quite do justice to the complexities explored by these authors.

15. Massimo and Shore 1963 (summary, pp. 212, 247–248, 369, 439–440; annotation, pp. 220, 349, 369–370, 441).

The Massimo and Shore article describes a study of the effects of an individual multidimensional counseling program on juvenile-delinquent, school-dropout males in three suburban areas of Boston. Because of its four dependent variables—recidivism, vocational adjustment, educational achievement, and personality adjustment—this study has multiple annotations and summaries in LMW.

The major strength of the study was its rigorous design. The assignment to treatment or control (no treatment) group was random, and a postrandomization check revealed that the two groups did not differ significantly on age, IQ, or socioeconomic level. The administration and scoring of the personality and educational achievement tests, both pretreatment and posttreatment, were done by an experienced psychologist who knew neither the treatment group of any boy nor the aims of the study. The high quality of this experiment was mentioned in the first LMW summary only.

The study has two weaknesses. First, its size was small: there were only 20 subjects in all. Second, the treatment involved many different facets—job placement and counseling, insight psychotherapy, remedial education, an informal, flexible, noncompulsory approach, and the enthusiasm and personality of the single therapist. Therefore, one cannot know which factors induced the changes that occurred. The small size was mentioned in the first LMW summary only and the multidimensional nature in the third only.

The experimental (E) subjects did better than the control (C) subjects on all four measures. The first two LMW summaries accurately report the findings; the third LMW summary points out the significant improvement made by the E's in educational achievement, but does not mention the fact that the improvement of the E's was significantly greater than the improvement of the C's on all four measures of educational achievement. In fact, the C's significantly declined on three of the four measures. The fourth LMW summary indicates that the E's improved in personality adjustment as measured by the TAT, but the C's did not. This conclusion is subtly misleading. Massimo and Shore's analysis (see p. 638) showed that the E group contained significantly more individuals who improved than did the C group. The LMW annotation corresponding to this summary (p. 441) gives an interpretation similar to that of Massimo and Shore.

All LMW summaries except the third (and all annotations) discuss a 2- and a 3-year follow-up. These are not mentioned in the Massimo and Shore article as given in the bibliography.

16. Molof 1967 (summary, pp. 251–252; annotation, p. 265).

Molof compared the effect of placement in a forestry camp with the effect of placement in an institution on recidivism in male youths; he found no difference. The LMW summary and annotation accurately describe this study, but are misleading in their discussion of its implications and its experimental quality.

The LMW summary considers simultaneously two studies of forestry camps, this one by Molof and another by Roberts. It states that the "total camp population was not representative of the institutional population and may, in fact, have been made up of slightly higher-risk" offenders than the institutions, and it concludes that the lack of difference in recidivism rates may therefore "indicate a positive contribution by the camps." Molof's introduction, however, emphasized the low-risk nature of the camp population. In his description of his own study samples, he pointed out the lack of difference in expected rates of recidivism (based on variables related to risk level) between those assigned to camp and those assigned to institution, although he did not perform statistical tests. Roberts's study has a separate annotation, and his forestry camp group may have been at higher risk of recidivism than his institutionalized group; this was not the case in the Molof study.

The experimental design of Molof's study does not deserve the high rating it receives in the LMW annotation. Although assignment to camp or institution was random, the assignment to the specific institution or camp was determined by a panel of one or two members of the Youth Authority Board or their representatives. Because the panel members were aware of the nature of the study, there were opportunities for biased selection. The LMW annotation does not mention this problem, but is otherwise accurate.

18. Shelley and Johnson 1961 (summary, pp. 174–175, 225, 426, 428, 448; annotation, pp. 182, 240, 430, 464).

Shelley and Johnson studied the effect of organized counseling services in two prison camps on personality change and the effect of the resultant personality change on recidivism. The study is annotated and summarized four times because of its two independent variables, individual counseling and group counseling, and its two dependent variables, personality change and recidivism.

The study had several major weaknesses. First, of the two prison camps studied, one had the organized counseling program and the other did not. Therefore, the treatment effect is confounded with intercamp differences, and it is not safe to ascribe the differences between E's and C's to the counseling program. The authors do not state the method of assignment to the two camps; presumably, it was not random. The authors state that they matched the E's and C's on age, intelligence, offense, and criminal history, but give no statistics as to how good the matching was.

Second, the "writer" (which one is not mentioned) administered the personality test, the TAT, himself (both pretreatment and posttreatment) and must have known who the E's and C's were. This lack of blindness may have biased the results.

Third, the influence of the treatment on recidivism cannot be inferred from this design. The authors measured the effect of the treatment on personality change and then the relationship between personality change and recidivism.

None of the LMW summaries mentions the first two weaknesses. In fact, the fourth summary gives the misleading impression that the counseling program took place at both camps. The first two summaries do note the third weakness, but the third summary calls the effort "a well-designed study" (p. 426) and indicates that it "warrants replication" (p. 428).

The time in treatment is 6 months. The article, however, states that the amount of counseling is equivalent to 52 hours of group counseling and 38 hours of individual counseling per year. All of the LMW summaries but the first give this information in such a way as to convey the idea that the treatment period was 1 year. The LMW annotations give the correct 6 months figure. LMW is modestly accurate on this study, but it attributes a considerably higher quality to the study than it should have.

19. Shoham and Sandberg 1964 (summary, pp. 52, 54–55; annotation, pp. 72–73).

Shoham and Sandberg studied the effect of probation on recidivism in Israel using an *ex post facto* design. The experimenters compared a systematic sample of those receiving a suspended sentence during 1955–1956 with a random sample of offenders convicted during that time period whose sentences were not suspended. The two groups were not comparable. Without reporting statistical tests or significance levels employed, the authors claimed that the groups did not differ in age, sex, or occupation, but did differ in national origin. Israeli courts tend not to impose suspended sentences on Israeli Arabs, and they tend to impose suspended sentences more often on Oriental and Sephardic Jews than on Ashkenazi Jews: the LMW summary recognizes this problem. But there is an additional problem, not mentioned in the LMW summary or annotation. The two groups may have differed also in the extent of their previous criminal records. At one point (p. 79), the authors stated that there was no significant difference in the two groups in the distribution of previous convictions. They also state (p. 83), however, that of those with four or more prior convictions, the median number of convictions for those receiving suspended sentences was five, less than that for the control group, seven. This statement would imply that the controls had worse criminal records, but is somewhat difficult to interpret.

The main finding of the study is that recidivism did not differ significantly in the two groups. The annotation reports that a *p*-value greater than 0.05 is associated with a χ^2 statistic for this finding. Such a statistic is not available in the original paper. In fact, the number in the control group is not even given. A table (p. 82) gives the success rate for each of a number of categories of age and number of previous convictions for the control group and for the suspended sentence group. There appears to be little difference between the groups, but insufficient information is provided to allow us to judge statistical significance.

The LMW summary gives an accurate summary of the table and points to the lack of information for statistical significance. It fails to point out that the higher success rate for those receiving suspended sentences compared with the controls in the category of offenders with more than four prior convictions may be misleading, as noted above. In that category, those given suspended sentences had fewer prior convictions than those sent to prison. The annotation also fails to mention this point.

20, 21, and 22. Warren *et al.* 1966a (summary, pp. 421–422, 548; annotation, p. 425) 1966b (summary, pp. 29–37; annotation, pp. 73–80) 1967 (see below).

The first two articles (1966a, 1966b) are reports on the same study, the California Community Treatment Project. Delinquent youth, both male and female, were classified into one of nine groups, based on their interpersonal maturity level, and then randomly assigned to either institutional treatment followed by standard parole or to one of a variety of community-based treatments, differentially adapted to maturity level, and small case load parole supervision. Various measures of recidivism and changes in personality test scores were the dependent variables. The community-based treatment was found to be superior and cheaper for many maturity-level categories.

The LMW summaries and annotations for this study are the longest and most detailed we examined, and they are quite accurate. In particular, they point out the two major flaws of the study. First, the recidivism measure was contaminated because the correctional officials were aware of the identities of control and experimental subjects. Thus their decisions on parole revocation, suspension, discharge, etc., could be biased. Indeed, as is noted by LMW, the experimental subjects committed more offenses and more severe offenses prior to revocation or unfavorable discharge, and the control subjects had their parole revoked or were unfavorably discharged for less serious offenses than the experimental subjects.

Second, the study design makes the findings difficult to interpret. No delinquents were assigned to community-based treatments thought inappropriate to their maturity level. Therefore, it is impossible to tell to what degree differences between control subjects and experimental subjects are due to differences between institution and community-based treatment and to what degree to the selection of an "appropriate" treatment for the experimental subjects.

The major failing of the LMW summaries, and, to a lesser extent, the annotations, is that they present the data in an oversimplified fashion. Because the study took place in two communities, Sacramento and Stockton, and used both boys and girls, an appropriate analysis would involve data in the form of a five-way breakdown—community by sex by maturity level by treatment (experimental or control) by outcome. Although the source documents do not show an analysis based on such a breakdown, they usually present broken-down frequencies so that readers may draw their own conclusions. The LMW summaries and annotations present the maturity level by treatment by outcome table of findings and emphasize overall treatment differences. Such collapsing may well be inappropriate, and LMW seems unaware of any potential problems.

Warren (1966b) contains some information on a closely related experiment in San Francisco, which is not discussed by LMW. Thus our initial examination of the materials suggested the potential relevance of Warren (1967), which deals solely with the San Francisco study. Since this material is summarized and annotated separately, however, we chose not to include an evaluation as part of this entry.

23. Adams 1966.

Adams (1966) describes "Project 00718," a set of research projects done at the Los Angeles County Probation Department starting in 1962. The LMW review annotates and summarizes three of the studies described therein. All the studies are reported in detail in other publications, and Adams's article presents only summaries. Therefore, the information it gives is frequently insufficient for an adequate critical assessment, but the LMW summaries and annotations accurately reflect the available information.

23a. "Experimental Assessment of the Las Palmas Program" (summary pp. 242, 244; annotation, p. 254).

Adams compared detention in Las Palmas, a multidimensional milieu-therapy institutional program for female juvenile delinquents, with a control treatment (detention in Juvenile Hall) and found a slight and statistically insignificant reduction in recidivism.

The LMW summary and annotation are basically accurate. Although recognizing its *ex post facto* nature, the annotation categorizes the design as having neither matching nor random allocation of subjects to treatment. In fact, however, the article states that the project staff employed group matching procedures in finding a suitable set of control subjects. The nature of these matching procedures, however, is not specified. A comparison of previous detection records in the two groups was made, but no differences were found. The LMW summary and annotation do not mention this comparison.

23b. "Community Program for Girls" (summary, pp. 26, 27, 29; annotation, p. 62).

Adams studied the effect of probation case load size on recidivism in delinquent girls and found that case loads of 15 were more successful and less costly than the usual case loads of 50 girls.

The LMW summary and annotation are basically accurate. Neither, however, discusses the poor quality of the design of the control group. Matching, rather than randomization, was used in assigning the girls to the two levels of case load, and the two groups differed in age, ethnic characteristics, number of detentions, total days detained, and the average duration of detention, albeit in different directions in terms of risk on different variables. The size and the statistical significance of these differences were not mentioned, nor were data provided from which they could be assessed. The LMW summary and annotation report the basic findings and, in addition, give some test statistics not reported in the article itself.

23c. "Intensive Probation Services for Boys" (summary, pp. 26, 27, 28, 29; annotation, pp. 62–63).

Adams studied the effect of case load size on recidivism in juvenile delinquent males and found that 15-boy case loads resulted in less recidivism than 75-boy case loads.

The LMW summary and annotation are basically accurate, but contain minor errors. First, neither mentions that this study was still in progress at the time of writing and the findings were therefore preliminary. Second, this study did use randomization in assigning boys to the case load conditions; the LMW summary mentions that five of the studies involving youthful offenders used randomization, but does not indicate which ones. The LMW annotation gives this project's design a high rating but does not explicitly mention the randomization. Third, Adams reports only summary statistics on the recidivism measures. No statistical assessment is given, and the LMW annotation and summary reflect this omission.

Two of the measures given, the proportion of each group ever redetained in Juvenile Hall (41.2 percent of the experimental group and 44.2 percent of the control group) and the proportion of each group placed outside their homes in camps or institutions (26.1 percent of the experimental group and 42.5 percent of the control group), may be analyzed by categorical data methods. When that is done, one finds that the former is not significant ($\chi^2 = 0.22$, df $= 1$, $p > 0.50$) but that the latter is ($\chi^2 = 7.18$, df $= 1$, $p < 0.01$). Insufficient information is available on the third measure, length of time of detention, to assess its statistical significance. Otherwise, the LMW summary and annotation are accurate.

24. Adamson and Dunham 1956 (summary, p. 212; annotation, p. 218).

Adamson and Dunham attempted to answer the question: Does referring a juvenile delinquent to a court-affiliated clinic for treatment influence the probability that he will be rearrested when he becomes an adult? They based their conclusions on data from a random sample of cases treated by the Wayne County Clinic in each of four years: 1930, 1935, 1940, and 1948. The three major findings are discussed in the LMW summary and in the annotation.

First, despite increases over time in the number of clinic staff per juvenile referred, there were no significant differences in recidivism rates among the four years studied. Both the LMW summary and the annotation handle this finding adequately.

Second, a comparison of those receiving psychiatric treatment with those not receiving psychiatric treatment revealed no significant differences in recidivism rates.

Both the LMW summary and the annotation state that this was a comparison of treatment with no treatment. The clinic, however, contained social workers and psychologists as well as psychiatrists, and it seems unreasonable to assume that those who received no psychiatric treatment received no treatment at all. The original article is ambiguous on this point. The table from which the recidivism rates were taken (Table 4,

p. 318) treated all four years as one sample. The potential dangers in this collapsing of data are mentioned neither in the LMW summary nor in the annotation. Adamson and Dunham discuss the problem of the *ex post facto* nature of the comparison of psychiatric treatment with no treatment. They recognize that treatment condition and risk level were confounded, since the poorest risks were most likely to receive treatment. The LMW summary does not mention this problem, but the annotation does label the study as *ex post facto*.

Third, among those receiving psychiatric treatment, the recidivism rate was inversely proportional to the amount of treatment, classified as "none," "limited," "moderate," and "intensive."

Table 6 (p. 319) presents the recidivism rates for various categories of treatment level. Like Table 4, it treats all four years as one sample. Neither the LMW summary nor the annotation mentions this problem. The comparison is *ex post facto*. Quite possibly, different types of delinquents receive different amounts of treatment and confounding has occurred, as Adamson and Dunham point out. The LMW summary is silent on this point, but the annotation correctly describes the research design. About 50 percent of the cases receiving "moderate" and "intensive" psychiatric care come from the most recent sample, 1948, and many of them were not old enough at the time of the study to have adult rearrest records. Therefore, the recidivism rates quoted for those groups receiving more psychiatric treatment may be artificially depressed. Neither the LMW summary nor the annotation mentions this fact.

The LMW treatment of this study is reasonably accurate but not sufficiently critical.

25. Brick, Doub, and Perdue 1959 (summary, p. 477; annotation, p. 482).

Brick, Doub, and Perdue did a series of studies to investigate the effect of chemotherapy on prison inmates. Their 1959 project dealt with the effect of meprobamate on neurotic inmates. Personality change was measured by pretreatment and posttreatment administration of the Rorschach test.

The LMW summary describes the study as not classically designed but methodologically sound. Since it involved random assignment of subjects to treatment or control groups, the use of a placebo for control, and pretreatment and posttreatment personality testing, it should meet the definition of a classically designed study. Our assessment of the research design agrees with the rating in the LMW annotation.

But the study has a serious methodological problem mentioned in neither the LMW summary nor the annotation. Counter to the authors' contention, the study was not double-blind because the meprobamate and placebo pills were of different colors. This procedural error may well have contaminated the results of the experiment.

The LMW summary and annotation accurately report the findings of this study, namely a greater reduction in neuroticism among experimental than among control subjects. (They neglect to mention that this difference was statistically significant.) The LMW treatment of the study was too uncritical.

28. Gersten 1952 (summary, p. 443; annotation, p. 458)

Gersten studied the effect of group therapy on personality adjustment in institutionalized male juvenile delinquents. The personality adjustment was measured by pretreatment and posttreatment administration of the Wechsler-Bellevue Intelligence Scale, the Stanford School Achievement Test, Maller's Personality Sketches, the Haggerty-Olson-Wickman Behavior Rating Schedules, and the Rorschach Test.

The LMW summary and annotation contain two flaws. First, the research design is not of sufficiently high quality to warrant the commendation given in the LMW summary or the high rating given in the annotation. Randomization does not appear to have been used. Instead, each experimental subject was paired with a control on age and IQ, and the two groups were matched on educational, socioeconomic, racial, and family background variables. The author does not state how these variables were defined, nor does he present any information on the composition of the resulting groups relevant to the matching variables. The author does not directly discuss the question of the blindness of administration and scoring of the tests, but his description of his experimental methods leads us to believe that none of the tests were treated in a blind fashion.

Second, the LMW summary and annotation accurately report the major conclusions of Gersten's article, but our reanalysis of the original data does not support all of these conclusions. Table 1 (pp. 44–45) presents the pretherapy and posttherapy scores for all the experimental and control subjects on all measures but the Rorschach Test. When we used the difference between pretreatment and posttreatment scores as a measure of improvement and compared the two groups via a series of t-tests, we found no significant differences (at the 0.05 level) in improvement on any of the four measures. The original data may not have been presented accurately, however, since several averages we calculated do not agree with those reported by the author. Gersten claims to have found a significant difference in improvement in IQ ($p < 0.05$) and Stanford Test scores ($p < 0.01$), but no significant differences on the other two measures between the groups. The LMW summary and annotation accurately repeat the results reported by Gersten.

The LMW discussion of this article was basically accurate but uncritical.

29. Gerstenlauer 1950 (summary, p. 443; annotation, pp. 458–459).

Gerstenlauer studied the effect of group psychotherapy on institutionalized juvenile delinquent males, measuring changes in IQ, educational achievement, and personality. The LMW summary introduces this as one of two studies (of a group of five) in which "most confidence can be placed" since "subjects were matched with controls." The article itself, however, is a brief (four-paragraph) abstract of a talk given by Gerstenlauer at the fifty-eighth annual meeting of the American Psychological Association. It merely outlines the study. Insufficient information is given for any confidence to be placed in the study. The LMW annotation describes the group therapy as "traditionally oriented" and the LMW summary calls it "dynamically oriented," but the article itself merely states that it was "activity-interview group therapy." The LMW annotation claims that independent experts rated the Rorschach tests, and the summary says that experts did so, but the article itself does not mention who did the rating.

Both the LMW annotation and the summary give an unwarranted impression of high quality for this study, but accurately report the actual findings. (It would be hard to misreport a total of four paragraphs!)

30. Grant and Grant 1959 (summary, p. 504; annotation, pp. 507–508).

Grant and Grant studied the effect of a milieu therapy program for adult Navy and Marine male offenders on "later duty success." They examined three factors: the maturity level of the therapy group (high, low, or mixed high and low), the effectiveness of the therapy group leader, and the condition of a stable or a changing group leadership.

The study is seriously flawed by the absence of a control group. All the subjects were given milieu therapy in some group under some combination of the three factors described above. There is therefore no way to tell if the milieu therapy itself had any effect. The LMW summary and annotation do not mention this point, but do accurately convey the major findings reported by the article. But Grant and Grant made two errors in their data analysis: they employed analysis-of-variance techniques for categorical data, and they treated the individual subject as the unit of analysis whereas the therapy group itself forms the more natural unit. Our reanalysis of their data reproduces none of the effects they discuss. Specifically, the much-emphasized interaction between supervisory effectiveness and subject's maturity level disappears. The LMW summary and annotation do not mention these statistical errors.

The LMW discussion of this study is accurate, but fails to be critical of serious shortcomings and faulty analyses.

31. Hulin and Maher 1959 (summary, p. 11; annotation, p. 417).

Hulin and Maher studied the relationship between time served and attitudes toward the law, both personal and abstract, in a group of maximum security state penitentiary inmates. They found a significant ($p < 0.05$) negative correlation between time served and positiveness of attitude for both personal and abstract attitudes.

The LMW summary handles this study very well. It points out the danger in trying to assert a causal relationship on the basis of a correlation. The study is *ex post facto* and therefore possibly confounded. It is also quite probable that the inmates with more negative attitudes served more time because of those attitudes (i.e., they may have been denied parole) rather than vice versa. The summary concludes with a few pages of well thought-out criticism of the general area of attitude research on prison inmates.

The LMW annotation is also quite accurate. It errs only in the "time in treatment" category. It reports the range of the set of means of time served for the four different groups of offender types. The range of actual time served, however, must be greater than the range of the means.

The LMW treatment of this study is accurate and thoughtful.

34. McWalter 1962 (summary, p. 330; annotation, pp. 331–332).

McWalter compared the effect of electroconvulsive therapy (ECT) with the drug chlorpromazine on Scottish prison inmates with anxiety-depression.

The LMW summary and annotation give the study a better rating than it deserves. The summary calls it "carefully executed." The annotation suggests that the research design involved either randomization or matching: actually, however, alternate patients were allocated to ECT or chlorpromazine treatment. The dependent variable, length of stay in the prison hospital, has several problems. Nurses, the prison medical officer, a psychiatrist, and the patient himself all provided input into the decision on patient improvement, which determined time of release. Because all of them knew the treatment used on the patient, there is the possibility of bias. Since ECT treatment is considerably more unpleasant than chlorpromazine, a patient receiving that treatment might "recover" more quickly simply to avoid the treatment. The LMW summary and annotation do not mention these confounding influences on the dependent variable.

McWalter categorized each patient as an introvert or an extrovert. His data lend themselves to a two-way factorial analysis of variance (treatment by personality type) with unequal cell sizes. When we analyzed the data in this way, we found that both main effects were significant, but that the interaction was not. Patients receiving ECT spent significantly fewer days in the hospital than patients receiving chlorpromazine ($p < 0.01$). Extroverts were hospitalized a significantly shorter time than introverts ($p < 0.05$). McWalter's analysis was based on a series of t-tests, and he came to substantially the same conclusion as we did. The LMW summary accurately reports these findings. The LMW annotation reports a reanalysis of the data that disagrees with ours regarding the significance of the personality variable.

The LMW treatment of this study was accurate but uncritical.

38. Persons 1965 (summary, pp. 308, 438; annotation, pp. 310, 441).

Using a sample of inmates in a federal prison, Persons studied the effect of individual psychotherapy on personality change and on institutional adjustment.

The study was well designed. The subjects were a random sample of the prison population and were randomly assigned to one of the two treatment conditions: experimental, which was individual psychotherapy, or control. The personality tests, the Taylor Manifest Anxiety Scale, the Delinquency Scale, and the Personal Experience and Attitude Questionnaire, were administered both pretreatment and posttreatment to both groups. Although the high quality of the design is not specifically mentioned in either LMW summary, both annotations give it a top rating.

The study has several flaws, however, and these are mentioned neither in the LMW annotations nor in the summaries. First, the treatment is insufficiently described. There is no description of the nature of the individual psychotherapy, other than the fact it occurred twice a week for 10 weeks and used an eclectic approach. Second, after each interview, the experimental subjects completed Snyder's Client Affect Scale. Presumably, the control subjects did not do so. Therefore, it is possible that the experimental subjects showed greater improvement in the personality measures not because their personalities actually changed more, but because they had had greater exposure to personality-type tests during treatment. Third, Persons does not mention whether the scoring and the administration of the personality tests was blind. The pretreatment testing occurred prior to randomization and therefore was necessarily blind. Presumably, posttreatment testing was not blind.

The measure of institutional adjustment, number of disciplinary reports issued by the institution's staff, was presumably not blind. The summary deals well with this problem.

The LMW treatment of this study was basically accurate but insufficiently critical.

COMMISSIONED
PAPERS

Assessing Outcomes of Medical Care: Some Lessons for Criminal Offender Rehabilitation

ALLYSON ROSS DAVIES

INTRODUCTION

Many reviews of the literature on the effectiveness of programs to rehabilitate criminal offenders suggest that such programs have had little or no effect on reducing criminal behavior following imprisonment (see, for example, Bailey 1966, Conrad 1975, Lipton *et al.* 1975, Lundman *et al.* 1976, Robison and Smith 1971). When evaluations yield such results, three explanations, perhaps not mutually exclusive but very different in their implications for future policy in criminal justice, may be offered.

The first explanation is that rehabilitation programs, almost irrespective of their different intervention strategies, settings, or prisoner

Allyson Ross Davies, M.P.H., is a health services researcher, The Rand Corporation.

NOTE: I would like to thank the Panel chairman, Lee Sechrest, and John Conrad, senior fellow, Center on Crime and Justice, the Academy for Contemporary Problems, for their helpful comments on an earlier version of the paper. I would also like to thank two Rand colleagues: Robert H. Brook, M.D., Sc.D., who directed the research on which this paper is based, for his review and comments, and Joan Petersilia, for her review, comments, and helpful suggestions as to appropriate citations in the criminal justice literature.

populations, actually have failed to achieve their intended outcome,[1] namely, restoration of the criminal's ability to function in a society that does not condone criminal behavior. Those that take this position are likely to reject the "medical model" of criminal behavior, which holds that such behavior is akin to disease and can be effectively treated by some intervention designed to restore the criminal to noncriminal behavior patterns. Having abandoned the treatment option of rehabilitation, advocates of this interpretation may argue in favor of some type of punishment that will remove the criminal from society for a "just" and specified length of time, through such means as flat-term or mandatory sentencing (see Fogel 1975, Twentieth Century Fund, Inc. 1976, von Hirsch 1976).

The second explanation for the lack of positive results in criminal offender rehabilitation is that the types of interventions tried thus far have not been successful, but that others not yet tried may prove so. Those that espouse this interpretation may argue, for example, that rehabilitation programs should be more carefully matched to the types of offenders "most likely to benefit" from them, much like medical treatments are tailored to the specific characteristics of a particular patient and disease.[2] Thus, advocates of this position have not given up the "medical model," nor the treatment option, but are searching for new types of rehabilitation.

The third explanation for the lack of positive results in criminal offender rehabilitation may be that the evaluation techniques were themselves faulty, and therefore no conclusions should be drawn. Proponents of this viewpoint may argue, for example, that an evaluation did not take into account all aspects of the rehabilitation effort in measuring its effectiveness, did not control for differences within the

---

[1] This discussion assumes throughout that the primary objective, and therefore the primary outcome measure, of criminal offender rehabilitation programs is reduction or elimination of further criminal behavior on the part of the offender. The variety of rehabilitation programs that have been attempted imply a variety of "secondary" outcomes for measurement. For example, appropriate outcomes for measuring the effectiveness of a vocational training program mounted as part of a rehabilitation effort would include acquisition of new job skills, finding and holding a job following release from prison, and many others in addition to a measure of reduction or elimination of further criminal behavior.

[2] Research is being carried out at The Rand Corporation in Santa Monica, California (Joan Petersilia, principal investigator) on the issue of tailoring rehabilitation programs to fit the characteristics of the offender by identifying "those most likely to benefit" from specific types of programs.

prisoner population that might have confounded the measurement of actual outcomes, or (more seriously) did not appropriately define or measure the outcome or outcomes of interest. Advocates of this interpretation are likely to propose a policy of finding or developing better or more appropriate methods of evaluating the effectiveness of rehabilitation programs. Such methods would enable them to obtain empirical evidence of the success or failure of different types of rehabilitation programs in achieving the desired outcomes. Depending on the nature of the evidence, results of such evaluations could be used to guide policy decisions regarding whether the "medical model" of criminal offender rehabilitation should be abandoned, what types of rehabilitation programs are effective and should be promoted, and what new rehabilitative techniques might be tested. For one side of the issue, see Adams (1975, 1976); for the other side, see Martinson (1976).

This paper was prepared for those who want to develop potentially better or more appropriate methods of evaluating the outcomes of criminal offender rehabilitation programs. It describes a method of evaluating the quality of medical care interventions that is based on information about patient outcomes[3] and highlights certain features of the method that might make it relevant to problems of measuring outcomes of criminal offender rehabilitation programs. The author is a health services researcher with only cursory familiarity with the literature on criminal rehabilitation and specific problems associated with evaluation of such programs. The paper is directed to an audience composed of those in the criminal offender rehabilitation field who are familiar with such programs and their evaluation; the way in which the method described herein might be translated to that field is left open to those with the greater familiarity.

In its broad outline, the outcome evaluation model described in this paper is similar to the comparative evaluation model termed "real outcomes versus expected outcomes," by Adams (1975). Briefly, the model involves developing expected standards of performance—on the basis of data from previous interventions, expectations defined by professionals or society at large, or some combination of these—against which to compare the performance of the program being evaluated.

---

[3] Developmental research on this method was done by The Rand Corporation under Contract No. HRA 230-75-0112, National Center for Health Services Research, U.S. Department of Health, Education, and Welfare. The description is based on the final contract report (see Brook *et al.* 1976).

BACKGROUND

Prior to describing the evaluation method itself, some background information and definition of terminology are necessary. Assessments of medical care traditionally rely on one or more of three basic types of information about medical care: structure, process, and outcome. Structural measures are concerned with innate characteristics of facilities or providers in the medical care system. Process measures are concerned with what a provider does to and for a patient and how well a patient is moved through the system. Outcome measures concern what happened to the patient as a result of care, in terms of treatment, palliation, cure, or rehabilitation. In criminal offender rehabilitation, structure might refer to characteristics of the parole, prison, or probation systems and their personnel; process to what these systems are designed to do to and for criminal offenders; and outcomes to such variables as recidivism, vocational success, and the offender's adjustment to the outside community.[4]

Information on outcomes is generally considered to be the most valid for purposes of quality assessment, given that the purpose of medical care is to maintain or improve health status. Thus, judging quality in terms of outcomes achieved is considered the most direct way to evaluate medical care. To date, however, most attempts to evaluate quality have focused on the structure or process of care, particularly the latter. These studies share the common assumption that adequate resources and technology (structure) contribute to adequate treatment (process) that in turn results in favorable health status (outcome). But there is a major problem in measuring quality through use of process variables alone: the relationship between the medical care process and health status is not always direct. In many cases, it may be so confounded by intervening variables—such as patient compliance— that adequate treatment may not result in good outcomes. On the other hand, apparently poor treatment may result in good outcomes if the process measures selected are invalid or incorrectly measured. Therefore, those in medical care evaluation have turned their attention to developing methods of evaluation that rely directly on information about the outcomes of care. As will be seen, there are also problems in determining how much of the outcomes achieved can be attributed to or explained by the quality of medical care intervention.

---

[4] See Adams (1975) for a more extensive listing of outcome criteria that have been used to evaluate rehabilitation programs.

USES OF THE OUTCOME METHOD IN QUALITY ASSESSMENT

In general, three ways in which the outcome method is used in quality assessment are relevant to evaluation of criminal offender rehabilitation programs:[5]

1. To monitor prospectively the quality of care within a single program as it is delivered, both to arrive at a value judgment about current quality and to intervene and change the care process when necessary to avoid adverse outcomes for present patients; and

2. To monitor retrospectively the quality of care:

   a. to identify problems within a delivery system (or, for example, a single rehabilitation program) in outcomes that result from poor process and to change those processes to achieve closer-to-optimal outcomes for future patients; or

   b. to do a comparative evaluation of different aspects of the delivery system (or, for example, of two different approaches to rehabilitation of criminal offenders) in order to make value statements that will support policy decisions.

Although their purposes are dissimilar, both monitoring and policy-relevant quality evaluation use the outcome method in essentially the same way. Only one distinction must be made: the stringency with which effects of factors outside the influence of the medical care system (or rehabilitation system) on outcomes are controlled for when outcome data are analyzed. Depending on the purpose, some type of control is necessary to conclude that differences in outcome are actually attributable to differences in type of care delivered, rather than to differences in patient- and disease-related characteristics (or offender- and offense-related characteristics) that cannot be altered by the inter-

---

[5] A major use of outcome information in medical care, not discussed here, is in studies to determine the efficacy of various types of treatment interventions (e.g., drug efficacy studies, comparative evaluation of surgical procedures in treatment of breast cancer, etc.). The use of outcome information to evaluate the *quality* with which the intervention is applied presumes that the efficacy of the intervention has been tested *or* that there is at least some level of agreement among clinicians as to what outcomes can be expected following a particular intervention. Medicine, like criminal offender rehabilitation, has not yet documented the efficacy of all its interventions; hence, determination of "expected outcomes" based on professional opinion becomes a major factor in development of outcome-based evaluation designs.

vention being evaluated, such as case-mix, sociodemographic characteristics, prior severity of disease (or offense), etc.

For monitoring purposes, constraints of time, budget, and expertise usually make it difficult to control for external factors, and the evaluation method itself, without such controls, is probably sensitive enough to detect major problems in quality and indicate where changes are necessary to achieve better outcomes. If the purpose of outcome evaluation is to reach policy-relevant conclusions (e.g., that certain types of physicians provide better care than others, or that extra-institutional rehabilitation programs are more effective than those in corrections institutions), far more careful control of external factors is required.

To control for such factors and make fair comparisons and value judgments, two things are necessary. First, the factors that affect outcomes and are not influenced by quality of the intervention must be identified. A major problem in this step is deciding what is and what is not within the purview of the medical care (or rehabilitation) system. Identifying these factors requires knowledge or expert guesses as to the strength and direction of their effects on outcomes. Second, appropriate statistical techniques must be selected to make necessary adjustments for differences among populations being compared. Two different techniques have been recommended. The first is to attempt to divide the population into homogeneous groups using as grouping variables those factors known or believed to be predictive of prognosis. This is the method most commonly used in medical care quality assessment when such controls are employed. A major problem is that there are few widely accepted systems for grouping patients according to prognosis. The second technique is one of a variety of multivariate statistical techniques, such as linear multiple regression, Tobit, and Logit. These techniques seem to be the most promising because they require no *a priori* hypotheses concerning how multiple external factors should be aggregated to produce valid and reliable prognostic grouping systems.

DETAILS OF THE METHOD

Once the outcome method has been chosen as appropriate for a quality-of-care assessment, the disease condition for study must be selected, outcome criteria identified, and standards of care established. Outcomes of care are than measured and a value judgment made as to whether the care is of good or poor quality in relation to the standards established. For purposes of this discussion, a "criterion" is the variable that is measured as an outcome (e.g., mortality), and a "standard" is a statement of the expected level of attainment on a given criterion, assuming a specified level of quality of care (e.g., assuming care of optimal quality, the mortality rate should be no higher than x percent).

SELECTION OF CRITERIA AND STANDARDS

The outcome criteria chosen for measurement can be either selective concepts (e.g., mortality, morbidity) or a more general concept such as overall health status. Most studies of quality of care to date have used specific outcome criteria rather than general health status indices. In part, this approach reflects the still preliminary conceptual development of overall indices and in part, the traditional focus of medical care process on specific aspects of disease rather than a patient's general health.

When the selective approach is taken in developing outcome criteria, measures of mortality and incidence of surgical procedures are most commonly used; when measures of morbidity are used, they are most frequently measures of one or more aspects of physiological functioning (e.g., blood pressure). This is similar to the state-of-the-art of measuring outcomes of rehabilitation programs for criminal offenders: as noted, the most common measure is one of recidivism (although definitions vary widely). In developmental work on the outcome method, the bias has been to recommend use of a broad range of outcome criteria, including indicators of physical, mental, and psychosocial health in addition to physiologic status, based on the belief that medical care is (or should be) directed at improving the overall health of the individual, and that assessment of its quality should hold it accountable for overall health (Brook *et al.* 1976). Use of multiple outcome criteria also allows the evaluator to see what types of outcomes are affected positively and negatively by the intervention, thus providing information useful to later evaluators in their selection of outcome criteria. Following similar reasoning, the use of multiple outcome criteria may well be essential to the success of evaluations in criminal justice.

Because few outcome studies have used a broad range of criteria to assess quality of medical care, however, there is little information available to determine the relative usefulness of either the selective or the comprehensive approach. Should efforts be concentrated on measuring a narrow range, or should resources be used to measure a comprehensive range of criteria at a less detailed level? The answer will depend to some extent on whether the intercorrelations between the criteria selected are high or low. Given the paucity of knowledge of the efficacy of medical care (and of rehabilitation programs), it cannot be assumed that achievement of optimal outcomes on one dimension will necessarily mean that all possible outcomes are optimal. For example, will a program that produces a low recidivism rate also assure that former offenders will be successful vocationally or adjust satisfactorily to the outside community? Unless this assumption holds, measurement of only a few outcome criteria may bias results. If many criteria are used, however, it may increase the likelihood of including those that are actually unassociated with the effects of the intervention (or increase the number of deficiencies found in care), thus complicating the decision as to which is most important to change first.

Lack of experience with the use of a comprehensive range of outcome criteria in quality assessment, however, contributes to problems in setting standards for a comprehensive set of criteria. For example, because most criteria (other than physiological criteria) have not been studied frequently in relation to specific diseases, the only information available for standard-setting is a physician's feeling as to whether and to what extent medical care can affect such outcomes as psychosocial health. Until greater experience is available, the range of outcome criteria should probably be limited to those for which enough is known regarding whether to attribute outcomes to the level of quality of care (or rehabilitation), to the natural history of the disease (or criminal behavior), or to some proportion of both. Other criteria, for which there is less available information, might be used as trial criteria, to obtain further information for subsequent evaluations.

TIME OF MEASUREMENT

A major consideration in applying the outcome method is the point in time during or after the intervention at which standards should be applied and outcomes actually measured. The time chosen will depend on the use of the outcome information: if it is used for both prospective monitoring and quality assessment, the time must be as close to the intervention as possible so problems can be identified and rectified quickly. If outcomes are to be used in retrospective evaluation, consideration of the specificity of the measure must also guide the choice of time. For example, if recidivism were to be the criterion, it should be measured when the effects of the rehabilitation program are likely to explain more of the variance than could be explained by the effect of maturation.

Other factors that will guide choice of time in certain cases are the criterion itself and what is known about the problem under consideration and its treatment. For some criteria, the effects of treatment or rehabilitation in achieving optimal outcomes are cumulative. Thus, if the effect of an intervention of optimal quality is to prevent occurrence of some adverse outcome (and an intervention of average or poor quality does not prevent it), the later the time chosen, the greater the likelihood of detecting significant differences in outcomes among patients treated by interventions of different quality. In other cases, the purpose of an intervention is to achieve an outcome as rapidly as possible, and an intervention of poor quality may not achieve this outcome as promptly as would one of optimal quality. In such cases, the earliest time at which maximum benefits should be achieved by an intervention of optimal quality should be chosen time.

Such considerations have infrequently been taken into account, at least explicitly, in measurement of outcomes for quality-of-care assessment. In any case, there are obvious problems in both medical care and criminal offender rehabilitation, related to lack of documentation of maximum benefits, adequate control of intervening variables, and obtaining agreement of those who set standards. Estimates of the sensitivity and specificity of outcome criteria and times at which maximum benefits can be expected must be subjected to rigorous pretesting prior to their use in an actual quality-of-care assessment or in evaluation of rehabilitation programs.

IMPLICIT AND EXPLICIT STANDARDS

Standards used in outcome assessment can be either implicit or explicit. If they are implicit, the outcomes to be examined are generally agreed to, but not established *a priori*. In medical care evaluations, physician-judges are asked to determine whether patient outcomes were improvable or unimprovable; their own unenunciated opinions of what optimal medical care can achieve thus become the standards. If they are explicit, specific outcome criteria are agreed to and established *a priori* for the population as a whole or defined subgroups (e.g., groups within specific prognostic categories). Depending on the available clinical literature, the amount of prior research on outcomes of interest, and the degree of consensus regarding what optimal care can achieve, explicit outcome standards can be based on empirical findings, estimates derived from clinical experience, or a combination of both. This approach can be time-consuming, but it has the advantage that the standards can be subsequently applied by nonphysicians to make the quality assessment by comparing documented outcomes to *a priori* standards.

The difference between implicit and explicit standards in rehabilitation assessment can be seen in the following example: in one assessment program, judges would examine records of treated offenders to determine whether in the judges' opinions offenders had been rehabilitated; in another program, rehabilitation would be defined as staying off welfare, earning as much or more than people at the thirtieth income percentile, and avoiding convictions for at least 2 years, and treatment records would be reviewed against that definition. As in medical care, application of implicit standards requires at least a modicum of expertise, while application of explicit standards is more nearly a clerical task.

Quality-of-care studies are using explicit standards more frequently now than 5–10 years ago, although there is still noticeable reluctance to publish the actual standards used. This is a problem, because if the standards are not valid, studies that demonstrate some or no deficiencies in care may not have reached valid conclusions. In part, this reluctance may relate to hesitation on the part of the profession in promulgating and being held accountable for specific standards of care.

JUDGMENTS

After criteria and standards are selected, outcomes are measured using information from medical records or patient interviews and compared to standards. The results of this comparison must be analyzed and some judgment made about the relative level of quality observed. In many cases, the value of achieving any particular outcome is implied in the criteria and standards selected. Those criteria selected presumably represent those outcomes (from a range of possible outcomes) that are the most important to achieve, for which medical care intervention can make the most difference, and that tell the most about the quality of care delivered. Standards thus contain an implicit definition of what medical care of optimal quality can be expected to achieve.

The values that are implied in selected criteria and standards need to be made explicit, both in assessments of the quality of medical care and in the evaluation of criminal offender rehabilitation programs. This is particularly true because the professionals whose care or programs are being assessed are probably the same people who will be involved in setting criteria and standards. These criteria and standards may not reflect public priorities and values or may prove too expensive in terms of the public's willingness to pay for achievement of such standards. For example, it might be found that the public does not value extra-institutional rehabilitation programs more than institutional programs and that optimal quality may not be that which avoids imprisonment for the criminal offender. If the professionals who set the standards do not share the public's values (and they may not), quality assurance of rehabilitation programs based on such standards will not prove cost-beneficial in the public's eyes. The issue of consonance between professional and public values is an important one in evaluating the effectiveness of criminal offender rehabilitation programs. This is particularly true because while society may view reduction of disability (rather than complete cure) as an acceptable outcome of medical care intervention, it may be less willing to accept anything short of elimination of criminal behavior as the outcome of a rehabilitation program.

CONCLUSIONS

This paper has described, in brief outline, a method of evaluating the quality of medical care based on information about patient outcomes that appears to be relevant to the problems of measuring outcomes and effectiveness of programs designed to rehabilitate criminal offenders. Its basic features are common to most evaluation techniques, although the labels applied to them may differ: definition of goals and objectives (criteria and standard setting), measurement of outcomes, comparison of actual to expected outcomes, and value judgments about the results of that comparison. Several aspects of the method may make it particularly useful to evaluative research on criminal offender rehabilitation programs, including: (1) use of multiple outcome criteria to evaluate a program; (2) the opportunity to make explicit the expected standards of program achievement; (3) consideration of the sensitivity and specificity of outcome variables being measured in choosing the times at which to measure them; and (4) emphasis on making values used in judging the worth or quality of the actual outcomes explicit and consonant with those held by the public. These aspects of the evaluation method described are important ones in assessing quality of medical care; because many criminal offender rehabilitation programs are based on the "medical model," the method may prove adaptable and useful to their evaluation.

REFERENCES

Adams, S. (1975) *Evaluative Research in Corrections: A Practical Guide.* Washington, D.C.: U.S. Department of Justice.

Adams, S. (1976) Evaluation: a way out of rhetoric. Pages 75–91 in *Rehabilitation, Recidivism and Research.* Hackensack, N.J.: National Council on Crime and Delinquency.

Bailey, W. (1966) Correctional outcome: an evaluation of 100 reports. *Journal of Criminal Law, Criminology and Political Science* 57:153–160.

Brook, R. H., Davies-Avery, A., Greenfield, S., Harris, L. J., Lelah, T., Solomon, N. E., and Ware, J. E., Jr. (1976) *Assessing the Quality of Medical Care Using Outcome Measures: An Overview of the Method.* (R-2021/1-HEW) Santa Monica, Calif.: Rand Corporation. Also published in (1977) *Medical Care* 15(9)(Supplement):1–165.

Conrad, J. P. (1975) Lessons of a Little Knowledge. Paper presented at the Conference on the Criminal and Society: Should We Treat or Punish?, Dec. 18–19. Available from the Academy for Contemporary Problems, 1501 Neil Ave., Columbus, Ohio, 43201.

Fogel, D. (1975) *We Are the Living Proof: The Justice Model for Corrections.* Cincinnati, Ohio: Anderson Publishing Company.

Lipton, D., Martinson, R., and Wilks, J. (1975) *The Effectiveness of Correctional Treatment.* New York: Praeger Publishers.

Lundman, R., McFarland, P., and Scarpitti, F. (1976) Delinquency prevention: assessment of reported projects. *Crime and Delinquency* 22:297–308.

Martinson, R. (1976) Evaluating in crisis: a postscript. Pages 93–96 in *Rehabilitation, Recidivism and Research.* Hackensack, N.J.: National Council on Crime and Delinquency.

Robison, J. and Smith, G. (1971) The effectiveness of correctional programs. *Crime and Delinquency* 17:67–80.

Twentieth Century Fund, Inc. (1976) *Fair and Certain Punishment: Report on Criminal Sentencing.* Task Force on Criminal Sentencing. New York: McGraw-Hill.

von Hirsch, A. (1976) *Doing Justice: The Choice of Punishments.* New York: Hill and Wang.

Methodological Considerations in Evaluating Correctional Effectiveness: Issues and Chronic Problems

EVA LANTOS REZMOVIC

The criminal justice system of the late 1970s is in the midst of growing debate over its ability to rehabilitate offenders. Some people, including 63 percent of the nation's top prison administrators, contend that correctional programs can reduce recidivism (Serril 1974). Research, however, has failed to find convincing evidence for this claim. Concomitantly, the research itself has been the subject of controversy: Do treatment programs fail to rehabilitate or has low-quality research precluded the detection of rehabilitative effects?

Twelve years ago, the President's Commission on Law Enforcement and Administration of Justice (1967, p. 273) reported that, although more than $4 billion is expended on the criminal justice system annually:

The expenditure for the kinds of descriptive, operational, and evaluative research that are the obvious prerequisites for a rational program of crime control is negligible. . . . There is probably no subject of comparable concern to which the Nation is devoting so many resources and so much effort with so little knowledge of what it is doing.

Seven years ago, based on a review of 100 correctional research studies, Logan (1972, p. 380) concluded: "none of these studies can be

---

Eva Lantos Rezmovic is a doctoral candidate, Division of Methodology and Evaluation .Research, Northwestern University.

described as adequate. There is not one study that meets all of the criteria . . . as the minimal methodological requirements of a scientifically sound test of effectiveness."

Today, the vital need for conducting sound evaluations persists. In response to the need for knowledge of program effects, funding agencies at the federal, state, and local levels are now applying increasing pressure on correctional agencies to evaluate the extent to which their program goals have been achieved. But attempts to form a coherent body of knowledge on the effectiveness and lack of effectiveness of correctional rehabilitation programs continue to be impeded, largely because of the shortcomings of the evaluative studies undertaken.

This paper discusses some of the methodological problems that have beset evaluations of correctional programs. Of particular interest are those methodological problems that can jeopardize the interpretability of findings from such evaluations. Implicit in this discussion is the realization that optimal conditions for scientific study of social phenomena almost never exist. As Rossi and Wright (1977, p. 13) note: "Indeed, the art of evaluation research may be appropriately described as an effort to make do with considerably less than one ideally would desire." Nevertheless, investigators should be able to formulate better research hypotheses, design more valid and powerful tests of experimental programs, use more sensitive dependent measures, implement better quality controls for monitoring programs, and draw more warranted conclusions than those evidenced in many reports of summative correctional program evaluations. Reasons these aspects of research are important and the implications of ignoring them are addressed in the following sections.

EVALUATION DESIGNS

TRUE EXPERIMENTAL TESTS OF TREATMENT EFFECTIVENESS

In designing evaluations of rehabilitation programs, investigators can exercise varying degrees of control over the experimental situation. The more control investigators have in designing and executing an evaluation, the greater their ability to make causal statements about program impact. In general, strength of methodology varies directly with extent of experimental control. Sound evaluations of correctional treatment programs require, in basic terms, that one administer treatment to one group of offenders and make outcome measurements of posttreatment behavior, and withhold treatment from (or provide alternate treatment to) a comparable group of offenders and secure outcome measurements on them.

Under the most favorable conditions, a treatment is available to a limited number of offenders. Since the value of the treatment is unknown and since the supply of eligible offenders exceeds the treatment's availability, a random procedure for assigning offenders to treatment may be justified. Some situations allow for random assignment even when there is no excess of "treatable offenders"—for example, if two or more treatments are available and the relative effectiveness of these treatments is of interest. When these types of situations arise, a true experimental test of the program's effectiveness should be undertaken.

True experiments, involving random assignment of subjects to experimental and control conditions, provide the most secure and valid means of assuring that the results of a study are due to the manipulated variables, rather than to systematically biasing factors. Randomization accounts for the fact that people differ in many ways and that these differences can affect the outcome variable under study. By relying on chance to determine experimental or control group membership, the probability that all relevant characteristics will be evenly distributed across groups is maximized. It is because of this equalizing effect that randomized experiments increase the confidence one can have in the causal relationship between treatment and effect and reduce the plausibility of alternative explanations for this relationship. That failure to randomize can result in extraneous sources of variance accounting for the findings has been substantially documented by Boruch (1975b), Campbell (1969, 1971), Campbell and Boruch (1975), Campbell and Erlebacher (1970), Campbell and Stanley (1966), and Gilbert *et al.* (1975), among others. Primarily because there are many more threats to the validity of nonrandomized experiments than randomized experiments (see Campbell and Stanley 1966 and Cook and Campbell 1976 for a list of these threats), results from randomized studies provide a framework for obtaining the least equivocal evidence for estimating program effectiveness.

Given the inferential persuasiveness of their results, randomized experiments are too infrequently done, although there have been some at each stage of the criminal justice process. For example, some recent experiments have been conducted in schools (Reckless and Dinitz 1972); in courts (Berger *et al.* 1975, Stapleton and Teitelbaum 1972); on probation (Lohman *et al.* 1965); in institutions for juveniles (Adams 1970, Jesness 1971); in prisons (Kassebaum *et al.* 1971); on work release (Waldo and Chiricos 1977); on parole (Havel 1965); and in the community (Empey and Lubeck 1972, Lenihan 1977, Palmer 1974). By randomizing, these studies maximized their ability to control for at least seven of the most common threats to internal validity: history, maturation, testing, instrumentation, regression, selection, and attrition. Randomization assured the pretreatment equivalence of the experimental and control groups so that conclusions about posttreatment differences would be robust to competing explanations of outcome.

Despite their infrequent use, true experiments are generally agreed to be the best evaluation model available. It must be pointed out, however, that randomization is not a panacea. While the importance of having comparable experimental and control groups cannot be overstated, failure to attend to other methodological requisites can undermine the power afforded by the experimental model. Some of these other methodological considerations will be discussed later; the salient point here is that randomization is most often a necessary, but not sufficient, precondition to deriving valid conclusions from program evaluations.

QUASI-EXPERIMENTAL TESTS OF TREATMENT EFFECTIVENESS

When conditions preclude the use of true experiments, some quasi-experimental techniques may be practical alternatives for assessing program effectiveness. The advantage of quasi-experimental designs is that they seem to be easier to implement—whether for legal, ethical, political, or logistical reasons—than true experiments; their disadvantage is that they are less efficient and produce more equivocal results. When an experiment is not randomized, a decrease in experimental control is accompanied by an increase in the need to make assumptions about the underlying nature of the data. Since these assumptions are often unverifiable, results from quasi-experiments are often vulnerable to dispute. Findings from many nonrandomized evaluations are subject to competing explanations that are not discountable on the basis of either empirical data or common sense (Boruch 1975b, Bernstein and Freeman 1975). Therefore, the tradeoff between ease of implementation and inferential strength of results must be carefully weighed.

Nonequivalent Control Group Design

One of the stronger quasi-experimental designs is the nonequivalent control group design. This design is appropriate if randomization is not feasible, if randomization fails to produce equivalent comparison groups (which can always occur by chance, but is unlikely if sample sizes are large), or if randomization breaks down after the beginning of an experiment (as in the Provo experiment [Empey and Erickson 1972]). In such situations, the aim is to find a nontreated group of offenders, maximally similar to the treated group, with which the posttreatment behavior of the experimentals can be compared. Depending on the research question, the comparison group may consist of other offenders in the same institution (e.g., work release versus non-work-release clients), offenders in other institutions (e.g., vocationally trained versus untrained clients), or noninstitutionalized offenders (e.g., probated versus imprisoned clients).

To ensure that the treated group is as similar as possible to the comparison group, a matching technique is frequently employed. The two groups are usually matched on variables presumed to be related to outcome in an attempt to maximize their pretreatment equivalence. Offenders' age, race, sex, education, socioeconomic status, and offense history are some of the more commonly used matching variables. If a comparison group is found for which the variables correspond to those of the treated group, it becomes easy to believe that the only remaining difference between the two groups is that one received treatment and the other did not. This, however, is a fallacy. If the matching techniques fail to account for all initial differences that have a bearing on treatment outcome, a study's findings will be systematically biased. The only instance in which estimates of treatment effects will not be biased is when the residual differences between comparison groups are unrelated to the way that treatment affects offenders' behavior. This is often a moot point, however, because we generally do not know all the attributes on which offenders should be matched. Therefore, we cannot know whether matching has succeeded or not in accounting for all relevant *a priori* differences between groups.

The major problem with matching is that it can introduce regression effects into research results. "*Regression effect* refers to the phenomenon that the values of variables tend to move toward the mean on subsequent evaluations" (Anderson *et al.* 1975, p. 321). One situation in which this occurs is when experimental and control groups are selected on the basis of extreme pretest scores. For example, if the most corrigible offenders are selected for treatment (as determined by scores on a personality test) and a comparison group is selected by matching the pretest scores of its members with those of the treated group, regression effects will bias the results. If the comparison group is somehow "better off" (e.g., more motivated and less crime-prone) than the experimental group, the treatment will appear to have exerted a harmful effect when it actually may have had no effect. This spurious result will occur because of measurement error on the pretest. The posttest scores will contain less measurement error, and the groups will regress toward their respective means on the second test. Consequently, the experimental group will appear to be less corrigible than it really is, the comparison group will appear to be more corrigible than it is, and a pseudo-negative treatment effect will be observed.

While the regression problems produced by matching are less intuitively clear when groups are matched on qualitative variables and when recidivism is the criterion of effectiveness, the same logic applies. In such a case, the variables on which groups are matched are those that are believed to predict recidivism (i.e., age, race, sex, offense history, etc.). Since the dependent variable is recidivism, the aim of the matching is to control for the probability of recidivating without treatment. Again, however, if not all attributes that correlate with recidivism are included in the matching, regression effects will appear. The two groups will differ in probability of recidivating, and due to the matching on selected variables, the recidivism rates of the groups will regress toward their respective means. (See Campbell and Erlebacher [1970] for a detailed discussion of how regression effects may occur and how they may bias evaluation results.)

The direction of bias produced by regression is readily apparent in some evaluation reports. For example, as part of the evaluation of Southfields, a milieu therapy program for delinquents, treated youths were compared with probated youths (Miller 1970, p. 310):

In an attempt to compensate for the lack of random assignment, . . . control groups [were restricted] to boys who met the basic criteria for admission to Southfields. Furthermore, [an effort was made] to match . . . by race and by number of previous arrests.

That the research results disappointingly revealed the probated group to have lower recidivism rates than the treated group should not have been surprising. If juvenile court judges succeeded in placing the more disturbed youths in Southfields, which appeared to be the case, then matching introduced regression biases into the results. Clearly, matching on only two variables was inadequate to control for all pre-existing group differences. Because of the imperfections of matching, the observed outcome was partly a function of the treated youths' regression toward their higher recidivism level and the probated youths' regression toward their lower recidivism level. Even if the treatment had had some rehabilitative value, regression effects could have affected the findings to show an advantage for the nontreated group.

Various statistical techniques are used almost as often as matching to equate nonequivalent groups. Partial correlation and multiple regression analyses are sometimes employed; analysis of covariance is used most frequently. It is often not recognized, however, that these statistical techniques are subject to the same biases that are present in matching. Because of imperfect measurements, statistical analyses, like matching, yield biased estimates of treatment effects. (The problems associated with covariance analysis are discussed below, in "Statistical Issues.")

What can be done to alleviate the interpretation problems caused by regression artifacts? The best procedure is to select a natural, intact comparison group that is similar to the treated group, and avoid matching. Even if the groups differ, the comparison group can be very useful in ruling out most hypotheses that compete with treatment as explanations of outcome. Certainly, if a treated group outperforms a comparison group that has a higher initial probability of success, the argument that the treatment was rehabilitative would be persuasive.

The nonequivalent control group design, if used properly, can produce meaningful evaluation results. Despite some problems, using a nonequivalent control group is highly preferable to not using a control group. The design certainly allows one to rule out a number of threats to validity, and extra efforts can be taken to be aware of and to measure uncontrolled sources of variation.

Interrupted Time-Series Design

The interrupted time-series design also ranks among the more powerful quasi-experimental techniques. This design, which involves a series of periodic measurements before, during, and after a treatment has been introduced, has two very good features: it controls for most of the common threats to internal validity, and it necessitates less interference with ongoing program operations than do most other evaluative techniques. While there are few instances of its application in criminal justice, it has potential as a meaningful evaluative device when more rigorous control cannot be exercised.

Schnelle and Lee (1974) evaluated the effects of a change in prison policy using interrupted time-series analysis. The intervention in this study consisted of a new type of disciplinary action whereby prisoners who were behavioral offense problems in a medium-security prison were transferred to a maximum-security prison after a given date. The dependent variable was the mean number of daily offenses for 7 months before and 23 months following the intervention. Schnelle and Lee's time-series analysis indicated that the intervention did exert a behavioral effect; that is, the percentage of prisoners who committed two or more offenses per month was lower for the entire 23-month period following the policy change. The investigators interpreted this as supporting the hypothesis that the intervention exerted a behavioral effect, but there were many threats to the validity of the Schnelle and Lee study. For example, external events that coincided with the intervention posed as a historical threat to internal validity; the possibility of unreliable record keeping posed as an instrumentation threat; and the introduction of the intervention during a month in which offense rates were unusually high posed a regression threat. Such threats to the validity of conclusions from time-series designs are fairly common. To reduce their plausibility, the evaluator should be very familiar with the experimental setting and attuned to external events that may influence the study's results. Through substantive knowledge of the experimental setting, alternative explanations for outcome may be rendered less plausible.

When only one time-series is being analyzed, history is the major threat to validity. If two series are being analyzed, however, with one serving as a control series, all major threats to internal validity are controlled. The multiple time-series design, consequently, may be the quasi-experiment that is the closest approximation to the true experiment that is currently available. Given its inferential strength and its unobtrusive nature, program evaluation using time-series methodology should be more frequent. Correctional institutions and agencies regularly maintain records on offender populations, and these are veritable storehouses of information. To date, the information contained in such archival records has been virtually untapped by correctional evaluators.

Recurrent Institutional Cycle Design

Another potentially useful quasi-experimental design—but one that has received very little attention—is the recurrent institutional cycle design. Campbell and Stanley (1966) refer to this as a patched-up design because it combines the features of several weak designs into one that has fewer threats to validity than its weak constituents. The patching-up process can involve any number of makeshift operations and comparisons that will buttress the weak foundations of a study. As Campbell and Stanley note (1966, p. 57): "The result is often an inelegant accumulation of precautionary checks, which lacks the intrinsic symmetry of the 'true' experimental designs, but nonetheless approaches experimentation." Patching up an originally weak design offers two benefits: specific threats to validity may be ruled out through a conceptual reformulation or extension of the study design, and treatment effects may be tested in several different ways instead of only one.

A patched-up design is particularly appropriate for settings in which the same programs are repeatedly presented to new groups of offenders. Suppose, for example, that a prison is interested in determining the ameliorative effects of psychotherapy on inmate behavior. It is hypothesized that if psychotherapy is effective, the rate of rule infractions among treated offenders should decrease. To test this hypothesis, the rule infraction rates of a group that has completed psychotherapy may be compared with those of a second group that is about to begin treatment. The claim that psychotherapy is effective would be supported if the posttreatment behavior of group 1 compared favorably with the pretreatment behavior of group 2. This conclusion would be tenuous, however, because several alternative explanations may also be able to account for the findings. For example, if rule infraction rate were correlated with change in seasons, growing older, or administrative changes in the prison, improved behavior may be caused by these external sources of variation instead of by the treatment. To strengthen this study's design, the posttreatment infraction rates of group 2 could also be measured. Now we would be able to test the treatment's effects in three different ways: (a) group 1 following treatment versus group 2 prior to treatment (group 1 should be superior); (b) group 1 following treatment versus group 2 following treatment (infraction rates should be the same); and (c) group 2 prior to treatment versus group 2 following treatment (infraction rates should have declined). Comparison (a) strengthens the study's conclusions by eliminating administrative changes as a rival explanation of treatment effects: such changes would affect all inmates in a prison, not just those involved in treatment. If comparison (b) yields a significant difference between the posttreatment behaviors of the two groups, however, selection effects may be biasing the results. That is, initial differences between the groups, such as age, may moderate the effectiveness of the treatment. If this were a realistic threat to validity, the investigator could test its plausibility through the addition of new comparison groups. For example, among those inmates who have not yet received psychotherapy, two groups could be formed: one whose ages correspond to those of group 1, another whose ages correspond to group 2. If age, instead of psychotherapy, accounted for the posttreatment differences between groups 1 and 2, then comparisons between treated and untreated corresponding age groups should show no difference.

The basic strength of this design is that several nonequivalent groups may be patched on to a study in order to rule out specific threats to validity. The inelegance of the resulting design is more than compensated for by the gain in inferential strength afforded by multiple exemplars of the treatment. Given that most rehabilitation studies involve poor study design (Lipton *et al.* 1974, Logan 1972), the general methodological quality of many evaluations may be enhanced simply by "looking around" for confirmatory evidence. While each piece of evidence is inadequate by itself, a combination of them can produce a convincing finding.

Regression-Discontinuity Design

Finally, correctional researchers are advised to consider the regression-discontinuity design when randomization is not feasible. This design is particularly appropriate in settings in which meritocratic rather than democratic criteria must dictate who will receive a treatment (Riecken *et al.* 1977, p. 121):

> The basic situation is a common one: An ameliorative program is in short supply; a basic decision that it should go to the most needy; a desire to see the program scientifically evaluated. For this situation, if random assignment among equally eligible subjects is ruled out, the Regression-Discontinuity design is probably the best one available and thus should frequently be used.

The essential requisite to using this design is an explicit ordering of eligibility on a continuous measurement scale. For example, when juvenile institutions receive Title I funds to create special education programs, the "most needy" youths are generally those who are furthest behind in academic achievement. Evaluating the effects of a Title I program may then proceed by: (1) obtaining a pretest measure of achievement on the institution's youths; (2) setting an explicit cutoff point for treatment eligibility (e.g., youths who score 2 or more years behind expected grade level receive the Title I program; youths who score less than 2 years behind receive the standard program); and (3) obtaining a posttest measure of achievement for both recipient and nonrecipient groups. While the posttest need not be identical to the pretest, it must be a valid measure of program effects and must correlate with the criterion of eligibility. Program outcome will then be evaluable as a function of the discontinuity in regression lines at the cutting point.

The logic of this design can best be illustrated graphically, as in Figure 1. If there were no difference in the effectiveness of the Title I

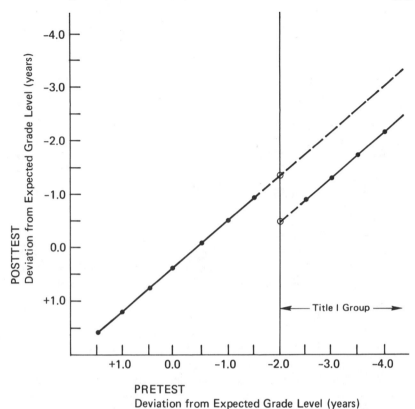

FIGURE 1   Regression-discontinuity analysis.

program versus the standard education program, there would be no
discontinuity in the regression lines of the treated and untreated
groups. Under the null hypothesis, those who performed worse on the
pretest would also have performed worse on the posttest (this condition is indicated by the extrapolated dashed line). But if the Title I
program had a greater ameliorative effect, then the type of discontinuity depicted in Figure 1 would occur: the intercept of the treated
group's regression line is lower than that of the nontreated group. The
magnitude of this effect is reflected by the magnitude of discontinuity
in the intercepts of the regression lines.

According to Campbell (1969, p. 422):

it is the dimensionality and sharpness of the decision criteria that is at issue,
not its components or validity. The ratings [eligibility] could be based on

nepotism, whimsey, and superstition and still serve. . . . [I]f the decision criteria is utterly invalid, we approach the pure randomness of a true experiment.

Once the eligibility criterion is set, however, it is important to adhere to the specified cutting point. If cases are admitted to the program on any other basis, those cases should be eliminated from the data analysis in order to control for selection bias. Quantitative ordering of eligibility and maintenance of the integrity of the design are the two key ingredients to applying this design.

CASE STUDIES, ONE-GROUP BEFORE-AFTER DESIGNS, AND *EX POST FACTO* ANALYSES

These three designs are the weakest forms of evaluation. For generating hypotheses about the nature of treatment and its effects, they have heuristic value. For providing meaningful evidence on the causal relationship between treatment and effect, they are almost wholly inadequate. They are mentioned briefly here because they are widely used in correctional research and because this use should be discouraged.

In a case study approach, treatment is administered to a group of offenders and outcome measures of behavior are taken later. What these "outcomes" mean, however, is unclear. Without a pretreatment measure of behavior, we cannot know whether posttreatment behavior improved, worsened, or remained unchanged. Whatever the findings, it is impossible to gauge their directionality. Case studies "have such a total absence of control as to be of almost no scientific value" (Campbell and Stanley 1966, p. 6).

In a one-group before-after design, the dependent variable is measured at two times: prior to and following treatment. While this improves on the case study by allowing the evaluator to determine amount and direction of change, its weak features far outweigh this strong point. The major fault of the design is the absence of a comparison group. Without a comparison group, it is impossible to determine what the outcome would have been without treatment. Unless the posttreatment behavior of treated offenders can be compared with that of a nontreated group, there is little confirmatory evidence to support the claim that treatment caused outcome. Seasonal changes, aging, staff turnover, and changes in record-keeping procedures are only some of the external variables that have been found to masquerade as treatment effects with this type of design.

Ex post facto studies also suffer from highly inadequate experimental control. As the name suggests, these studies are undertaken either after a treatment program has begun or after it has ended. Evaluators who must resort to employing this methodology are well advised to recognize its limitations, however. Knowledge of what, besides treatment, transpired between the onset of a program and the measurement of an outcome will almost always be incomplete. Archival records, which may be in error, incomplete, or only marginally relevant to research interests, must often be relied on. Finding an adequate comparison group is also a chronic problem, since belated efforts to generate equivalent sources of comparison rarely succeed. Again, matching and covariance analysis cannot adjust the bias inherent in comparisons between nonequivalent groups. The well-known Highfields experiment (McCorkle *et al.* 1958) on the effects of milieu therapy on delinquent youths is one study that has been amply criticized on these grounds (Sherwood and Walker 1959). In sum, *ex post facto* studies allow so little control over the experimental variables that inferences based on them must be treated with strong reservations.

NATURAL EXPERIMENTS

Opportunities to conduct rigorous evaluations of treatment programs can arise even in the absence of planned randomization. In particular, a researcher may find instances in which offenders are normally assigned to treatment on a random basis. In such a situation, useful information can be gained by conducting a "natural experiment." According to Boruch (1975a, p. 35): "[I]t is intuitively appealing to regard some processes in society as naturally random, and to capitalize on the intuition to develop procedural approximations to true experiments." The natural experiment is a procedural approximation to the true experiment because the least fallible way of ensuring randomness is to use a predetermined random methodology for assigning subjects to experimental and control groups. The natural experiment, however, can have one advantage over the true experiment: because the experimental setting is in no way artificial or contrived, the possibility that the study's findings are mediated by subjects' reactivity to the experiment itself is minimized.

Shelley and Johnson's study (1961) of the impact of individual and group counseling on antisocial attitudes and recidivism exemplifies a naturally randomized process. They describe the following situation (p. 351):

A combination of special circumstances offered an unusual opportunity to evaluate the effects of a counseling program in changing social attitudes.

Temporarily there were two camp facilities for youthful offenders, essentially similar as to program, with the difference that for a period of six months one had an organized counseling program and the other did not.

Since the criteria for assigning offenders to the two camps were identical, a natural experiment could be undertaken. Unfortunately, the investigators undermined the power of the design afforded them by matching a subset of offenders in the two camps on age, intelligence, offense, and previous criminal history. By matching, a natural experimental design was transformed into a nonequivalent control group design with all its accompanying threats to validity. For example, if race affects magnitude of antisocial attitudes, the observed outcomes may have been due to differences in the racial composition of the two groups rather than to the counseling service; but race was not included as a matching variable. Therefore, while the populations of the two camps may have been equivalent, it is questionable whether the study samples were. (It should be noted that matching prior to randomization is an asset because it increases the statistical power of the analyses. It is when matching is done after random assignment, or in place of it, that biased estimates of effects can result.) Natural experiments can provide powerful tests of program effects if evaluators take advantage of inherently natural processes.

INDIRECT EXPERIMENTS

The flexibility of the experimental model of evaluation is generally not well understood. It is commonly thought that unless individuals are randomly placed in experimental and control groups, a true experiment cannot be implemented. Although this is often the case, a randomized design may sometimes be employed even when randomization cannot be done directly. In such cases, an indirect experiment may be feasible (Zeisel 1968). The methodology of the indirect experiment can be easily understood through the example set by the Manhattan bail bond project (Ares *et al.* 1963, Botein 1965, Sturtz 1967). The hypothesis of the Manhattan bail bond study was that criminal defendants with substantial ties to the community could be released on their own recognizance (ROR) and still appear for trial on their appointed court dates. Whether bail was more effective than ROR in ensuring court appearance was not directly testable, however, since random assignment to bail and nonbail conditions would have been unlawful. Instead, the following procedure was adopted: On the basis of interviews and reviews of records, project staff identified 363 defendants as sufficiently rooted in the community to be eligible for ROR. This sample was then randomly divided into experimental and control groups. All members of the experimental group were recommended to the judge for ROR; members of the control group were not recommended. While the staff's recommendations were accepted in the majority of cases, it was the judge who determined whether bail should be set. Based on this design, the experiment was able to show conclusively that ROR did not increase the likelihood of failure to appear for trial. The Manhattan bail bond study is noteworthy for at least two reasons: since the program is currently operating in numerous jurisdictions across the country, the experiment is an exemplary case of a rigorous evaluation that exerted policy impact; also, the experiment demonstrates how a problem that is not amenable to formal, randomized experimentation can be reformulated to accommodate a more tractable, high-quality methodology.

STATUS OF CORRECTIONAL EVALUATION

Reviews of the correctional research literature tend to confirm Bernstein and Cardascia's conclusions (1975, p. 4): "If past evaluation efforts are any guide, future evaluations are likely to be inadequate in design, inept in execution, and uninterpretable in the findings produced."

In a near-exhaustive investigation of correctional rehabilitation research, Lipton *et al.* (1975) reviewed more than 900 studies of treatment effectiveness. Covering the period from 1945 to 1967, only 231 of the studies were considered sufficiently interpretable even to be included in the survey. Yet, despite this winnowing out of more than 75 percent of available research, serious methodological flaws were still rampant in the remaining 231 studies. For example, 8 percent of the included studies used no comparison group and 29 percent were *ex post facto* analyses. Random assignment of subjects was used in less than 35 percent of the 231 studies—and this is a very liberal estimate since distinctions were not always made between randomized and nonequivalent control group designs. Considering all of the more than 900 studies initially examined by the authors, the opportunity for making maximally valid judgments about treatment effects was jeopardized in over 90 percent of the studies before they were even completed.

Since earlier, less extensive surveys of correctional program evaluations had already indicated the use of randomized experimental designs to be infrequent, the findings of the Lipton *et al.* review are not completely surprising. Based on a survey of 100 studies of treatment effectiveness, Bailey (1966), for example, reported that 22 percent of the studies used experimental designs. Since the 22 percent included any kind of design that incorporated a control group (e.g., random, matched, nonequivalent cohort, and retrospective control groups), it is likely that the percentage of true randomized experiments was much smaller. In a separate survey of 100 evaluations of treatment programs (which include a 41 percent overlap with Bailey's sources), Logan (1972) found that 23 percent used a true experimental design. Perhaps most interesting about Logan's survey is that, while his period of coverage extended from 1934 to 1967, more than half of the 23 studies cited as using randomized designs were conducted in California during one 10-year period, 1957–1967.

Most recently, Dixon and Wright (1974) reviewed some of the post-1965 research literature in the areas of delinquency control, prevention, and treatment. They found (p. 11):

Ninety-five of these (350) articles and reports contained some form of empirical data about project efforts. Fifty percent of these studies used some form of comparison groups, of which about half (28% of the total) used a randomized or matched subjects design.

The state of the art of correctional evaluation may be characterized as tenuous and confusing. Reviews of the literature have not only reported the bulk of research to be nonexperimental, but also to provide disappointingly little and inconsistent evidence for the effectiveness of rehabilitative programs (Bailey 1966, Bennett 1973, Kassebaum *et al.* 1971, Martinson 1974, Robison and Smith 1971, Slaikeu 1973, Ward 1973). In light of the methodological deficiencies inherent in the designs of many studies, it is not surprising that attempts to identify effective methods of rehabilitating offenders continue to founder. Clearly, the design of an experiment is directly related to the interpretability of its results. Interpretability is also affected by measurement issues.

MEASUREMENT OF OUTCOME

OPERATIONALIZATION OF THE RESPONSE VARIABLE

A recurrent question in correctional research concerns the evaluative criteria necessary for reliable and valid measurement of treatment outcome. Dependent variables can and have been defined in such different ways that interpretation of program effects is confounded by a diversity of measurements of the same criterion. This problem is most salient in studies of recidivism, but it also affects other outcome variables. For example, exactly what does "institutional adjustment" mean? It has been variably defined as the absence of rule infractions, disciplinary lock-ups, or criminal behavior. Cooperating with institutional staff, becoming involved in prison activities, and scoring well on attitude tests are other indices of institutional adjustment. It is clear that use of such diverse measures can obscure interpretation of treatment effects. Two studies can draw very different conclusions if they use differerent combinations of these measures as the response variable. Certainly, it is not incongruous to expect that offenders who commit rule infractions may not commit criminal offenses; that offenders who cooperate with staff may not want to engage in prison activities; and so on. Even if two programs are equally effective, this fact can be easily camouflaged by differences among studies in how the dependent variable is defined.

There is little doubt that inconsistencies in defining and measuring outcome have affected attempts to integrate a meaningful knowledge base of correctional research. In discussing the problems of measuring recidivism reliably, the National Advisory Commission on Criminal Justice Standards and Goals stated (1973, p. 529): "Unless . . . measurements are based on standard criteria, reviews cannot be valid, nor can comparisons be made when necessary." The extent to which such standard criteria have been absent in correctional research is readily apparent in even a cursory perusal of the Lipton *et al.* (1975) volume. While numerous practical and methodological impediments to conducting meaningful evaluations may sometimes be beyond the control of an evaluator, defining the criterion to be measured should not. There is need for greater agreement on the operationalization of criteria and not simply on the labels attached to them.

SENSITIVITY OF RESPONSE VARIABLE

Beyond the issue of defining the outcome variable lies another one concerning the sensitivity of its measurement. There is considerable variability of the extent to which different studies measure program impact. Differential sensitivity of outcome measures can lead to different conclusions about program effects, so that even if two studies define a criterion identically, there is still no assurance that their conclusions about a program's worth would be the same. In evaluating a vocational training program, for example, one study may use employment as the dependent variable, while another study may use both employment and percentage of time employed as the dependent variables. The two studies may agree that the experimental and control groups do not differ in employment rates, but the second study may also find that experimental subjects retain jobs for a longer period of time than control subjects. The consequent conclusion of "no detectable treatment effect" by one study and "partially successful treatment effect" by the other would be due to the nature of the measurement processes rather than to the program.

The problem of using differentially sensitive outcome measures has been one of the chronic obstacles to obtaining reliable estimates of treatment effects. In the quest for discovering large effects, many researchers have neglected the potential benefits of measuring effectiveness in terms of what everyone really knows it to be—a continuous variable. Offenders have been dichotomized into recidivists and non-recidivists, adjusters and nonadjusters, achievers and nonachievers, etc. Similarly, programs have been dichotomized into successes and failures, despite the multidimensionality of all of the criteria. Such a dichotomous classification scheme has very limited value for yielding precise measurements of correctional results.

Perhaps the current despair over not knowing what works to rehabilitate offenders is due more to a failure to perceive what works than to the fact that nothing works. It seems axiomatic that if the extent and nature of changes resulting from a program are crudely measured, there is little basis on which to improve overall program effectiveness. To make measurement and evaluation more sensitive to true program effects, there need to be more systematic attempts to focus on both primary and secondary research goals, to use multiple dependent measures for assessing multiple program outcomes, and to detect offender-treatment interactions in addition to main effects. Although the results of such attempts may not answer the comprehensive question, "What works?", they could certainly help administrators and researchers turn their efforts in more appropriate directions.

LENGTH OF FOLLOW-UP PERIOD

One of the most difficult questions for correctional researchers to answer has been simply stated by Glaser (1973, p. 99): "How long a period suffices for adequate observation?" Desire for immediate knowledge of program effects, limitations of time and resources, and difficulties in keeping track of the individuals under study are some of the factors that have precluded long-term follow-ups on offenders. Although there is evidence that some treatment effects dissipate over time while others are manifested only after a latency period, the length of follow-up is often determined by two practical considerations: data accessibility and program funding. The problem that this raises is that estimates of the magnitude and direction of treatment effects can be a direct function of when the measure of the dependent variable is taken.

While most researchers probably believe that long follow-up periods are likely to produce more accurate findings than short ones, one of the biggest problems accompanying long follow-ups is attrition. Especially in correctional research, it is not unusual to lose track of 30–60 percent of the subject sample within 2 years. The question that arises is: What is the use of doing long follow-ups when attrition may produce such an unrepresentative final sample that a study's findings may be uninterpretable? Unfortunately, there are no ready answers to this question. Nevertheless, some constructive steps can be taken, including: (1) devising better techniques for minimizing attrition in the first place; (2) ascertaining the reasons for attrition when it occurs; and (3) developing better statistical methods for estimating the size and direction of attrition-produced bias (Riecken and Boruch 1974).

These steps will help in getting good follow-up data—regardless of how long the follow-up period is. There is also the more fundamental need for better theory. The literature is replete with pleas for developing theories that can link short-term effects to long-term effects. Until such theories are developed and tested, both short-term and long-term follow-ups are needed. Short follow-ups can provide immediate feedback, while long follow-ups can check on the durability of early effects. In the absence of good theories, such repeated testing of program effects may be our best available default option.

STATISTICAL ISSUES

Decisions about treatment effectiveness and ineffectiveness ultimately rest on the results of statistical analyses. However, just as threats to internal validity becloud meaningful interpretation of research results, so do threats to statistical conclusion validity (Cook and Campbell 1976). The extent to which statistical results are to be believed as reflecting the true relationship between treatment and outcome depends on the appropriateness with which statistical tests are applied. Because of a variety of oversights, statistical tests have not been sufficiently sensitive to detect the existence of treatment effects. The resulting biases of inference have greatly undermined the accumulation of knowledge about the effectiveness of rehabilitation programs. This section discusses some of the major statistical considerations that are generally ignored in correctional research.

POWER

If statistical analyses fail to reject the null hypothesis (the working hypothesis that posits that the posttreatment behavior of experimental and control groups will not differ), the finding may mean that the treatment had no rehabilitative effect. But failure to find statistically significant treatment effects may also be due to low statistical power. The power of a significance test is the probability of detecting a treatment effect given that the treatment is, in fact, effective. Despite its critical influence on estimates of treatment effects, statistical power is "infrequently understood and almost never determined" (Cohen 1977, p. 1). The implication of failing to determine whether statistical tests have sufficient power is that we often cannot distinguish programs that do not rehabilitate offenders from programs that are too weak to yield significant results even if the treatment works. Some of the factors mediating statistical power are significance levels, sample size, and experimental control.

Significance Levels: Type I and Type II Errors

The significance level of a statistical test is the probability level that prescribes the point for rejecting the null hypothesis. As a matter of convention, researchers are accustomed to setting significance levels at 0.05. If the significance level of a statistic exceeds 0.05, it is generally concluded that the treatment had no effect (i.e., the null hypothesis is not rejected). If the significance level is equal to or less than 0.05, it is generally concluded that the treatment was effective (i.e., the null hypothesis is rejected). In corrections, as in other areas of research, there is little indication that evaluators recognize that there is nothing sacred about 0.05 (Skipper *et al.* 1970). In fact, using a 0.05 test may be antithetical to the purposes of the research. For example, if exploratory studies that seek to identify promising rehabilitation techniques set a stringent level of significance, the likelihood of discovering effective treatments is minimal. By setting higher significance levels, say 0.15 or 0.20, the power to discern effective programs can be increased. Since increased power is accompanied by an increased risk of accepting an ineffective program, however, there can be no unilateral rules for setting significance levels. They must be determined by the expected costs of drawing incorrect conclusions. In particular, the evaluator must weigh the relative costs of committing Type I versus Type II errors of inference. (A Type I error is the rejection of a null hypothesis that is true, and the probability of its occurrence is equal to the signficance level; a Type II error is the failure to reject a null hypothesis that is false.) Since Type I and Type II errors are inversely related to one another, "it is *the nature of the problem* under study which ought to dictate which type of error is to be minimized" (Skipper *et al.* 1970, p. 157). If the costs are high of erroneously concluding that a treatment is effective, the evaluator must safeguard against Type I errors by setting low significance levels (e.g., 0.05, 0.01, or even 0.001, depending on the magnitude of risk allowable). Conversely, if the costs are high of erroneously concluding that a treatment is not effective, Type II errors should be reduced by setting higher significance levels.

Viewed in the context of statistical power, the prevalent "nothing works" doctrine in corrections is based on weak foundations. Just as programs have been dichotomized into successes and failures and offenders into recidivists and nonrecidivists, so we have come "to internalize the difference between .05 and .06 as 'right' vs. 'wrong,' 'creditable' vs. 'embarrassing,' 'success' vs. 'failure' " (Skipper *et al.* 1970, p. 156). Through blind reliance on arbitrary levels of significance, a continuum of possible conclusions is generally reduced to rejecting or not rejecting the null hypothesis. In an unknown number of cases, correctional evaluators have sacrificed the power to detect useful rehabilitation programs by being overcautious to avoid a mistaken inference that a treatment was effective when this was not true. In studies such as Lenihan's (1977), where the consequences of a Type I error could result in vast expenditures of financial assistance to ex-offenders, the need to protect rigorously against chance findings was justified. With less expensive, nonthreatening correctional programs, however, it may be worse to fail to detect a worthwhile program than to implement an innocuous one. While the information accrued in this way would not be conclusive, it could be of great heuristic value in providing some much needed direction to correctional research. For those rehabilitation methods that survive the rigor of subsequent tests and replications, correctional knowledge will be richer.

Sample Size

The need to weigh Type I errors against Type II errors becomes pointless if research studies are based on sample sizes that are too small to yield meaningful conclusions in the first place (Chandler 1970, Meehl 1970). There is a direct relationship between small sample size, low statistical power, and inability to obtain statistically significant treatment effects. When study samples are small, "a difference reflecting a genuine effect might not be statistically significant, or might even be reversed by sampling fluctuations" (Riecken *et al.* 1977, p. 117).

Again, the "nothing works" doctrine in corrections can be faulted for failing to discriminate between high- and low-power studies. While errors of measurement and sampling preclude perfect power, the results of small sample studies are particularly imprecise and easily produce spurious results. Determining the pervasiveness of "no effect" findings due to small research samples would be a major contribution to correctional knowledge. It is suspected, however, that the experience of Berger *et al.* (1975) in evaluating a volunteer program for juvenile probationers is not unique. The final evaluation report concluded (p. VII-1):

The data indicate that the program did not accomplish general reductions in delinquent behavior among those probationers it served. None of the literally hundreds of analyses of data suggest that the delinquency of the participants in the program declined relative to the controls. One would have expected that, if only [by] statistical chance, some apparently reliable data would indicate that some set of participants became less delinquent in some way under some conditions. But even while we are certain that some of the reliable results that we report must be statistically spurious just by chance, still none of the results in hand point to a positive change in participants relative to the controls.

Contributing to the perplexity of these results was the additional finding that experimental youths actually increased their delinquent behavior. Taking this report at face value, it may be thought of as contributing evidence for the "nothing works" doctrine. Upon closer scrutiny, however, it may be seen that the purported reliability of results is highly questionable. There were 94 subjects in the final study sample: Can a program be reliably evaluated on the basis of 94 subjects who are divided among three comparison groups? What, if anything, do research results signify when some analyses are performed on subgroups of only three, four, and five people? Assuming that the volunteer program actually had a small rehabilitative effect on delinquent behavior, the probability of detecting that effect with 94 subjects, using an F test, was less than 0.20. That is, the probability that the investigators committed a Type II error, if there was actually a small, positive treatment effect, was more than 80 percent. When the beneficial effects of a treatment are very small, a study with three groups requires approximately 160 subjects in each to have a 50-50 chance of correctly rejecting the null hypothesis at the 0.05 level of significance (Cohen 1977).

The importance of conducting research with large enough samples to be able to detect treatment effects cannot be overstated. Correctional researchers should, as standard practice, incorporate power analyses into the design stage of program evaluations. Methods are now available for easily determining the power of statistical tests for a given level of significance, sample size, and magnitude of expected treatment effect (see Cohen 1977). If the number of offenders available for a particular research study is too small to permit powerful tests of effects, every effort should be made to increase the sample size. Even if this temporarily increases research costs, the resulting increase in the validity of the results will make it a worthwhile investment. If nothing can be done to increase a sample size, researchers should at least report the power of their statistical tests along with the results. Minimizing the drawing of unwarranted conclusions from research findings should be the responsibility of the individual researcher.

Experimental Control

Having little control over experimental variables can also produce highly equivocal results, regardless of how large the study sample is. Lack of experimental control may be a function of several factors: variations in treatment implementation, unreliable outcome measures, heterogeneous subject samples, and extraneous influence operating in the experimental setting (Cook and Campbell 1976). Each of these factors contributes to statistical instability by inflating the error variance associated with research results. And as error increases, statistical power decreases.

It should be noted that these threats to statistical conclusion validity are unrelated to evaluation design. The best designs are vulnerable to these threats and cannot compensate for tests that are low in power. Until issues of statistical power are adequately dealt with, the chances of finding that something works will continue to be mediocre.

"PROVING" THE NULL HYPOTHESIS

The purpose of statistical tests is to test the null hypothesis (H_0). When a treated group of offenders is compared with an untreated group, the null hypothesis postulates a no-effect outcome of treatment. The aim of an experiment, however, should be to reject the null hypothesis and conclude that treatment was effective. If no treatment effects are found, the only legitimate conclusion that can be drawn from the research is that the data do not warrant a rejection of the null hypothesis. It is not legitimate to conclude that the null hypothesis is true.

Despite the fact that the logic of statistical inference clearly indicates that the null hypothesis cannot be proved, some correctional research studies are deliberately designed to accept the null hypothesis. For example, pretrial diversion is less expensive than court trials, and probation is less expensive than imprisonment. If it can be shown that these less expensive programs do not result in higher rates of recidivism than the traditional programs, why not replace the old programs? The reason is that statistics cannot confirm the validity of a no-difference finding. The conclusion "that there is *no* difference is always strictly invalid, and is functionally invalid as well unless power is high. The high frequency of occurrence of this invalid interpretation can be laid squarely at the doorstep of the general neglect of attention to statistical power . . ." (Cohen 1977, p. 16).

The potentially harmful effects of attempting to prove the null hypothesis can be illustrated via the matrix presented in Figure 2. Cells A and C represent the conventional experimental approach in which, even though the null hypothesis assumes no difference, the study hopes to show that the new program is superior to the old: that is, it hopes to reject H_0 and conclude that the alternative hypothesis, H_1, is

EXPERIMENTAL PROGRAM

		H_0: New = Old H_1: New better than old (Underlying assumption: H_1 is true)	H_0: New = Old H_1: New worse than old (Underlying assumption: H_0 is true)
DECISION	Accept H_0	A	B
	Accept H_1	C	D

FIGURE 2   Decision alternatives in hypothesis testing. (Note: The author wishes to acknowledge the help of Paul M. Wortman in developing this figure.)

correct. If the new program is not found to be superior (A), the old program is retained. If the new program is found to be superior (C), it replaces the old program. Neither of these decisions has harmful policy implications. Similarly, decisions arising from cell D are innocuous because a new program that is less effective than the old one will not be adopted.

It is programmatic or policy decisions based on cell B that can pose a threat. If the new program is assumed to be as effective as the old and H_0 is accepted, the old program may be replaced by the new, less-expensive one. But if the experimental tests used to decide that the two programs are equivalent have low statistical power, the consequences of implementing the new program are unknown. Possibly, the experiment failed to detect that the new program was actually harmful (e.g., produced an increase in crime rate when offenders were probated rather than imprisoned). The long-term costs of committing such a Type II error may be high. In situation A in Figure 2, accepting H_0 would not be harmful, except in the sense that a mediocre program may be retained when better programs, as yet unknown, exist. In situation B, however, there is the risk of replacing a mediocre—and even a workable—program with one that may be damaging.

Since even nonsignificant findings can have policy implications in corrections, program evaluation must minimize errors of inference. Experimental control and statistical power must be clearly and demonstrably high before a finding of no difference is deemed adequate justification for program changes.

ANALYSIS OF COVARIANCE

Because randomization has not been feasible (or not attempted) in many research studies, evaluators have relied heavily on the nonequivalent control group design. Usually, treatment effectiveness is measured in terms of the observed outcomes plus a number of background variables (i.e., covariates) that are presumed to affect the outcome. It is generally thought that these covariates can be used to statistically control for sources of variation that would not have been present if the experimental and control groups were equivalent to begin with. The belief is that if the right covariates are selected (i.e., those that correlate with treatment outcome) and if the effects of these covariates are partialled out, then treatment effects can be estimated without bias because the comparison groups will have been equated. But the comparison groups will not be equivalent if either of the following conditions obtain: the groups differ significantly on some (or all) of the measured covariates; or the groups are equivalent on the measured covariates, but there are unmeasured covariates related to treatment outcome on which they do differ.

Analysis of covariance (ANCOVA) has often been used to statistically adjust for initial differences between nonequivalent groups. A fact that is generally ignored, however, is that ANCOVA was designed for use in randomized experiments for greater precision in estimation of treatment effects. In these situations, ANCOVA can reduce the magnitude of experimental error, thereby providing a more powerful test of treatment effects than does the conventional analysis of variance. When ANCOVA is used without random assignment, however, adjusting for pre-existing group differences may not be possible.

The major problem with the use of ANCOVA in nonrandomized experiments is that covariates contain errors of measurement. That is, the variables are not measured with perfect reliability. The reliability of offense history, for example, is often questionable because self reports may be inaccurate, records may be incomplete, and offenders may not be apprehended for all the crimes that they commit. The effect of the unreliability is often to underadjust for pre-existing differences, thus making the treatment appear worse than it really is (Campbell and Boruch 1975, Campbell and Erlebacher 1970, Reichardt 1979).

The ANCOVA estimates of treatment effects are incorrect because the least-squares estimators of the regression slope are biased when there is measurement error in the covariate. Although this problem has been recognized, there is little agreement on how to deal with it. At one extreme, practitioners such as Nunnally (1975, p. 134) argue that "at the present stage of knowledge about the use of COVARAN [covariance analysis], it is a *distinct mistake* to employ this method of analysis with quasi-experimental designs." A more optimistic approach is taken by Porter (1967), who argues that the bias in ANCOVA can be corrected. Porter suggests using a measure of within-group pretest reliability to correct for the bias in the regression slope estimate.

A number of other techniques for statistically correcting for pre-existing group differences have also been recommended. For example, Kenny (1975) suggested using standardized gain score analyses, Sherwood et al. (1976) suggested a multivariate matching technique, and Magidson (1977) suggested using structural equation models.

While alternative strategies are being developed, ANCOVA is likely to remain a widely used technique for analyzing data from nonequivalent control group designs. But disagreement persists about the type of correction that should be applied to ANCOVA to enable it to fully adjust for group nonequivalence. Currently, the only concensus that exists is that the available corrections are applicable for specific situations in which the true score variance of the covariates is known. In summary then, evaluators must be aware that conventional ANCOVA produces biased estimates of treatment effects in nonrandomized studies, that corrections to ANCOVA are not generally applicable, and that data from a nonequivalent control group design must be analyzed with great care. (See Campbell and Boruch [1975] for a discussion of conditions under which statistical biases can appear; see Reichardt [1979] for a general review of ANCOVA-related problems and the strengths and weaknesses of the suggested alternatives.)

STATISTICAL VERSUS PRACTICAL SIGNIFICANCE

Given a large enough sample size, statistical significance can be found in practically any research study. It is likely that small treatment effects will be statistically significant with large study samples and that large treatment effects will not be significant with small study samples. Discovering that rehabilitative treatments produce statistically significant results, therefore, is insufficient for concluding that rehabilitation works—just as insufficient as using nonsignificant results to conclude that rehabilitation does not work.

A treatment effect that attains a desired significance level "is only one link in a chain of methodological evidence that the results are substantially as claimed; to offer it as the only piece of evidence is misleading" (Selvin 1970, p. 100). Despite such cautions, the mistake of equating statistical significance with practical significance is frequently made. That these two are not interchangeable has been repeatedly observed in studies that use multiple regression analyses. With a large number of subjects, it is almost certain that the independent variables will account for a significant portion of variance in the dependent variable. For example, with 300 offenders, one may easily find that treatment, age, race, and years of incarceration combined are significant predictors of success on parole. If the mutliple correlation (R) is .4, however, only 16 percent of the variance (R^2) in parole success is explained by the predictors; 84 percent is not. This may be a statistically significant finding: Is it also of substantive importance? This is a matter that only decision-makers, not statistics, can address.

The problem of failing to distinguish between the two types of significant results is pervasive. We generally find that evaluation results are reported in terms of t, F, and χ^2 values along with their associated degrees of freedom and levels of significance. These statistics provide a statement of the conditional probability that experimental and control groups differed on the dependent variables. Less often reported is the strength of the relationship between independent and dependent variables or the magnitude of difference between groups. Even if these are reported, the question of how substantively significant these findings are is usually bypassed. Yet answering this question is one of the major purposes of research. As Lykken states (1970, p. 279):

[T]he finding of statistical significance is perhaps the least important attribute of a good experiment: It is *never* a sufficient condition for concluding that a theory has been corroborated, that a useful empirical fact has been established with reasonable confidence—or that an experimental report ought to be published. The value of any research can be determined, not from the statistical results, but only by skilled, subjective evaluation of the coherence and reasonableness of the theory, the degree of experimental control employed, the sophistication of the measuring techniques, the scientific or practical importance of the phenomena studied, and so on.

If correctional theory were better developed, it could guide evaluators and decision makers in determining which statistically significant results have little practical relevance and which statistically nonsignificant results can have important practical relevance. Even without fully developed theories, however, researchers, program administrators, and treatment personnel usually have some idea of what a "good" outcome would be. Expectations of what constitutes trivial or important treatment effects should be stipulated before research is undertaken. Researchers should state in advance what job retention rates should be in work-release studies, what court appearance rates should be in ROR studies, the extent to which treatment should reduce recidivism, etc. Only when such substantively determined criteria are set can the confusion between statistical and practical significance be disentangled and a coherent synthesis of correctional knowledge be formed.

TREATMENT SPECIFICATION AND MONITORING

Before we can legitimately conclude that a method of correctional treatment has been shown not to work, there is a great deal we need to know beyond experimental design and outcome criteria. This third face of evaluation involves the assessment of the integrity of the treatment program itself (Quay 1977, p. 1).

To many evaluators charged with discovering treatment effects, the contents of the program being evaluated are a black box. In part, this is due to a failure to recognize (or if recognized, a failure to act on) the need for treatment specification as a mechanism for understanding evaluation results. In part, it is also due to the difficulty of describing programs that are complex, variable, or vague. In either case, the study that fails to describe the nature of the treatment seriously truncates its own information yield.

If a treatment is inadequately specified, it can be of little use in linking effective and ineffective program elements to outcome. A case in point is the experimental study by Berger *et al.* (1975) of a volunteer program for juvenile court probationers. In a report of more than 400 pages of text and appendixes, no more than a few paragraphs are devoted to describing the program. Consequently, despite an 18-month evaluation effort using an exemplary research design, the nature of the relationship between the program's characteristics and its inability to reduce delinquent behavior remains unknown. Slaikeu's review (1973) of 23 evaluation studies on group treatment of offenders found that all of them lacked adequate description of treatment practices and, further (p. 89), that "beyond labeling the treatment as psychotherapy or counseling, few researchers go on to say precisely what this means to them. The studies are notably lacking in clear definition of treatment."

A related important factor in understanding evaluation results is the intensity of the treatment. Rarely is there sufficient monitoring of treatment implementation to be able to gauge the treatment intensity. In fact, some studies provide no empirical evidence that the treatment was implemented at all. In looking at 236 federally funded evaluations, Bernstein and Freeman (1975) found that 22 percent of the studies took no steps to determine whether program specification and program implementation corresponded with one another. There are also reports of failure to implement treatment. Berger *et al.*, for example, report (1975, p. VII-2) that "from a quarter to a third of the probationers who were supposed to receive some service never did. For various reasons, they were never contacted by a volunteer probation officer, or they got no tutoring, or they never participated in counseling." Even among those who did receive service, some youths met with their volunteers immediately after referral, while others met up to 4 months later. Clearly, such variations in the treatment delivery directly affect the overall findings of an evaluation. The mere existence of a treatment says nothing about how well, how often, and to whom it is administered.

Reckless and Dinitz's (1972) experimental evaluation of a delinquency prevention program was also confronted with the problem of how to interpret treatment outcome as a function of treatment input. The results found the program to be ineffective, but the question of "why" was not answerable. One hypothesis suggested that the treatment program may not have been intensive enough to impel attitude or behavior changes in the youths. Had there been periodic monitoring and measurement of treatment delivery, the reasons for the program's inability to produce the expected changes may have been better understood.

The experiment by Kassebaum *et al.* (1971) on the effectiveness of group counseling with prisoners found no significant treatment effects, but did provide a wealth of information on treatment components. This substantive information was then able to provide valuable insight into the reasons for the nonsignificant findings. Some of the factors that characterized treatment in this study were as follows: counseling sessions were often superficial and ineptly handled; the sessions bored some participants; staff and client turnover was high; offenders were less interested in the program than in impressing the parole board with their participation; offenders distrusted the motives of the program and considered group leaders to be incompetent (Quay 1977). Given these types of conditions, can a treatment program realistically be expected to work?

If treatment integrity is lacking, conclusions about the value of rehabilitative techniques can be an artifact of the particular experimental setting in which the study was conducted. That is, if the program is an incomplete, diluted, or corrupted representation of the conceptualized treatment, it is not valid to conclude that the treatment is ineffective: the treatment has not really been tested. At present, it is impossible to know how often correctional studies have concluded that treatment was ineffective when they should have concluded that shortcomings in treatment implementation precluded the drawing of conclusions about its value. One suspects that the current despair over "nothing works" could be alleviated to some extent if we could distinguish program failures from treatment failures through substantive knowledge of program events.

Finally, description and monitoring of control conditions are also necessary to meaningful interpretation of evaluation results. As Riecken and Boruch note (1974, p. 142):

Statistical tests of program effectiveness will, in the last analysis, be made *relative* to the control conditions; without good specification of what those conditions are, neither the experimenter nor the program manager can attach much substantive meaning to program effects.

There are at least three reasons for specifying what the treatment is and for monitoring its implementation. First, knowledge of intended and actual program operations is an aid to asking the right research questions. Second, a well-specified and adequately monitored treatment program provides a more powerful experimental test. It facilitates answering the question "why"—whether the program succeeds or fails. (See Bernstein and Cardascia 1975, Hall and Loucks 1977, Quay 1977, and Riecken and Boruch 1974 for the types of information necessary to describe treatment and assess the integrity of its implementation.) Third, if a treatment is found to be effective, sufficient documentation of program elements will facilitate its replication at other sites. Although the current concern of correctional evaluators is that "nothing works," an important question is what they would do if something did work. It is likely that they would be hard-pressed to repeat past performances if there is little accurate and coherent description of what treatment was delivered.

EXTERNAL VALIDITY

Implicit in the evaluations of most treatment programs is the desire to generalize the research findings to persons and situations not included in the study. In order for such findings to apply to offenders in other prisons, or even to the rest of the offenders in the institution in which the study was conducted, an experiment must possess external validity. External validity is the extent to which experimental results are generalizable to different offenders, settings, staffs, and times.

Meaningful assessment of rehabilitative effectiveness requires not only that evaluation results be internally valid, but also that these results be generalizable. For example, if a psychotherapy program is evaluated on the basis of a highly select sample of offenders (e.g., middle-aged rapists) and if the program is found to be ineffective, little would be learned about psychotherapy as a rehabilitative technique. It would be invalid to conclude that psychotherapy does not rehabilitate offenders because the treatment was given only to rapists. It would also be invalid to conclude that psychotherapy fails to rehabilitate rapists, since only middle-aged rapists were included in the study. Even the conclusion that psychotherapy is ineffective for middle-aged rapists would be tenuous. Idiosyncratic characteristics of the study sample, general prison morale, or the personalities of the psychiatrists may have interacted with the treatment in ways that could disallow generalizing the study's results beyond the narrow, confined setting in which the treatment took place.

To implement a study that will be externally valid, there is one basic methodological requisite: the sample used in the research must be representative of the target population to which generalizations will be made. To demonstrate that a study is externally valid, there is an additional methodological requisite: the study must be repeated in another setting on another sample of offenders and the same findings obtained. Unfortunately, correctional research studies rarely fulfill either of these criteria. Instead, correctional programs have been evaluated in a diversity of institutional settings with a diversity of subject samples, and there has been almost no attempt to replicate research findings.

Given that circumstances, rather than research questions, often determine the composition of the sample in criminal justice research, it is not generally possible for evaluators to sample representatively from the target population. Therefore, researchers must be particularly attuned to factors that may threaten their study's external validity. Among the most common threats to external validity are: the interaction of offender characteristics and treatment; the interaction of setting and treatment; the interaction of history and treatment; the interaction of treatments when there are more than one; and the interaction of the time of measurement and treatment effects.

Interaction of offender characteristics and treatment If a treatment is more effective for some types of offenders than for others and if the study does not look for such differential effects, research results may be generalizable only to subgroups in the target population. The importance of focusing on offender by treatment interactions was clearly demonstrated in Adams's PICO study (1970). In this randomized experiment, the effects of individual psychotherapy were evaluated on delinquents judged to be "amenable" or "nonamenable" to treatment. The results showed that treated amenable delinquents not only recidivated less than treated nonamenable delinquents but also that the treatment had an adverse effect when administered to nonamenable delinquents. Had Adams not differentiated his sample in these ways, a finding of "no treatment effects" and a serious delimitation of external validity would have been likely.

Interaction of setting and treatment If treatment effects obtained in one correctional setting cannot also be obtained in other correctional settings, then research findings must be very narrowly construed.

Evaluators must be aware of features of the experimental setting that are unique to a particular study site to determine if these unique features can affect research findings. If they can, this threat to external validity should be stipulated in the final report and considerable caution should be exercised in using the study's results to make inferential leaps.

Interaction of history and treatment If treatment effects obtained at one time cannot also be obtained at another time, then external events that coincide with the experiment may make the results unique. Beyond being alert to extraneous factors that might produce this interaction, evaluators should conduct reviews of the relevant literature. If earlier findings support present ones, then the plausibility of a history-and-treatment interaction is diminished.

Interaction of treatments and treatments If multiple treatments are administered to offenders (e.g., vocational training, academic education, and counseling), research results may not be generalizable to situations in which only one of the treatments is given. Often, there is little that the evaluator can do to control for this threat to external validity. If the multiple treatments are given sequentially, however, its components should be analyzed separately so that the effects of the first treatment could be estimated separately from those of subsequent ones (although this presumes that treatment effects are immediately observable).

Interaction of time of measurement and treatment effects If treatments have differential effects over time and if the measurement lag is not in synchrony with the causal lag, then generalization of treatment effects to other times may be invalid. This threat may be lessened if outcome measures are taken at several times.

While there are numerous other threats to external validity, the five noted above illustrate some of the factors that researchers and policy makers should be cognizant of in interpreting research results. More thorough reviews of factors that can jeopardize the external validity of experimental results have been provided by Bernstein *et al.* (1975), Bracht and Glass (1968), Campbell and Stanley (1966), and Cook and Campbell (1976).

Some threats to external validity can be ruled out on empirical or logical grounds; others cannot. Therefore, replication of studies is the single most conclusive way of verifying the generalizability of research findings. Replication, however, requires that administrators and researchers know exactly what it is that is being replicated: this emphasizes again the need to have accurate descriptions of rehabilitative treatments. While the retrospectively evaluated Highfields program was cited earlier as a poor example of research methodology, and while the Southfields evaluation was also criticized on methodological grounds, both experiments are notable: the Highfields study because its detailed description of treatment components enabled its replication and the Southfields study because it capitalized on an opportunity to evaluate a replica of the Highfields program. Such replications are all too infrequent. That too few replications have been undertaken in corrections to be of use in identifying consistently effective and noneffective rehabilitation techniques is highly regrettable.

THEORY

Well-developed theories of correctional treatments could have tremendous potential for upgrading the quality of rehabilitation research. Unfortunately, while much has been written about the need to base research on a more theoretical framework (Adams 1975, Cressey 1958, Glaser 1973, 1974a, 1974b, 1975, Gottfredson 197$\it{z}$, Lejins 1971, Lejins and Courtless 1973, Lipton *et al.* 1975, Nelson and Richardson 1971, Reed 1974, Schulman 1961, Wilkins 1964), little has been done about it. In fact, little has changed since Cressey's observation (1958) that the labeling of a program as rehabilitative is less grounded in theoretical expectations of effective practices than in the tautological belief that rehabilitation is whatever it is that the program does. As to which program is selected as a rehabilitative model in a particular setting, intuition plays a major role. For example, Cressey writes (1958, p. 760):

In our society, education is a Good Thing, and schools must be maintained in prisons and justified as corrective ("good" men are educated; therefore, to make bad men good, educate them), whether or not there is any scientific evidence of their effectiveness.

Inadequate theory development has been cited as the key deficiency in correctional research (Glaser 1974a, p. 144):

The primary cause of a poor yield from criminal justice evalution may well be a poverty of theory more often than a dearth of methodological skill. Because of atheoretical formulation of questions, our research answers are useless, or their utility is not recognized, or the reasons for their utility or non-utility are not discerned.

Theories of crime causation and rehabilitation do exist. For example, delinquent and criminal behavior can be conceptualized within the framework of psychogenic, social, physiological, constitutional, or economic theories (Gottfredson 1972), and at least some rehabilitation techniques can be conceptualized within the framework of behavior modification, symbolic interactionist, or sociocultural relativity theories (Glaser 1974a). The major problems, however, are that (1) theories are often insufficiently developed to be of practical use in guiding correctional practice and research, and that (2) even when there are well-developed theories, research fails to capitalize on them. To date, there is little evidence that correctional research proceeds in a theory-testing, knowledge-building direction. Therefore, while "[w]e are not wholly ignorant of the precursors to anti-social conduct or of requirements for its modification . . . the needed comprehensive system, building upon presently available knowledge and earlier theory, has not yet been developed" (Gottfredson 1972, p. 69).

If theories were used to guide correctional research, they could have significant impacts on almost all aspects of research methodology. Research questions could be formulated in terms of testable hypotheses suggested by theory as plausible areas of investigation; outcome measurements could focus on program subgoals that are posited by theory as directly affecting final outcome; length of follow-up measurements could be based on theoretical assumptions of when treatment effects should appear; and the expected relationship between short- and long-term effects could be better stipulated and tested. Perhaps more importantly, theories could help point out what dependent variables should be measured. Despite the heavy emphasis on rehabilitation as a recidivism-reducing technique, and the prevalent findings that treatments do not affect recidivism, we cannot blanketly dismiss these treatments as nonrehabilitative. With little *a priori* theory of what treatment outcomes should be observable, positive effects on attitudes, prison adjustment, job earnings, job retention, family relationships, or offense latency and seriousness may be easily overlooked. Whether recidivism is to be the criterion of effectiveness or not, theory-based testing of rehabilitation strategies would provide a much more efficient way of accruing knowledge than the current trial-and-error procedures.

Partly due to its atheoretical orientation, much of correctional research can be characterized as dealing in circumstantial evidence (Levine 1973). Failure to specify the links between program input and program outcome, when combined with inadequate monitoring of treatment implementation, strongly detracts from the meaningfulness of studies that claim to have directly tested treatment effectiveness. These studies do yield data, but, as Kaplan states (1964, p. 268):

[t]he word "data," . . . is an incomplete term, like "later than"; there are only data *for* some hypothesis or other. Without a theory, however provisionally or loosely formulated, there is only a miscellany of observations, having no significance either in themselves or against the plenum of fact from which they have been arbitrarily or accidentally selected.

CORRECTIONAL POLICY VERSUS KNOWLEDGE

It may be said that correctional research has two goals: to discover what works; and to have an impact on the correctional process by effecting change in the operations of the system or the behavior of offenders. Except when administrators and researchers have common purposes, as in administrative experiments (Campbell 1967, Thompson 1974), the accomplishment of the first goal has been in the domain of evaluators while the accomplishment of the second goal has been in the domain of administrators and legislators.

When it comes to formulating program policy decisions, evaluation results are clearly only one of many sources of input. Furthermore, what weight will be attached to evaluation findings in future decision-making processes is an empirical question. According to Rossi and Wright (1977, p. 6): "As techniques improve in quality and timeliness, and as policy makers' understanding of the activity increases, evaluation research will become an increasingly important element in the policy process." The question that we are now confronted with is: What is the soundest way for evaluators to assess and effect changes in the corrections system?

It has been a tenet of this paper that strong experimental design, based on qualitative knowledge of the processes under study, is a necessary tool for discovering what programs work and for estimating the size and direction of program effects. Once the data are in, interpretation of their meaning, the writing of a coherent, noncryptic report of findings, and the dissemination of results become important extensions of the evaluative effort. At present, there is an obvious need to develop effective methods for communicating evaluation results and for persuading administrators to at least consider these results (Weiss 1972). According to Gottfredson (1972), improving research utilization is one of the major challenges confronting correctional evaluators.

While discussion of utilization per se is tangential to the concerns of this paper, the interface between research methodology and decision making does merit some attention. In particular, it is relevant to consider Adams's (1975) views on why rigorous evaluation results may be less appropriate as input to policy decisions than as input to a scientific knowledge base. According to Adams, not only has correctional research been largely nonexperimental, but studies with weak designs seem to have greater impact than those with strong designs. These considerations, when combined with the present nature of decision making and the application potential of different research methods, suggested to Adams that the utility of experimental designs may be overrated (p. 16):

There are obviously types of questions that can best be answered by experiments, but they may not at this time be the most important questions. It would appear that in the next decade or two, at least, evaluative research in corrections may call for greater flexibility and resourcefulness than for rigor and certainty.

The arguments that suggest an advantage to research that lacks "rigor and certainty" are debatable, and there have undoubtedly been many reactions—both pro and con—to these arguments. Recognizing that Adams's main interest was to stimulate thought on an important topic and that a useful service has been performed by doing so, the premise and expediency of advocating weak research methodology should be questioned.

At this time, there is no empirical evidence to either refute or affirm the notion that "level of impact correlate[s] negatively with strength of design" (Adams 1975, p. 15). Adams's suggestion was based on judgments about the two most extreme cases (i.e., a field survey and a randomized experiment) in a selective review of six studies. The impact of studies that fell between these two extremes did not seem to contribute to the concluding inference. Hence, aside from questions of statistical power if analyses are based on small sample sizes, there is the problem of no analysis having been performed to substantiate the assumption of negative correlation. In order to perform this type of analysis, it would be necessary to define "impact" and to develop a scheme for rank ordering the "strengths" of the experimental, quasi-experimental, pre-experimental, and nonexperimental methodologies currently in use.

If it is true that weak designs have greater impact, how could this be explained? It is difficult to believe that nonexperimental studies have more influence on policy makers because their designs are nonexperimental. It would seem more likely that, given the relative scarcity of carefully controlled experimental studies in corrections, evaluators have had little to offer as formal input to policy decisions other than the equivocal inferences drawn from weakly designed studies. Probabilistically, with a short supply of rigorous studies and an abundant supply of weak studies, weak studies would be expected to be more widely used and to have had greater effects in policy decisons.

Again, assuming that weak designs have greater impact, what should the implications of such a finding be? Should it impel evaluators to jettison the experimental method in favor of techniques that produce equivocal, but influential, results? Or should it rather signal the need to know why findings from controlled experiments fail to be used in the decision-making process? It may be that experiments are too slow in yielding information that is useful to decision makers, that experiments address irrelevant issues, that final reports are too long or too complex for administrators to be able to use, that administrators are unaware of the specific advantages of experimental results, or that administrators are simply not informed about the findings of experimental research. While any of these possibilities may be true, it is true that a dearth of information on the subject precludes their verification, and that none of them is intrinsic to the experimental method. (Boruch [1975b] provides an excellent discussion of some of the commonly encountered objections to controlled field experiments.) Before resorting to doing low-quality research, we need to first know what factors inhibit the usefulness of high-quality research, and we should also be convinced that these problems are untractable.

Lobenthal's (1974) position on the issue of impact takes a more political perspective (p. 72):

[It is unfair to] retrospectively [judge] intrinsic research qualities according to outcomes which are later determined by political vagaries and other intervening or extraneous forces. . . . [I]t is plainly a matter of clout rather than a scientific attribute inherent in the research when someone who is well placed in the agency or the legislature picks up the cudgels and goes to bat for a programmatic reform consonant with the research findings or recommendations.

Because evaluation takes place in a context where methodological, bureaucratic, and political forces act together to produce a given decision, the basis for reliance on weakly designed studies may appear to be methodological when it is, in fact, ideological (Williams and Evans 1969).

It has also been argued that despite their flaws, weakly designed studies are better able to deal with the important problems in corrections and so they should have greater impact. In considering this argument, it should be noted that bibliographies have been compiled on hundreds of social programs that have been evaluated with randomized designs (Boruch *et al.* 1978) including programs in the economic, judicial, mental rehabilitation, education, law enforcement, communications, medical, and offender rehabilitation areas. In criminal justice, the Manhattan bail bond experiment (Ares *et al.* 1963, Botein 1965, Sturtz 1967) and Lenihan's (1977) LIFE project on the recidivism-reducing effects of financial assistance to ex-offenders are exemplary cases of rigorous evaluations that addressed important issues and exerted considerable influence on decision makers. At the very least, such findings indicate that a blanket dismissal of experiments as being unable to deal with important problems is not substantiated by the available evidence.

Finally, let us briefly consider alternatives. Adams suggested that field surveys, case studies, and time-series experiments may be preferable to controlled experimentation because of their greater influence on the operations of the corrections system. Certainly, there is no reason to fault such studies if legal, ethical, political, or logistical factors preclude the use of studies with stronger designs. When rigorous methodologies can be employed to assess program effectiveness, however, the value of relying on such approaches is questionable.

Field surveys can be very useful as screening devices to indicate which programs are worthy of further study (Rossi 1971). Experimentation, after all, is a confirmatory procedure that is appropriate when there is reason to believe that a program is effective. If used as the first of a two-stage process, surveys can help avert the wasteful expenditure of time and money on experiments that are probably unnecessary. If used as a confirmatory method by itself, however, a survey has so many sources of variation left uncontrolled that heavy reliance on its results becomes a precarious exercise. For example, the California probation subsidy program (California Youth Authority 1974, 1975) was a large-scale, high-impact study based on a field survey. The program was found to be highly successful in diverting offenders from state correctional facilities and, consequently, in reducing the operating costs of correctional agencies and the amount spent on incarcerating offenders. There have been questions, however, about the extent to which the subsidy program was the causal factor in reducing institution commitments. Several other factors have been cited as competing explanations for the findings of the study: (1) In some counties, diverse social pressures to restrict commitment rates within upper and lower bounds may have exerted a stronger influence on commitments than did the subsidy program; (2) commitment rates were decreasing even before the introduction of the subsidy program; (3) population growth was changing; (4) crime rates were changing; (5) community alternatives to imprisonment were becoming more popular; and (6) sentencing policies may have been affected by increasing collaboration between judges and correctional administrators and the use of presentencing diagnostic reports (Bennett 1973, Kuehn 1973).

There is no question that the subsidy program had an impressive effect on the California corrections system. The question is: If an experimental test of the program had been feasible, should it not have been carried out in order to produce less equivocal evidence on the program's effects and greater confidence in the *raison d'être* of the resulting policy decision? If Adams can be interpreted literally, the answer quite possibly may be no. But to implement weakly designed studies for the sake of having an impact on policy decisions—when a better procedure is available—has very limited ultimate value for either furthering our knowledge of correctional programs or enhancing our credibility.

Residual uncertainty stemming from other, high-impact, loosely designed studies can be equally great. Time-series analyses, though they can be powerful quasi-experimental techniques, may leave several questions about program effects unanswered, as described earlier. Case studies are most susceptible to rival explanations, and as Campbell and Stanley (1966, p. 7) note: "the many uncontrolled sources of difference between a present study and potential future ones which might be compared with it are so numerous as to make justification in terms or providing a bench mark for future studies . . . hopeless." Thus, while it is true that experimental research cannot at this time answer the most important questions, neither can its quasi-experimental and nonexperimental counterparts.

CONCLUSIONS

The problems involved in conducting correctional research are multifaceted and complex. There exists as Adams has said (1975, p. 3):

a great deal of confusion over objectives, criteria, and methods, disagreement over whether evaluative research shows programs to be "efficacious" or not, and in the latter case, controversy over whether the inefficacy should be attributed to the research or to the correctional program.

Differential lack of rigor in applying methodological tools has resulted in a vast, confusing literature on the effectiveness of correctional rehabilitation programs. There are many problems with drawing reliable conclusions about "what works" given the disparity of methodological approaches to the same problem, differences among researchers in defining their criteria, and differences in measuring the same criteria—all under varying conditions and with different populations.

Weak experimental designs and lax methodologies are among the strongest obstacles to determining which rehabilitation methods are effective. Because of this, evaluators need to strive for as much scientific rigor as possible under the constraints of a given situation. Obviously, when there is pressure for immediate action, it makes little sense to undertake rigorous program evaluation. But many of the questions to which correctional administrators seek answers have existed for a long time, and they defy any ready solutions. Given that there is no imminent panacea to major problems, controlled systematic study has much to contribute. The advantages of randomized experimental tests should be particularly considered. If an experiment is not randomized, conclusions about treatment effects are frequently jeopardized by plausible alternative explanations, and arguments for the causal relationship between treatment and effect must too often rely on unsubstantiated assumptions. If an experiment is randomized, the probability of nontreatment variables accounting for the outcome is minimized, and so the validity and credibility of the results can be much greater than those obtained from quasi-experimental and nonexperimental studies.

Advocacy of randomized studies has met with a number of objections. One is that it is inappropriate or impractical to conduct true experiments in field settings. The available evidence, however, fails to support that contention. In corrections, as well as other fields, there have been successful randomized experiments. Boruch's continuously expanding bibliography of true experimental evaluations points to the validity of his conclusion (1975b, p. 110): "Given the number, quality, and variety of field experiments which we have been able to identify, the *general* contention that experiments are impractical is a bit underwhelming." Conversely, however, a general contention for the feasibility of randomized studies is also unjustified, since we know that they cannot always be carried out (see, for example, Clarke and Cornish 1972). But there has been very little examination of factors that may be associated with where, when, and why strong evaluations can be undertaken. At present, we need information on what conditions enable and prohibit the implementation of strong evaluations. We may well find that Glaser was correct when he observed (1971, p. 39) that "rigorously controlled experiments are possible in corrections more often than is usually assumed."

Another objection often raised against randomized studies is that they are costly and slow. In considering the validity of this argument, we are again faced with a dearth of information. Reports on the relative costs of different methodologies are so scarce that there is little evidence to either affirm or refute this contention. True experiments need not be either costly or slow if the treatment program is short and if the treatment has immediate effects. They can be time-consuming and expensive if programs are of long duration and if long-term effects are of interest—but this is true for any evaluation, experimental or otherwise.

Finally, Boruch (1975b) and Gilbert *et al.* (1975) have written about the inadequacy of considering only absolute costs. According to these investigators, the costs of conducting weak evaluations are likely to be higher, in the long run, than those of strong evaluations, because ". . . the cost of wrong decisions (or no decisions) based on equivocal data can be high" (Boruch 1975b, p. 113) when money is repeatedly invested into programs whose effectiveness is not clearly established.

When conditions prevent randomization, quasi-experimental techniques are definitely useful alternatives. It is a fallacy, however, to think that statistical control can compensate for experimental control. Regardless of what type of evaluation design is used, statistics cannot compensate for deficiencies in theory, measurement, power, or treatment integrity. As Glaser says (1965, p. 6): "It is a statistical maxim, in most behavioral science problems, that with strong data you can use weak [statistical] methods; the strong methods . . . are useful primarily to squeeze a suggestion of relationship out of weak data."

Clearly, a strong experimental design cannot stand alone—it needs to be followed by careful implementation, measurement, analysis, and interpretation of the treatment program. The valid and clear conclusions that can be derived from well-designed and well-executed program evaluations have much to offer for both offenders and policy makers.

REFERENCES

Adams, S. (1970) The PICO project. In N. Johnston, L. Savitz, and M. E. Wolfgang, eds., *The Sociology of Punishment and Correction.* New York: Wiley.

Adams, S. (1975) *Evaluative Research in Corrections: A Practical Guide.* National Institute for Law Enforcement and Criminal Justice, Law Enforement Assistance Administration. Washington, D.C.: U.S. Department of Justice.

Anderson, S. B., Ball, S., Murphy, R. T., and associates (1975) *Encyclopedia of Educational Evaluation.* Washington, D.C.: Jossey-Bass.

Ares, C. E., Rankin, A., and Sturtz, H. (1963) The Manhattan bail project: An interim report on the use of pretrial parole. *New York University Law Review* 38:67–95.

Bailey, W. C. (1966) Correctional outcome: an evaluation of 100 reports. *The Journal of Criminal Law, Criminology and Police Science* 57:153–160.

Bennett, L. A. (1973) Should we change the offender or the system? *Crime and Delinquency* 19:332–342.

Berger, R. J., Crowley, J. E. Gold, M., and Gray, J., with Arnold, M. S. (1975) *Experiment in a Juvenile Court: A Study of a Program of Volunteers Working with Juvenile Probationers.* Ann Arbor, Mich.: Institute for Social Research, University of Michigan.

Bernstein, I. N., and Cardascia, J. (1975) *Strategies and Designs for Criminal Justice Evaluation.* Paper presented at the meeting of the American Sociological Association, San Francisco, Calif.

Bernstein, I. N., and Freeman, H. E. (1975) *Academic and Entrepreneurial Research.* New York: Russell Sage.

Bernstein, I. N., Bohrnstedt, G. W., and Borgatta, E. F. (1975) External validity and evaluation research: a codification of problems. *Sociological Methods and Research* 4:101–128.

Boruch, R. F. (1975a) Coupling randomized experiments and approximations to experiments in social program evaluation. *Sociological Methods and Research* 4:31–53.

Boruch, R. F. (1975b) On common contentions about randomized field experiments. In R. F. Boruch and H. W. Riecken, eds., *Experimental Testing of Public Policy.* Boulder, Colo.: Westview.

Boruch, R. F., McSweeny. A. J., and Soderstrom, E. J. (1978) Randomized field experiments for program planning, development, and evaluation: an illustrative bibliography. *Evaluation Quarterly* 2:655–695.

Botein, B. (1965) The Manhattan bail project: its impact in criminology and the criminal law process. *Texas Law Review* 43:319–331.

Bracht, G. H., and Glass, G. V. (1968) The external validity of experiments. *American Educational Research Journal* 5:437–474.

California Youth Authority (1974) *California's Probation Subsidy Program. A Progress Report to the Legislature, 1966–1973.* Sacramento, Calif: California Youth Authority.

California Youth Authority (1975) *California's Probation Subsidy Program. A Progress Report to the Legislature, Report No. 2.* Sacramento, Calif: California Youth Authority.

Campbell, D. T. (1967) Administrative experimentation, institutional records and nonreactive measures. In J. C. Stanley and S. M. Elam, eds., *Improving Experimental Design and Statistical Analysis.* Chicago, Ill.: Rand McNally.

Campbell, D. T. (1969) Reforms as experiments. *American Psychologist* 24:409–429.

Campbell, D. T. (1971) Methods for the Experimenting Society. Paper presented at the meeting of the American Psychological Association, Washington, D.C.

Campbell, D. T., and Boruch, R. F. (1975) Making the case for randomized assignment to treatments by considering the alternatives: six ways in which quasi-experimental evaluations in compensatory education tend to underestimate effects. In C. A. Bennett and A. A. Lumsdaine, eds., *Evaluation and Experiment.* New York: Academic Press.

Campbell, D. T., and Erlebacher, A. (1970) How regression artifacts in quasi-experimental evaluations can mistakenly make compensatory education look harmful. In J. Hellmuth, ed., *Compensatory Education: A National Debate*. Vol. 3 of *Disadvantaged Child*. New York: Brunner/Mazel.

Campbell, D. T., and Stanley, J. C. (1966) *Experimental and Quasi-Experimental Designs for Research*. Chicago, Ill.: Rand McNally.

Chandler, R. E. (1970) The statistical concepts of confidence and significance. In D. E. Morrison and R. E. Henkel, eds., *The Significance Test Controversy*. Chicago, Ill.: Aldine.

Clarke, R. V. G., and Cornish, D. B. (1972) The controlled trial in institutional research. *Home Office Research Studies*. London: Her Majesty's Stationery Office.

Cohen, J. (1977) *Statistical Power Analysis for the Behavioral Sciences*. New York: Academic Press.

Cook, T. D., and Campbell, D. T. (1976) The design and conduct of quasi-experiments and true experiments in field settings. In M. D. Dunnette, ed., *Handbook of Industrial and Organizational Psychology*. Chicago, Ill.: Rand McNally.

Cressey, D. R. (1958) The nature and effectiveness of correctional techniques. *Law and Contemporary Problems* 23:754–771.

Dixon, M. C., and Wright, W. E. (1974) *Juvenile Delinquency Prevention Programs: An Evaluation of Policy Related Research on the Effectiveness of Prevention Programs*. Institute for Youth and Social Development, George Peabody College for Teachers, Nashville, Tenn. Available from National Technical Information Service, Springfield, Va.

Empey, L. T., and Erickson, M. L. (1972) *The Provo Experiment: Life and Death of an Innovation*. Lexington, Mass.: D. C. Heath.

Empey, L. T., and Lubeck, S. G. (1972) *The Silverlake Experiment*. Chicago, Ill.: Aldine.

Gilbert, J. P., Light, R. J., and Mosteller, F. (1975) Assessing social innovations: an empirical base for policy. In C. A. Bennett and A. A. Lumsdaine, eds., *Evaluation and Experiment*. New York: Academic Press.

Glaser, D. (1965) Correctional research: an elusive paradise. *Journal of Research in Crime and Delinquency* 2:5–8.

Glaser, D. (1971) Five practical research suggestions for correctional administrators. *Crime and Delinquency* 17:32–40.

Glaser, D. (1973) *Routinizing Evaluation: Getting Feedback on Effectiveness of Crime and Delinquency Programs*. Center for Studies of Crime and Delinquency, National Institute of Mental Health. Washington, D.C.: Department of Health, Education, and Welfare.

Glaser, D. (1974a) Remedies for the key deficiency in criminal justice evaluation research. *Journal of Research in Crime and Delinquency* 11:144–154.

Glaser, D. (1974b) The State of the Art of Criminal Justice Evaluation. Paper presented at the second annual meeting of the Association for Criminal Justice Research, Los Angeles, Calif.

Glaser, D. (1975) Maximizing the impact of evaluation research on corrections. In E. Viano, ed., *Criminal Justice Research*. Lexington, Mass.: D. C. Heath.

Gottfredson, D. M. (1972) Five challenges. *Journal of Research in Crime and Delinquency* 9:68–86.

Hall, G. E., and Loucks, S. F. (1977) A developmental model for determining whether the treatment is actually implemented. *American Educational Research Journal* 14:263–276.

Havel, J. (1965) *Special Intensive Parole Unit, Phase IV: The Parole Outcome Study*. Research Report No. 13. Sacramento: California Department of Corrections.

Jesness, C. (1971) The Preston typology study: an experiment with differential treatment in an institution. *Journal of Research in Crime and Delinquency* 8:38–52.

Kaplan, A. (1964) The Conduct of Inquiry: Methodology for Behavioral Science. San Francisco, Calif.: Chandler.

Kassebaum, G., Ward, D. A., and Wilner, D. M. (1971) *Prison Treatment and Parole Survival.* New York: Wiley.

Kenny, D. A. (1975) A quasi-experimental approach to assessing treatment effects in the nonequivalent control group design. *Psychological Bulletin* 82:345–362.

Kuehn, L. L. (1973) *An Evaluation of the California Probation Subsidy Program.* Ann Arbor, Mich.: University Microfilms.

Lejins, P. P. (1971) Methodologies in the evaluation of correctional programs. In *Proceedings of the 101st Congress of Correction of the American Correctional Association.* College Park, Md.: American Correctional Association.

Lejins, P. P., and Courtless, T. F. (1973) A general model for justification and evaluation of correctional programs. In *Proceedings of the 103rd Congress of the American Correctional Association.* College Park, Md.: American Congressional Association.

Lenihan, K. J. (1977) *Unlocking the Second Gate: The Role of Financial Assistance in Reducing Recidivism among Ex-Prisoners.* R&D Monograph 45. Employment and Training Administration, U.S. Department of Labor.

Levine, M. (1973) The randomized design provides circumstantial evidence. *International Journal of Mental Health* 2:51–58.

Lipton, D., Martinson, R., and Wilks, J. (1975) *The Effectiveness of Correctional Treatment: A Survey of Treatment Evaluation Studies.* New York: Praeger.

Lobenthal, J. S. (1974) Evaluative research in corrections—a practical guide. *Federal Probation* 38:72–73.

Logan, C. H. (1972) Evaluation research in crime and delinquency: A reappraisal. *Journal of Criminal Law, Criminology and Police Science* 63:378–387.

Lohman, J. V., Wahl, G. A., and Carter, R. M. (1965) *The San Francisco Project.* Berkeley: University of California.

Lykken, D. T. (1970) Statistical significance in psychological research. In D. E. Morrison and R. E. Henkel, eds., *The Significance Test Controversy.* Chicago, Ill.: Aldine.

Magidson, J. (1977) Toward a causal model approach for adjusting for preexisting differences in the nonequivalent control group situation: a general alternative to ANCOVA. *Evaluation Quarterly* 1:399–420.

Martinson, R. (1974) What works—questions and answers about prison reform. *The Public Interest* (35):22–54.

McCorkle, L. W., Elias, A., and Bixby, F. L. (1958) *The Highfields Story: An Experimental Treatment Project for Youthful Offenders.* New York: Holt.

Meehl, P. E. (1970) Theory testing in psychology and physics: a methodological paradox. In D. E. Morrison and R. E. Henkel, eds., *The Significance Test Controversy.* Chicago, Ill.: Aldine.

Miller, L. C. (1970) Southfields: evaluation of a short-term inpatient treatment center for delinquents. *Crime and Delinquency* 16:305–316.

National Advisory Commission on Criminal Justice Standards and Goals (1973) *Corrections.* Washington, D.C.: U.S. Government Printing Office.

Nelson, E. K., Jr., and Richardson, F. (1971) Perennial problems in criminological research. *Crime and Delinquency* 17:23–31.

Nunnally, J. C. (1975) The study of change in evaluation research: principles concerning measurement, experimental design, and analysis. In E. L. Streuning and M. Guttentag, eds., *Handbook of Evaluation Research,* Vol. 1, Beverly Hills, Calif.: Sage.

Palmer, T. (1974) The Youth Authority's community treatment project. *Federal Probation* 38:3–14.

Porter, A. C. (1968) *The Effects of Using Fallible Variables in the Analysis of Covariance.* Ann Arbor, Mich.: University Microfilms.

President's Commission on Law Enforcement and Administration of Justice (1967) *A Challenge of Crime in a Free Society.* Washington, D.C.: U.S. Government Printing Office.

Quay, H. C. (1977) The Three Faces of Evaluation: What Can Be *Expected* to Work. Paper presented at the National Conference on Criminal Justice Evaluation, Washington, D.C. To appear in L. Sechrest, ed., *Evaluation Studies Review Annual.* Vol. 4. Beverly Hills, Calif.: Sage.

Reckless, W., and Dinitz, S. (1972) *The Prevention of Juvenile Delinquency: An Experiment.* Columbus, Ohio: Ohio State University Press.

Reed, J. A. (1974) Program evaluation research. *Federal Probation* 38:37–42.

Reichardt, C. S. (1979) The statistical analysis of data from the nonequivalent control group design. In T. D. Cook and D. T. Campbell, eds., *The Design and Analysis of Quasi-Experiments in Field Settings.* Chicago, Ill.: Rand McNally.

Riecken, H. W., and Boruch, R. F., eds. (1974) *Social Experimentation: A Method for Planning and Evaluating Social Intervention.* New York: Academic Press.

Riecken, H. W., Boruch, R. F., Campbell, D. T., Caplan, N., Glennan, T. K., Jr., Pratt, J. W., Rees, A., and Williams, W. (1977) The priority score allocation design. In M. Guttentag and S. Saar, eds., *Evaluation Studies Review Annual.* Vol. 2. Beverly Hills, Calif.: Sage.

Robison, J., and Smith, G. (1971) The effectiveness of correctional programs. *Crime and Delinquency* 17:67–80.

Rossi, P. H. (1971) Evaluating social action programs. In F. G. Caro, ed., *Readings in Evaluation Research.* New York: Russell Sage.

Rossi, P. H., and Wright, S. R. (1977) Evaluation research: an assessment of theory, practice, and politics. *Evaluation Quarterly* 1:5–52.

Schnelle, J. F., and Lee, J. F. (1974) A quasi-experimental retrospective evaluation of a prison policy change. *Journal of Applied Behavioral Analysis* 7:483–496.

Schulman, H. M. (1961) *Juvenile Delinquency in American Society.* New York: Harper.

Selvin, H. C. (1970) A critique of tests of significance in survey research. In D. E. Morrison and R. E. Henkel, eds., *The Significance Test Controversy.* Chicago, Ill.: Aldine.

Serril, M. S. (1974) Is rehabilitation dead? *Corrections Magazine* 1:3–32.

Shelley, E. L. V., and Johnson, W. F., Jr. (1961) Evaluating an organized counseling service for youthful offenders. *Journal of Counseling Psychology* 8:351–354.

Sherwood, C. C., and Walker, W. S. (1959) Some unanswered questions about Highfields. *American Journal of Correction* 21:8–9, 25–27.

Sherwood, C. D., Morris, J. N., and Sherwood, S. (1975) A multivariate, nonrandomized matching technique for studying the impact of social interventions. In E. L. Streuning and M. Guttentag, eds., *Handbook of Evaluation Research.* Vol. 1. Beverly Hills, Calif.: Sage.

Skipper, J. K., Jr., Guenther, A. L., and Nass, G. (1970) The sacredness of .05: a note concerning the uses of statistical levels of significance in social science. In D. E. Morrison and R. E. Henkel, eds., *The Significance Test Controversy.* Chicago, Ill.: Aldine.

Slaikeu, K. A. (1973) Evaluation studies on group treatment of juvenile and adult offenders in correctional institutions: a review of the literature. *Journal of Research in Crime and Delinquency* 10:87–100.

Stapleton, W. V., and Teitelbaum, L. E. (1972) *In Defense of Youth: A Study of the Role of Counsel in American Juvenile Courts.* New York: Russell Sage.

Sturtz, H. (1967) Experiments in the criminal justice system. *Legal Aid Briefcase* 25:1–5.

Thompson, C. W. N. (1974) Administrative experiments: the experience of fifty-eight engineers and engineering managers. *IEEE Transactions on Engineering Management* EM-21:42–50.

Waldo, G. P., and Chiricos, T. G. (1977) Work release and recidivism: an empirical evaluation of social policy. *Evaluation Quarterly* 1:87–108.

Ward, D. A. (1973) Evaluative research for corrections. In L. E. Ohlin, ed., *Prisoners in America*. Englewood Cliffs, N.J.: Prentice-Hall.

Weiss, C. H. (1972) *Evaluation Research: Methods for Assessing Program Effectiveness*. Englewood Cliffs, N.J.: Prentice-Hall.

Wilkins, L. T. (1964) *Social Deviance*. London: Tavistock.

Williams, W., and Evans, J. W. (1969) The politics of evaluation. *Annals of the American Academy of Political and Social Science* 385:118–132.

Zeisel, H. (1968) Methodological problems and technique in sociolegal research: the indirect experiment. *Law and Society Review* 2:504–508.

Models of Criminal Recidivism and an Illustration of Their Use in Evaluating Correctional Programs

PETER SCHMIDT *and* ANN D. WITTE

INTRODUCTION

Evaluations of correctional programs, as well as many other types of social programs, have been greatly hindered in the past because of the costs and often the impossibility of using classical experimental designs. In many, if not most, correctional settings, random assignment of individuals to programs is not feasible because of moral, legal, and administrative considerations. In addition, in the rare situations in which random assignment has been possible, the costs of following up both a control and an experimental group have often proven substantial.[1]

In order to overcome the first difficulty, researchers in corrections

---

Peter Schmidt is a professor of economics, Michigan State University. Ann D. Witte is an associate professor of economics, University of North Carolina at Chapel Hill.

NOTE: The analysis contained in this paper was supported by a contract from the North Carolina Department of Correction. The statements and conclusions in the paper, however, are solely those of the authors and do not necessarily represent the opinions of the Department of Correction. We would like to thank Ross Mann, Ken Parker, and Jeff Williams for their help in conducting this evaluation.

[1] In one evaluation (Witte 1975) that used a quasi-experimental design in an *ex post facto* setting, the average cost of interviewing once and collecting information on the activities of a random sample of released inmates for an average period of 37 months was $250 per person.

have often resorted to quasi-experimental techniques. (For an excellent discussion of a number of quasi-experimental techniques, see Campbell and Stanley [1966]). Although such techniques are extremely valuable, they do not, in general, reduce the cost of evaluating correctional programs. (Indeed, they often increase it.) In addition, the use of such techniques makes it difficult to attribute any changes observed to program participation, since the group of individuals who participated in the correctional program usually differs significantly in a number of important ways from the comparison group that did not participate. With such designs, it is necessary to control for these other differences that may lead to changed behavior before one can attribute an observed change to program participation.

In order to adequately control for "other differences," the researcher requires two things: a model that indicates the factors that are likely to affect the outcome of interest; and a statistical technique that will allow control for the factors identified.

There are a number of difficulties in correctly using quasi-experimental designs. Correctional evaluators have tended to measure the outcome of correctional programs in simple dichotomous ways. For example, the most common measure of correctional outcome, recidivism, has usually been simply an indicator of whether or not an individual has returned to crime, measured in many ways (for examples, see Lipton *et al.* [1975]), by some set time after release. More complex measures of this correctional outcome, such as measures of the seriousness and frequency of criminal activity, have not, in general, been used because they tend to be either qualitative or limited (truncated or censored) in nature. Such variables make control for "other factors" much more difficult. But the concentration on simple dichotomous measures of correctional outcome has meant that the models of correctional outcome that have been developed deal with only such outcome measures: for example, there are relatively good models of simple dichotomous measures of recidivism, but poor models (or none at all) of more complex measures of criminal activity.

The authors in this paper develop models for a more complex measure of criminal activity, specifically, the length of time after release until reimprisonment. In addition, the authors show how the models developed can be used to evaluate correctional programs without use of a comparison group. The technique illustrated, the predicted versus actual technique, should help administrators of large, diverse correctional facilities, such as state prison systems, obtain more frequent and less costly evaluation than has been possible in the past.

The next section of the paper develops models of the length of time after release until return to prison, using the truncated lognormal distribution. The subsequent section evaluates an innovative vocational evaluation program for youthful offenders by using the models to predict expected recidivism and to compare this expected level with the actual level of those who participated in the program. The final section of the paper contains our summary and conclusions.

THE MODELS

The data set used to estimate the models described below consists of information on all individuals released from the North Carolina Department of Correction during the first 6 months of 1975 (January 1 to July 1). Information on the personal characteristics of these individuals was taken from the computerized inmate histories of the department. The postrelease criminal activity of these individuals was determined by a search of North Carolina Department of Correction records in February 1977.

There were 4,881 men and women released from the Department of Correction during the first 6 months of 1975, but the records of only 2,216 (45 percent) contained information on all major factors found to be related to participation in criminal activity in the past. Unfortunately, when one compares the characteristics of those for whom all information was available and those for whom it was not, one finds many significant differences. In general, more information tended to be available for those who had been in prison for shorter periods of time prior to the release. For a detailed comparison of intergroup characteristics, see Schmidt and Witte (1978). The difference in amount of information available reflects a (historic) increase in the quality and completeness of the department's inmate records. Fortunately, as described below, we were able to expand the sample and greatly increase its representativeness of groups normally participating in correctional programs.

The dependent variable considered in these models is the length of time in months from release until reincarceration in the prison units of the North Carolina Department of Correction.[2] This variable is denoted

---

[2] While a more geographically comprehensive measure of recidivism would be desirable, information on such a comprehensive measure is not regularly available, and hence the measure proposed seems practical and relevant to policy.

LTFPCV. From a statistical point of view, the unusual features of LTFPCV are that it is nonnegative (by definition) and positively skewed. The positive skewness results from the fact that most individuals who return to prison do so quite quickly, although some do not return for long periods, if ever. A further complication is that we cannot observe a value of LTFPCV longer than the length of the individual's follow-up period. Indeed, for individuals who do not return to prison in North Carolina during their follow-up periods, we do not observe any value of LTFPCV. Thus, an appropriate distribution for this dependent variable must be nonnegative, positively skewed, and truncated from the right by the length of the follow-up period.

In an earlier paper (Witte and Schmidt 1977), this dependent variable was analyzed using a different data set; comparison of a number of possible distributions indicated that a truncated lognormal distribution was most appropriate. We will therefore use the truncated lognormal distribution in our present analysis. The basic assumption is that LTFPCV follows a lognormal distribution whose mean is a linear function of various explanatory variables and that is truncated by the length of the follow-up period. The model is estimated by maximum likelihood. An explicit statement of the model and method of estimation can be found in Witte and Schmidt (1977) or Amemiya and Boskin (1974).

In order to check on the predictive accuracy of the models, we randomly divided our sample of 2,216 individuals for whom all information was available into two groups. The first group, containing 1,616 individuals, was used to estimate the models and constitutes the estimation sample. The second group, containing 600 individuals, was used to test the predictive accuracy of our models and constitutes the validation sample. Prediction outside the sample used in estimation is considered a rigorous test of model specification and is particularly appropriate here since the models are intended to be used for predictive purposes.

On the basis of past research on the determinants of criminal recidivism (see Service [1972] for a survey of this literature and Witte and Schmidt [1977] for previous work on this particular dependent variable), we hypothesized that the mean of LTFPCV was a linear function of 14 variables:

(1) a constant term (CNST);

(2) a dummy variable equal to one for nonblacks and equal to zero for blacks (RACE);

(3) a dummy variable equal to one if the individual's record indicated a serious problem with alcohol and equal to zero otherwise (ALKY);

(4) a dummy variable equal to one if the individual's record indicated use of hard drugs and equal to zero otherwise (JUNKY);

(5) a dummy variable equal to one if the release from the sample sentence (the sentence prior to release during the first 6 months of 1975) was supervised and equal to zero if it was not (SUPER);

(6) the number of convictions prior to the one leading to the sample sentence (CONVBS);

(7) a dummy variable equal to one for males and zero for females (SEX);

(8) age (in months) at release (AAR);

(9) a dummy variable equal to one if the sample conviction was for a crime against property and equal to zero otherwise (PROPTY)[3];

(10) a dummy variable equal to one if the sample conviction was for a crime against a person and equal to zero otherwise (PERSON)[4];

(11) a dummy variable equal to one if the sample conviction was for a felony and equal to zero otherwise (MF);

(12) a dummy variable equal to one if the individual was married at the time of release from imprisonment and equal to zero if not married (MS);

(13) a dummy variable equal to one if an individual participated in the North Carolina work release program and equal to zero otherwise (WR)[5]; and

(14) the number of years of schooling completed (SG).

The first step in our analysis was to estimate the specification containing all of the above variables on the 1,616 individuals in our estimation sample. When this was done, four variables were found to be insignificantly related to LTFPCV: ALKY, JUNKY, PERSON, and MS. The asymptotic t ratios—which are asymptotically distributed as $N(0, 1)$ under the null hypothesis that the associated coefficient is zero—for these four variables were -0.83, 0.61, -1.04, and 0.71, respectively, none of which is close to the usual critical points. Also, the likelihood ratio test of their joint significance yielded a test statistic of only 3.4, which does not approach the usual significance points of

---

[3] This crime category includes such offenses as robbery, breaking and entering, and larceny; it is as defined in Witte (1975, Appendix G) except that robbery is included in the property rather than the persons offense category.

[4] As defined by Witte (1975, Appendix G), with the exception noted in footnote 3.

[5] Work release, a program that allows men and women to work in the free community by day and return to prison at night, is the major rehabilitative program of the North Carolina prison system.

the χ_4^2 distribution. We therefore felt justified in dropping these four variables from our analysis.

While only 2,216 of the 4,881 individuals who were potential members of our sample had information on all the variables used above, an additional 1,632 individuals had information on all the variables used except ALKY or JUNKY. Since ALKY and JUNKY had now been dropped from the analysis, we expanded our usable sample from 2,216 to 3,848 individuals. This number is equal to 70 percent of the men and women released from prison during the first 6 months of 1975. This is an important improvement because the expanded data set is far more representative of the population of all releasees than the original data set was. In fact, the individuals who were excluded from the expanded data set tended to be short-term (mean value of time served during sample sentence was only 5 months), misdemeanant offenders, who would not normally have participated in correctional programs. Thus, the expanded data set should be quite representative of those releasees who are potential participants in the correctional programs that our models will be used to evaluate.

The 3,848 individuals in the expanded sample were randomly split into an estimation sample of 2,848 individuals and a validation sample of 1,000 individuals. In order to estimate our basic model, we randomly selected 1,000 individuals from the estimation sample. This was done because a sample of 1,000 is quite adequate to obtain reliable estimates and because estimation using 2,848 data points would have exhausted our budget for computer time.

Using this data set, we estimated the model containing all the explanatory variables used previously, except ALKY and JUNKY.[6] When this was done, the variables RACE, SUPER, MF, WR, PROPTY, and SEX turned out to be insignificantly related to LTFPCV. None of these variables had an asymptotic t ratio of more than 1.0 in absolute value, and the likelihood ratio test statistic for their joint significance was only 2.10, which is far less than the usual critical points of the χ_6^2 distribution. Therefore, these variables were dropped from the analysis.

The variables remaining in our specification are CNST, RULE,

---

[6] Note that the variables MS and PERSON were re-entered into the specification to see if the expansion of the data set might make them significant; it did. This points out the difference in using the expanded data set and the importance of using the most representative data set possible. It is even quite possible that if we had had values of ALKY and JUNKY for all the individuals in our expanded data set, these variables, too, would be significantly related to LTFPCV. Unfortunately, there is no way to check this possibility.

TABLE 1 Truncated Lognormal Analysis of LTFPCV (Sample of 1,000 Individuals from Enlarged Sample of 2,849 Individuals)

Variable	Coefficient	t Ratio
CNST	−179.1967	−1.58
RULE	−10.4744	−2.31
CONVBS	−12.0640	−2.09
AAR	0.8102	1.95
SG	25.8254	2.74
MS	131.0160	1.94
PERSON	291.4832	1.62

Estimated variance (σ^2) equals 2.6471.
SOURCE: Schmidt and Witte (1978, Table 3.2, p. 80).

CONVBS, AAR, SG, MS, and PERSON. The results for this specification are given in Table 1. These results indicate that the type of individual who is likely to return to prison soonest is young, single, and uneducated, has had many previous convictions and rule violations, and was in prison for a crime (the sample crime) that was not a crime against a person.

To test the predictive accuracy of our final model, we used it to predict the probability of recidivism during the follow-up period for the 1,000 individuals in our (new) validation sample. For the formula used to make these predictions, see Witte and Schmidt (1977, Appendix). Summing these predicted probabilities, one obtains the predicted (expected) number of individuals who will return to prison during their follow-up period. For the 1,000 individuals in our validation sample, the expected number of new prison convictions was 178.658; the actual number was 169. This is an overprediction of 5.7 percent. Using the appropriate test,[7] one obtains a test statistic of −0.82 for the difference between the actual and the predicted number reimprisoned. Under the

---

[7] Let $R_i = 1$ if the ith individual is a recidivist and $R_i = 0$ if not. Let P_i be the (predicted) probability of recidivism for the ith individual. Then, under the null hypothesis that these probabilities are correct, the central list theorem implies that

$$\frac{\sum_i R_i - \sum_i P_i}{\left[\sum_i P_i(1 - P_i)\right]^{1/2}} \rightarrow N(0, 1)$$

null hypothesis that our model is correct, the asymptotic distribution of this test statistic is $N(0, 1)$, and a value of -0.82 is clearly insignificant at normal levels of statistical significance. This is encouraging evidence as to the adequacy of the model.[8]

AN EVALUATION USING THE MODELS

As pointed out in the introduction, the models can considerably strengthen quasi-experimental designs used to evaluate correctional programs. They indicate what variables need to be controlled for in order to accurately attribute changes in criminal behavior to program participation and illustrate the use of statistical techniques that will allow this control for more complex measures of recidivism. The models can also be used directly to evaluate correctional programs; this use of the models is illustrated in this section.

THE PROGRAM

The program evaluated in this section began in January 1975 at Sandhills Youth Center, a unit of the North Carolina Division of Prisons that houses approximately 160 minimum-custody, honor-grade boys who are 16–18 years old. The program has been conducted by the staff of Sandhills Community College under grants from the U.S. Department of Labor.

Inmates are transferred to Sandhills Youth Center during the later stages of their incarceration in order to prepare for their release. The North Carolina Division of Prisons has two such prerelease centers for

---

[8] We also estimated separate models for five race-sex-age groups: (1) females; (2) nonblack male adults (≥ 21 years); (3) black male adults; (4) nonblack male youths; and (5) black male youths. We found that the overall model presented here predicted best for groups (3), (4), and (5), while the group specific model predicted best for groups (1) and (2). As we are concerned only with groups (4) and (5) in the evaluation presented here, we present only the overall model. For nonblack male youths, the test statistic for the accuracy of prediction of the overall model was -0.35, while that for the model estimated specifically for this group was 0.74. For black male youths, the comparable test statistics were 0.91 and -1.08.

To further test predictive accuracy, we predicted the number of recidivists in our validation sample for follow-up periods ranging from 2 to 25 months. In no case was the prediction generated by our models significantly different from the actual number of recidivists. Indeed, for only three follow-up periods (months 15, 16, and 17) did the test statistic for the accuracy of prediction exceed 1.00 (Schmidt and Witte 1978, p. 88).

youthful offenders, Sandhills and Burke, and inmates are assigned to the two centers on the basis of their expected county of release. Inmates expected to be released in the eastern part of the state (generally Charlotte and east) are generally assigned to Sandhills, and those expected to be released in the western part of the state are generally assigned to Burke. All inmates assigned to Sandhills Youth Center with 60 days or more remaining to be served on their sentences have participated in the Sandhills Vocational Evaluation and Job/Educational Development program since February 1975.

The program consists of three phases. During the first phase the inmate goes through a 3-week period of evaluation. The first week begins with an orientation to the program's purpose, facilities, personnel, and objectives. Next, the individual is given a number of tests (academic, personality, dexterity, interest surveys, etc.) designed to determine his level of academic achievement, vocational interest, and personal development. In addition, basic client data are collected. For examples of typical client and test data sheets, see Schmidt and Witte (1978, Chapter 5, Appendix A).

The second week of this evaluation phase includes counseling, interviews, and work sample endeavors. The work samples are a vital and unique portion of the program. They allow the program participant to sample a typical vocational situation. For example, in the auto mechanics work sample, an inmate is provided with an auto engine, mechanic's tools, and an illustrated manual. He is asked to perform various tasks with the engine, such as removing and gapping the spark plugs. He is observed to determine his ability and is asked about his interest after completion of the work sample. Work samples in machine shop work, drafting, electronics assembly, welding, carpentry, electrical work, auto mechanics, and drawing were available under the Sandhills program.

The third week of the evaluation phase consists of intensive interviews and counseling designed to develop a plan of action to remedy academic deficiencies, solve personality problems, and prepare the youth for an appropriate vocation. By the end of the third week, the vocational evaluator and the individual agree on an adjustment plan for services, and a formal evaluation meeting is held. In addition to the youth and his evaluator, the youth center psychologist, a local vocational rehabilitation counselor, and a job developer from the program are present. These latter individuals will be responsible for aiding the youth in carrying out his plan. For an example of a typical vocational evaluation resume and plan, see Schmidt and Witte (1978, Chapter 5, Appendix B).

Phase two consists of implementation of the adjustment plan and preparation for release. During this phase the youth works closely with the program's job developer in order to obtain an appropriate job or school placement on release. In addition to developing a job or school plan, the job developer checks to see that the young man makes satisfactory progress in completing his adjustment plan. The continual coordination and follow-up by the job developer are probably the reasons that most program participants received the recommended services (which is not usually the case in prisons); more than 90 percent of the recommended services were received (see Schmidt and Witte [1978, Table 5.1] for details). At the end of this phase the individual is released.

The final phase of the program consists of a follow-up for 90 days after release. During this phase the youth or a close associate is contacted once a month to determine if he is adjusting properly. Unfortunately, the follow-up phase usually consists of nothing more than monthly phone contact. For a typical case progress record, which illustrates better how the program operates, see Schmidt and Witte (1978, Chapter 5, Appendix C).

THE DATA

The data set used to evaluate the program at Sandhills Youth Center consists of information on 489 individuals who participated in the vocational evaluation and job/educational development program and who were released between February 21, 1975, and February 21, 1977. We were unable to obtain information on an additional 25 individuals who participated in the program and were released during this period, either because computer data could not be found or because the Department of Corrections' alphanumeric identifier could not be determined. We have no reason to believe that the omitted individuals differ systematically from those for whom we were able to obtain information.

Information on the personal characteristics of the 489 individuals was obtained from the computerized inmate histories of the North Carolina Department of Correction. The postrelease criminal activity of these individuals was determined by a search of North Carolina Department of Correction's records in June 1977.

METHOD OF EVALUATION

In order to evaluate the program, the number of individuals who would be expected to return to prison in North Carolina at various times after release is predicted for individuals who participated in the vocational training program using the (final) model of Table 1. We obtain our sequential predictions as follows. For any program group of size N under consideration, with varying follow-up periods, the predicted number of recidivists within m months after release is

$$\sum_{i=1}^{N} P_{im^*}$$

where, for each individual, m^* is the lesser of m or the length of the individual's follow-up period. The predictions for each month obtained by the above formula are compared with the actual number of recidivists for each month of the follow-up period, R_m, using the following test statistic:

$$\frac{\left[R_m - \sum_{i=1}^{N} P_{im^*} \right]}{\left[\sum_{i=1}^{N} P_{im^*} (1 - P_{im^*}) \right]^{1/2}}$$

Under the null hypothesis that the predicted probabilities are correct, the test statistic is asymptotically distributed as $N(0, 1)$.

Assuming that our models are adequate, which the previous section supports, any significant difference between predicted and actual recidivism may be attributed either to program participation or to some other difference in Sandhills Youth Center. For purposes of evaluation, the above method of sequential recidivism prediction is preferred to calculating a single test statistic for the group by considering only the maximum number of months each individual's activities were followed. Our reason for preferring the above method is that it allows us to explore potential effects on the timing as well as the rate of recidivism.

Table 2 shows the actual and predicted number of recidivists for the 476 program participants (of the total of 489) for whom all necessary information to use our model was available.[9]

---

[9] For the 13 individuals excluded, we lacked information on the number of previous convictions, CONVBS. The exclusion of these individuals, rather than, say, the use of an estimate of CONVBS, increased the appropriateness of our model, since this exclusion makes the group for whom recidivism is predicted quite like the group for whom our models were estimated.

TABLE 2   Actual and Predicted Number of Recidivists for All Sandhills Program Participants ($N = 476$)

Months After Release	Actual Number of Recidivists	Predicted Number of Recidivists	Test Statistic
2	3	9.741	−2.18
3	8	17.188	−2.26
4	17	24.902	−1.63
5	20	32.372	−2.26
6	25	39.418	−2.40
7	36	45.634	−1.50
8	49	51.200	−0.32
9	61	56.400	0.65
10	69	61.140	1.08
11	72	65.486	0.87
12	76	69.252	0.89
13	81	72.533	1.09
14	84	75.386	1.09
15	89	77.854	1.40
16	90	80.040	1.24
17	93	82.023	1.35
18	96	83.716	1.51
19	96	85.080	1.33
20	99	86.229	1.55
21	99	87.110	1.44
22	99	87.683	1.37
23	99	88.055	1.32
24	100	88.314	1.41
25	100	88.471	1.38
26	100	88.538	1.38
27	100	88.556	1.38

SOURCE: Schmidt and Witte (1978, Table 5.3, p. 128).

As can be seen in Table 2, participants in the vocational evaluation program had significantly lower (two-tailed test, 10-percent level) recidivism rates than predicted by our models for months 2, 3, 5, and 6. But there were no significant differences between actual and predicted numbers of returnees beyond 6 months. Indeed, what difference does exist is in the direction of more returnees than predicted, which, if significant, would indicate deleterious long-term effects of the program. While predictions for less than 3 or 4 months should be treated with some caution as they are to some extent strongly influenced by the form of distribution used, the prediction for months 5 and 6 should not be very much affected by that distribution, and the superior performance for Sandhills program participants can be attributed to some aspect of the Sandhills experience.

One question remains: Is this favorable performance due to program participation or to some other facet of the Sandhills experience? Unfortunately, this question cannot be unambiguously answered using the present evaluative technique. Indeed, this ambiguity points up a weakness in the present technique when applied to a prison unit or group specific program. If either the prison unit or the group differs significantly from the system norm in a way not controlled for by our model, unambiguous attribution is not possible. But favorable results are useful even in such situations, as they may, as in the present case, indicate the possible length of program effect and point up programs for which more costly experimental designs may be merited.

The results obtained above do not seem unreasonable. Considering the relatively perfunctory nature of the follow-up effort and its termination after 90 days, one would expect the maximum program effects to occur in the period immediately after release. Later atrophy of favorable effects could be due either to failure to find jobs in fields of training or failure to keep jobs that are obtained.

SUMMARY AND CONCLUSIONS

In this paper, we have developed models of a measure of the extent and timing of criminal recidivism. Specifically, we have developed models of the length of time after release until reimprisonment (LTFPCV), using the truncated lognormal distribution.

Our available data set was randomly split into samples used for estimation and validation, respectively. Results for our final specification, as given in Table 1, indicate that the type of individual who is likely to return to prison soonest is young, single, and uneducated, had many previous convictions or rule violations, and a sample crime that was not a crime against a person. This model was tested by using it to generate predictions for the 1,000 individuals in our validation sample. We predicted that 178.7 individuals would return to prison during their follow-up periods, while 169 actually did so. This is an overprediction of only 5.7 percent, and is statistically insignificant (asymptotic $N(0, 1)$ statistic equals 0.82) at usual significance levels. This is encouraging evidence as to the adequacy of the model.

The models developed in this paper can be used for a number of purposes. They can be used to explore the effect of changing offense mix, such as the recent dramatic rise in property offenses, on both the rapidity of return to prison and the number of offenders returning. Such predictions may allow correctional planners to more adequately predict expected prison populations.

The most likely use of such models, however, is to improve correctional program evaluation. If it is possible to use a quasi-experimental evaluation design, such models can be used to indicate the factors that it is necessary to control for and the way in which these factors may be controlled so that a change in behavior may be accurately attributed to program participation. If a quasi-experimental design is not possible, the models developed provide an alternative method of evaluating correctional programs. This alternative method of evaluation uses the models developed to predict the rate of recidivism (for various lengths of time after release) expected for a group that participates in a program and compares this prediction with the actual recidivism experienced by the group. *If the models are accurate,* any significant difference between predicted and actual recidivism may be attributed to program participation. The first phrase is important since this evaluative technique is only as good as the models on which it is based. We believe that we have presented convincing evidence for the adequacy of the models developed here, based on the accuracy of their predictions for random samples of individuals not included in the estimation of the models. This technique is most appropriate for evaluating programs that are in operation throughout a system. For programs specific to a unit or group, it is impossible to unambiguously attribute favorable performance to program participation, since other unit or group differences not reflected in the models may cause the observed effect. Even in this instance, however, the results of using this technique are useful to indicate potentially effective programs for which the expense of a true experimental design may be justified.

As an illustration of the use of the models developed in this paper, we evaluated an innovative vocational evaluation program for youthful offenders. As can be seen in Table 2, our model predicts significantly higher rates of recidivism than actually experienced for individuals who participated in the programs for the second, third, fifth, and sixth months after release. There are no significant differences between actual and predicted rates of recidivism beyond 6 months. Indeed, what difference does exist is in the direction of more returnees than predicted, which, if significant, would indicate deleterious long-term effects of the program.

Since the program evaluated was specific to a unit, we could not unambiguously attribute differences between actual and predicted recidivism rates to program participation. But the results obtained are useful in two ways. First, the marked increase in the difference between actual and predicted recidivism for 6 and more months after release indicates a rapid fall-off of any beneficial effects. This would seem to point up the desirability of strengthening and perhaps lengthening the follow-up phase of the program. Second, given the favorable results for the second, third, fifth, and sixth months after release, our results indicate that, particularly after implementation of a strengthened follow-up phase, the Sandhills vocational evaluation program may merit the expense and administrative and legal difficulties involved in conducting a full-scale experimental evaluation.

REFERENCES

Amemiya, T., and Boskin, M. (1974) Analysis when the dependent variable is truncated lognormal, with application to the duration of welfare dependency. *International Economic Review* 15:485–496.

Campbell, D. T., and Stanley, J. C. (1966) *Experimental and Quasi-Experimental Designs for Research*. Chicago, Ill.: Rand McNally.

Lipton, D., Martinson, R., and Wilks, J. (1975) *The Effectiveness of Correctional Treatment: A Survey of Treatment Evaluation Studies*. New York: Praeger Publishers.

Schmidt, P., and Witte, A. D. (1978) Determinants of Criminal Recidivism: Further Investigations. Report, under grant 77-04-B07-1013, to the North Carolina Department of Correction, Raleigh, N.C.

Service, P. (1972) *The Recidivism of Persons Released from Facilities of the North Carolina Department of Correction during January–July, 1968*. Raleigh, N.C.: North Carolina Department of Correction.

Witte, A. D. (1975) *Work Release in North Carolina: An Evaluation of Its Post Release Effects*. Chapel Hill, N.C.: Institute for Research in Social Science.

Witte, A. D., and Schmidt, P. (1976) Determinants of Criminal Recidivism. Report to the North Carolina Department of Correction, Raleigh, N.C.

Witte, A. D., and Schmidt, P. (1977) An analysis of recidivism using the truncated lognormal distribution, *Applied Statistics* 26(3):302–311.

Issues in the
Measurement of Recidivism

GORDON WALDO *and* DAVID GRISWOLD

Before definitions and measures of recidivism are discussed, several preliminary remarks are in order. First, the problem of measuring recidivism is fraught with all the hazards and difficulties that face the criminologist in attempting to measure "crime." There are numerous definitions and measures of crime, and thus far, the field of criminology lacks consensus on the questions of what is crime and how it is measured. There is no reason to assume that questions related to definitions and measures of recidivism can be more readily resolved.

Second, the criminal justice system has various goals that are frequently in conflict; the reduction of recidivism represents only one of those goals. For example, the goals of incapacitation and rehabilitation call for quite different strategies in approaching the problem of crime (see Governor's Special Committee on Criminal Offenders 1968, pp. 281–285).

Third, recidivism has traditionally been viewed as an important measure of the success of correctional programs, but additional measures have been used to evaluate the success of programs. Those other measures include personality change, attitudinal improvement, institutional adjustment, the development of vocational skills, employment

Gordon Waldo is a professor, School of Criminology, Florida State University. David Griswold is an assistant professor, Department of Criminal Justice, University of Nevada, Reno.

success, family stability, community crime rates, reduced costs, etc.[1] In some instances, these variables have been used as substitutes for recidivism when it could not readily be measured; in other situations these variables have been viewed as proximate variables to determine a program's ability to achieve stated goals. But if the overall program goal is rehabilitation (or specific deterrence), it would seem that the reduction of recidivism should be a long-range goal of any correctional program; it becomes, perhaps, the most impotant indicator of failure or success. For these reasons, indicators that are not specifically designed to measure reinvolvement in crime will be largely ignored.

Fourth, the concept of recidivism has tended to become reified. We should not lose sight of the fact that we are concerned with recidivism, at least in the context of evaluative research, only to the extent that it serves as a proxy for the success or failure of programs. The measurement of recidivism does not permit us to conclude that a program was successful for X percent of the population, but only that it was unsuccessful for Y percent. Since many other factors affect recidivism data, it is fallacious to conclude that nonrecidivism demonstrates rehabilitation or success (see National Advisory Commission on Criminal Justice Standards and Goals 1973, pp. 513–514).

Fifth, critics of the concept of recidivism argue that it is an inappropriate indicator since it is as much, or perhaps more, a measure of the response of the criminal justice system as it is a measure of the behavior of ex-offenders. This is a valid criticism if the intent is to establish a "true" recidivism rate for a group or to predict recidivism. It is permissible to use recidivism to measure success, however, if it is used as a relative or comparative measure rather than as an absolute or "true" indicator of the proportion of successes or failures. If our purpose is to evaluate the efficacy of the programs by comparing experimental and control groups, there is little reason to assume that the response of the criminal justice system will be different for the two groups. Any error in the measurement of recidivism should have a comparable effect on each group if the treatment did not generate a differential response pattern for the two groups, thereby producing an interaction effect between the treatment and the measure of recidivism. This is an important assumption and one that should be examined in any evaluative research, although it is seldom considered. An

---

[1] For example, in the studies evaluated by Lipton et al. (1975), less than half used indicators designed to measure further involvement in crime (National Advisory Commission on Criminal Justice Standards and Goals, 1976).

illustration for this point is found in a review of the Community Treatment Project in California (Lerman 1968, p. 224):

This important study may have exercised excellent control over the random selection of boys; unfortunately, the ideology of treating boys in the community spilled over into the post-experimental phase. The experimental and control groups appear to differ in the behavior of the parole agents with respect to revocation of parole—not in the delinquent behavior of the boys.

As important as this assumption is in the use of recidivism data for evaluation purposes, we are not able to dwell on it at any length at this time.

In contrast to the above arguments, other writers, such as Korn and McCorkle, see recidivism data as representing very important measures (Korn and McCorkle 1966, p. 24):

The analysis of recidivism rates is an extremely important function of the criminologist. They provide the most objective over-all basis for evaluating the effectiveness of law-enforcement programs . . . they are to the criminologist what the Geiger counter is to the geologist.

The National Advisory Commission stated (1973, p. 512): "Unlike any other social service system, corrections possesses in recidivism a criterion whose salience is universally agreed upon."

Finally, we would like to note that a large number of related topics are not addressed in this paper. Cost-benefit analysis, cost-effectiveness analysis, base expectancy rates, and predictive techniques all represent important topics in correctional evaluation, but they are beyond the scope of this paper. Nevertheless, it should be noted that since these techniques typically use recidivism data as a starting point, all of the measurement problems discussed in this paper have important consequences for these techniques as well.

DEFINITIONS OF RECIDIVISM

As is the case with any other concept used in scientific research, we are concerned with at least three levels of definition—the real definition, the nominal definition, and the operational definition (Hempel 1952). If the real definition refers to a "statement of the essential characteristics of some entity" (Hempel 1952, p. 2), then we are ultimately concerned with this definition of recidivism. Unfortunately, this level of meaning defies verbalization, much less measurement, but as DiRenzo noted (1966, p. 14), it is "a genuine proposition which must be either true or false."

NOMINAL DEFINITIONS

As we begin to communicate what we mean by recidivism, we move to the nominal level of definition, which reflects "an agreement . . . concerning the use of verbal symbols" (Hempel 1952, p. 2). Broadly speaking, recidivism means return to crime. But even with this definition, there is little consensus. The *American College Dictionary* defines recidivism as "repeated or habitual relapse into crime" or "the chronic tendency toward repetition of criminalistic or antisocial behavior patterns" while *Webster's Seventh New Collegiate Dictionary* defines it as "a tendency to relapse into a previous condition or mode of behavior." Unsatisfied with these dictionary definitions, we turned to introductory textbooks in criminology and corrections; surprisingly, there were few nominal definitions of recidivism. A haphazard sampling of 14 textbooks revealed that whereas all used the term recidivism, only three made any attempt to define it. Barnes and Teeters (1959, p. 58) defined it as "the proneness of many criminals to continue a life of crime." Korn and McCorkle (1966, p. 24) stated: "offenders who relapse are known technically as recidivists." Johnson (1974, p. 611) said: "The recidivist usually is defined as a person who, having been convicted, imprisoned, and released, again commits a crime." One of the most popular textbooks in corrections did not define the term but contained phrases such as: "The problem of recidivism or repeaters . . ."; "Recidivism, or repeated arrests, . . ."; and "Recidivism or repetition of crime . . ." (Fox 1972, pp. 73, 209).

Others frequently fail to define recidivism. For example, the President's Commission on Law Enforcement and Administration of Justice (1967) did not define recidivism or address any of the difficulties involved with the concept. The National Advisory Commission on Criminal Justice Standards and Goals (1973) had a discussion of recidivism, but the definition provided is an operational rather than a nominal one. Lipton *et al.* (1975) focused primarily on the measurement rather than the meaning of recidivism, although they include a definition (p. 12): ". . . the return of a person with a criminal record, or the commitment of a probationer to a penal institution for violation of the conditions of parole or probation or for the commission of a new criminal offense." It is not clear how a person on probation violates conditions of "parole," but that is perhaps a moot point for the moment. Wilkens provided a clearer definition (1969, p. 43): "The term recidivist . . . will simply mean that the offender, once treated-punished, has offended again and that the subsequent offense has been placed on his record." This last phrase concerning placement on the record undermines Wilkens's definition. Probably the most satisfactory nominal definition is in the *Preliminary Report, Governor's Special Committee on Criminal Offenders for the State of New York* (1968, p. 287), which defined recidivism as "an offense committed by a person who has previously been convicted or adjudicated for an offense." Because of difficulties associated with other definitions, we use this definition here.

The implications of several of the definitions mentioned go beyond the manner in which recidivism has traditionally been studied. For example, if the term "habitual" is used, it clearly implies something more than the definition we are using. Additionally, the terms "tendency toward repetition" and "proneness" imply something other than a behavioral referent for recidivism. A person might be considered a recidivist by these definitions if the individual had a "tendency" or was "prone" to commit crimes, even though a criminal act had not actually been committed. Returning to Wilkins's definition, it is not suitable because it excludes criminal behavior that is not recorded. While we may be forced to accept such a definition for operational purposes, it is an unacceptable nominal definition.

OPERATIONAL DEFINITIONS

At the level of operational definition, there is even greater disparity concerning the measurement of recidivism. There is considerable variation in terms of how it has been measured as well as disagreement over how it should be measured. The National Advisory Commission on Criminal Justice Standards and Goals stated (1973, p. 512): "The paradox of correctional measurement is the existence of a criterion variable that is easily recorded, simple to measure, and logically relevant but that also obscures research." The measurement of recidivism has varied in terms of the level of contact in the criminal justice system, the sources of data, the way the data are manipulated, the kinds of crimes (or rule violations) that are counted, and the length of the follow-up period.

In terms of the level of contact, some of the more common measures are: rearrest (Levin 1971, Waller 1974); reconviction (Glaser 1964, Greenberg 1975); reincarceration (Baer *et al.* 1975, Cowden 1966, Laulicht 1963); and technical violations of probation or parole rules. Also, individuals reincarcerated for a new crime and technical parole violators returned to prison are frequently combined and treated indiscriminately as recidivists, although this is not necessarily the case (Metzner and Weil 1963, Trudel *et al.* 1976).

The sources of data include institutional records for those reincarcerated in the same institution or in the same jurisdiction, rap sheets of the Federal Bureau of Investigation (FBI), police and court records, and self-reports of arrest, conviction, etc. For instance, Waldo and Chiricos (1974) used state institutional records, FBI rap sheets, and self-reports as sources of data. In examining several early recidivism studies, Glaser (1964) found that recidivism information was obtained from local, state, and federal records. Arrest data have provided additional recidivism measures, such as time to first rearrest, number of charges, arrest rate per month, and seriousness of crime for which arrested. Incarceration data have yielded similar measures, i.e., time prior to reincarceration and seriousness of new offense. Seriousness of new offenses has been measured by seriousness of crime indices (Rossi *et al.* 1974, Sellin and Wolfgang 1964) and in a cruder manner by length of sentence received.

The question of what infractions to include also creates measurement problems. The data range from the commission of any new crime (even the most minor misdemeanor) to the extreme of reincarceration for the exact crime for which the person was previously imprisoned. The medical analogy has provided the basis for the latter position. Johnson argued (1974, p. 613):

The evaluation of prisons as failures on the basis of recidivism is rather unusual when compared with other people-processing institutions. The medical patient's later appendectomy is not viewed as a failure of medical treatment for a broken arm, although the sources of criminal behavior are at least as varied as the forms of illness and injury requiring medical attention.

Tittle also spoke to the issue (1975, p. 402): "Being arrested for gambling cannot be accepted as evidence of recidivism for a burglar." The medical analogy has some merit, but evidence on plea bargaining suggests that we cannot look at the crime for which a person is convicted to determine whether or not the individual has committed the same crime again.

The problem is to decide which crimes are serious enough to constitute recidivism. The National Advisory Commission on Criminal Justice Standards and Goals stated (1973, pp. 512–513):

An offense above a determined level of seriousness must be charged against the system as a failure because the problem has not reduced the burden of crime. The problem lies in prescribing a level of seriousness that separates those criminal acts so minor or non-serious as not to merit public attention from those major or serious enough to be reported. . . . Ideally, some factor that combines the offense category and the sentence received should be utilized.

A related issue involves the treatment of technical violators of parole as recidivists. This is such a pervasive problem that it deserves separate comment. It is reasonably clear that a person who fails to report to his or her supervisor on time or who drinks alcoholic beverages is not a recidivist in the sense that the term has been defined above. The individual may represent a failure on parole, but the person is not a recidivist.

As Greenberg notes (1975, p. 554):

It appears for male parolees, and even more so for female parolees, the proverbially high rate of recidivism (as defined by returns to prison, the usual measure) is in large part an artifact created by the parole system itself, since many of the returnees were sent back to prison for behavior that is not forbidden to the general public, for suspicion of an offense where guilt was not provided in court, and at least sometimes when the parolee had already been tried and acquitted, or when the offense was minor and would not have resulted in imprisonment had the offender not been on parole.

The National Advisory Commission recognized this problem when it suggested that both kinds of information should be recorded but that they should be maintained separately.

The manner in which technical violations are defined confuses the issue even more. There is variation across jurisdictions concerning what constitutes a parole violation. In some instances, a person may be reincarcerated for a technical violation when the parole officer thinks the parolee is involved in a more serious crime. A more extreme case is one in which a crime has been committed that could be proved in court, but officials decide it is not worth the time and effort involved since the person could be reincarcerated as a parole violator for a longer period of time than if convicted of the new crime. In this case, the person is recorded as a technical violator and, therefore, not defined as a recidivist. It would appear, however, that the risk of misclassifying these kinds of cases is less than the error involved in treating all parole violators as recidivists.[2]

---

[2] Juvenile recidivism can also be distinguished from adult recidivism in several ways. One fundamental difference is that youths subsequently adjudicated delinquent for status offenses (acts that would not be defined as criminal if committed by adults) are sometimes defined as recidivists. Another marked difference is that juveniles referred to juvenile court are frequently considered recidivists, but perhaps reinstitutionalization in either a juvenile or an adult correctional facility is the most common criterion (Baer *et al.* 1975, Cowden 1966, Cymbalisty *et al.* 1975, Laulicht 1963).

LENGTH OF FOLLOW-UP

The length of the follow-up period has also varied considerably for different studies. Follow-up periods have been for as little as 6 months (Venezia 1972) and for as long as 10 years or more (England 1971, Unkovic and Ducsay 1969), although generally they have ranged from 1 to 5 years.[3] Some have suggested that 1 year may be sufficient because recidivism can be predicted with some accuracy; more recently, a 3-year time period has been recommended (National Advisory Commission on Criminal Justice Standards and Goals 1973). Others have argued that virtually all individuals are reconvicted within 5 years and that a longer follow-up period may be unreasonable (Hood and Sparks 1970, Mandel et al. 1965).

The issue of the appropriate period of follow-up is both an empirical and a logical one. Generally, it has been noted that the greatest risk of recidivism is during the first year or two. The proportions of recidivists over time are a function of the method used to compute the percentages. Many studies inflate the proportions of early recidivists because inappropriate methods are used to compute the rates (Berecochea et al. 1972). For example, if the interest is in determining at what point in time the risk of failure is greatest, the survivor cohort method best addresses this question.[4]

The question of follow-up is logically related to the issue of delayed treatment effect (versus the opposite condition of the extinction of a treatment effect). One argument is that the impact of a program may not be observed initially for it may take several years for the difference between the two groups to emerge. Another possibility is that an initial difference in favor of the treatment groups may disappear over a period of time (Lerman 1968). Both of these arguments suggest that a reasonably long follow-up period, at least 3 years, is necessary in order to determine the true impact of a program.

At least one writer (Kantrowitz 1975) suggests that for policy deci-

[3] The National Advisory Committee on Criminal Justice Standards and Goals (1976) has noted that 85 percent of the studies considered by Lipton et al. (1975) had follow-up periods of 3 years or less. In 25 percent of the studies, the follow-up period was less than the period of treatment, so these studies may tell us little about the performance of ex-inmates subsequent to treatment.

[4] Berecochea et al. (1972) compared three methods—the survivor method, the total cohort follow-up method, and the failure base method—and found that the proportions recidivating over time varied according to the method employed. They emphasize that the method used should be dictated by the question being addressed.

sions a 6-month period might be sufficient. He reanalyzed data from a parole violation study and concluded that the same decision could have been made at the 6-month interval as was reached at the 3-year interval. A shorter follow-up period would have the advantages of reduced cost and time in conducting evaluative studies. It is obvious that the "true" rate of recidivism will continuously increase as the follow-up period is extended because, by definition, it cannot decrease, only increase. For evaluative purposes, it is the comparative rather than the "true" rate of recidivism that is important. The data from an earlier study (Waldo and Chiricos 1974), however, do not clearly support Kantrowitz's conclusions (see Table 1). At the end of a 6-month period, the control group had a recidivism rate that was almost three times as great as that of the experimental group (4.3 versus 1.6 percent), but by the end of a 12-month period, the two groups had virtually identical rates (7.4 and 7.5 percent), and they varied slightly from period to period over the next 2 years. While the 6-month period for these data would have been grossly misleading, the 12-month period does produce the same conclusions about the relative effectiveness of the two programs as would be reached by the end of the thirty-ninth month. The problem, however, is that it is difficult to determine in advance the proper time for follow-up. Glaser addressed this time issue when he stated (1973, p. 100): "One clue that a short-run follow-up is significant in these cases is a progressive improvement in the success rate of the treated group as compared with the control or comparison group, with each additional interval of follow-up period"; however, he also said (p. 99): "There are no single answers to the above questions, because the answers depend upon the people-changing problem, the criteria of effectiveness, and the treatments to be compared."

Stollmack and Harris (1974) addressed a different issue concerning the follow-up period by using what is referred to as "failure-rate analysis." In most correctional programs, the members of the treatment group are exposed to the treatment at different times rather than at the same time. In order to standardize the length of time after release from prison and the exposure to risk of recidivism, researchers are usually forced to use the least common denominator for time out of prison. If the first person in the experimental group was released from prison on June 30, 1974, and the last person was released on June 30, 1975, then a 2-year follow-up would involve counting recidivism as of June 30, 1976, for the first case and June 30, 1977, for the second case. Stollmack and Harris argue that this forces one to ignore some of the data as well as to expose the two cases to different contemporaneous

TABLE 1 Number of Months Between Release and Return to the Division of Corrections for Experimental and Control Groups—Florida Sample

Number of Months	Experimental			Control		
	Frequency	Percent	Cumulative Percent	Frequency	Percent	Cumulative Percent
0–3	0	0.0	0.0	0	0.0	0.0
4–6	3	1.6	1.6	4	4.3	4.3
7–9	4	2.1	3.7	1	1.0	5.3
10–12	7	3.7	7.4	2	2.2	7.5
13–15	2	1.1	8.5	2	2.2	9.7
16–18	1	.5	9.0	2	2.2	11.9
19–21	8	4.3	13.3	4	4.3	16.2
22–24	4	2.1	15.4	3	3.2	19.4
25–27	0	0.0	15.4	0	0.0	19.4
28–30	2	1.1	16.5	2	2.2	21.6
31–33	2	1.1	17.6	0	0.0	21.6
34–36	0	0.0	17.6	0	0.0	21.6
37–39	3	1.6	19.2	0	0.0	21.6
Not reincarcerated within 39 months	152	80.8	100.0	73	78.4	100.0
TOTAL	188	100.0		93	100.0	

SOURCE: Waldo and Chiricos (1974, p. 239).

234

events occurring in their environments. Their method overcomes these difficulties and also avoids bias from disparate exposure times; however, the issue they have addressed is relatively minor in comparison with some of the other measurement problems.

It is relatively easy to determine how recidivism has been measured; it is more difficult to determine how it should be measured. There has been a continuing debate between law enforcement and correctional personnel concerning whether arrest or conviction data are more appropriate. The National Advisory Commission on Criminal Justice Standards and Goals attempted to resolve the issue (1973, p. 512):

. . . the use of arrests as the data for recidivism is subject to the objection that neither the behavior of the offender nor its significance has been verified by court action. . . . Recidivism should be measured by reconvictions.

The Commission went on to note (p. 513):

. . . the following definition should be used. Recidivism is measured by (1) criminal acts that resulted in conviction by a court, when committed by individuals who are under correctional supervision or who have been released from correctional supervision within the previous 3 years, and by (2) technical violations of probation or parole in which a sentencing or paroling authority took action that resulted in an adverse change in the offender's legal status.

Other social scientists, such as Lerman (1968), have argued for a position similar to that advocated by Sellin over 25 years ago (1965, p. 64):

It is still assumed by many criminal statisticians . . . that conviction statistics alone can furnish the basis for measuring criminality, but during the last two decades an increasing number of scholars . . . have come to the conclusion that a more satisfactory basis is to be found in the statistics of ''crimes known''. . . . The value of criminal statistics . . . decreases as the procedure takes us further away from the offense itself.

Glaser suggested still a different strategy (1973, pp. 22–23):

Success is too often measured as though it were an all-or-nothing matter. . . . Recidivism, for example, is measured in terms of one rearrest reconviction, or imprisonment. . . . Any measure . . . [that] classifies all research subjects as either successes or failures, is thereby limited in its sensitivity as an index of variations in the effectiveness of alternative programs and policies. . . . Probably the most sensitive criterion of the effectiveness of correctional endeavors with any group of offenders is the percentage of time they are confined during a follow-up period. . . . By reflecting severity of as well as number of penalties, the total amount of subsequent confinement time provides a crude index of differences in the extent of societal outrage at the conduct of various groups of released offenders.

The use of confinement rather than sentence imposed introduces an inadvertent source of bias that has been addressed by other researchers (Hopkins 1976). If a person is incarcerated for a portion of the follow-up period, this makes the individual a recidivist, but it also has the effect of removing the person from the "population at risk" when something other than a dichotomous measure of recidivism is used. If this position is combined with that advocated by Stollmack and Harris (1974), the complexity of handling the follow-up period is increased.

Another issue involves the probability of Type I and Type II errors because these errors vary according to the point in the criminal justice system at which recidivism information is obtained (Blumstein and Larson 1971). If Type I errors are those persons who have not committed a crime but are erroneously arrested or convicted and Type II errors are those persons who have committed a crime but are not arrested or convicted, the later the stage in the system at which recidivism is measured, the lower the probability of Type I errors and the higher the probability of Type II errors. In other words, using rearrest as a criterion would involve more Type I errors and fewer Type II errors than reconviction. To a large extent, then, the question becomes: Should Type I errors or Type II errors be minimized? While this may represent an alternative way of conceptualizing the problem, it fails to resolve the issue. The question concerns the risks attached to making each of the types of error. How much do we lose, and which risk are we willing to maximize? The criminal justice system operates on the basis of Type I and Type II errors when the question of guilt or innocence of the accused is considered and has presumably opted for increasing the risk of letting the guilty go free rather than increasing the risk of convicting the innocent (Feinberg 1971).

In spite of the National Advisory Commission's concern for adopting one clear and universally acceptable measure of recidivism, it is doubtful that it will be forthcoming in the near future. It is clear that the various operational definitions provide different proportions of recidivists; it is less clear that they lead to drastically different outcomes. For the moment, we might entertain the possibility that perhaps (to paraphrase Wilkens) when we know so little, we should not be overly hasty in restricting ourselves to one, and only one, measure of recidivism. A better strategy might be to use several different measures until we have a better understanding of the implications involved in using alternative measures.

NONTRADITIONAL MEASURES OF RECIDIVISM

At least two studies have sought to develop indices of recidivism (Mandel *et al.* 1965, Moberg and Ericson 1972). In the first study, a nine-item index was developed to measure the seriousness of recidivism (Mandel *et al.*, p. 60):

I. Convicted for commission of a felony.
II. Returned to custody as violator of parole for commission of an alleged felonious offense (not convicted).
III. Returned to custody as violator of parole rules for commission of a misdemeanor (convicted or not).
IV. Returned to custody as violator of technical parole rules only.
V. Convicted and sentenced for one or more misdemeanors (other than traffic), but not a parole violator.
VI. Convicted of one or more traffic violations resulting in fines of $100 or more, or jail or workhouse sentences of 30 days or more, or both.
VII. Charged or fingerprinted or "wanted" for a felony, even though no record of conviction is available.
VIII. Charged or fingerprinted for one or more misdemeanors (other than traffic), even though no record of conviction is available.
IX. No finding of recidivism.

A basic problem with the index is that no distinction was made between the behavior of parolees and that of expirees. (The index was developed from a study of parolees and expirees in Minnesota.) Specifically, an individual in category II was defined as a recidivist, while one in category VII was considered nonrecidivistic. Clearly, these two items are similar, and perhaps category VII could be interpreted as indicative of more serious behavior than category II. There is an additional problem of confusion between recidivism of releasees and parolees in the index. Separate classificatory schemes are necessary for the two types of offenders.

Moberg and Ericson (1972) expanded this classificatory scheme to 10 items, but their index applied only to parolees. A fundamental problem with both of these indices is that the ordering of items from most serious to least serious has a logical rather than an empirical basis. (They are not true scales because seriousness is based only upon the judgments of the authors and others.) It is questionable whether either of these indices even has face validity, not to mention predictive, concurrent, or construct validity.

Instead of relying on a dichotomy of success and failure, Glaser (1964) created several categories of relative success and failure, and he also included elements other than indicators of criminal behavior in his continuum. At one extreme there is clear reformation as evidenced by no further criminal associations; at the other is clear failure as indicated by return to prison for the commission of a felony. Marginal failures and successes fall between these two extremes.[5] Further refinement of Glaser's work would probably be of limited value because some of the variables are intended to measure behavior other than criminal activity.

The use of a seriousness-of-offense scale similar to that developed by Sellin and Wolfgang (1964) has also been advocated (Unkovic and Ducsay 1969). Such a scale has at least two advantages over dichotomous measures. The seriousness of offense for different individuals can be compared as well as the seriousness of offense for which a person was initially imprisoned and later reimprisoned. Still, there may be several drawbacks to a seriousness-of-offense scale (Moberg and Ericson 1972); for example, there may be inadequate information with which to score an offense. Such a scale is also primarily concerned with scoring offenses rather than offenders.

A COMPARISON OF RECIDIVISM MEASURES[6]

Traditionally, criminologists have observed that there may be problems with relying on official measures. As Erickson notes (1972, p. 389):

First, data derived from police and/or court records of arrests, court appearances may be less directly related to actual lawbreaking than to patterns of differential law enforcement, methods of gathering and reporting statistics and definitions of criminality. Second, any research which attempts to differentiate between delinquents and nondelinquents, criminals and noncriminals, which utilizes arrests, court appearances or convictions as the sole criterion of criminality may be biased in a number of ways and therefore, fail to distinguish "real" delinquents from nondelinquents.

Further, there is a paucity of research on the relationships between unofficial and official crime and delinquency. Erickson (1972) found that the gamma coefficients for the relationships between court records, self-reports, and estimates of future delinquency ranged from 0.6

---

[5] Actually, we have simplified Glaser's classificatory scheme, for he devised about a dozen gradations of success and failure.

[6] Much of the discussion, as well as the tables, in this section is from Griswold (1977).

to 0.9. In a similar study, Farrington (1973) found that self-report measures have some predictive validity, concurrent validity, and internal consistency but that their retest reliability was not great. Nevertheless, comparisons of measures may tell us little about the validity of a particular measure because there are no known valid measures to use as criterion variables (Nettler 1974).

In addition, there has been minimal effort in the comparison of various recidivism measures, although multiple measures are sometimes utilized. Data collected for an evaluation of work release by Waldo and Chiricos (1974) used 15 measures of recidivism. Variation is greatest between categories of data and least within categories. For example, with the FBI measures, all of those reincarcerated have also been recharged and rearrested; likewise, all of those recharged have also been rearrested.

The correspondence between reincarceration measures of the FBI and Florida Division of Corrections (FDC) are also of interest. About 69.7 percent of those reported reincarcerated by the FBI were also included in the FDC statistics. This is not surprising because the FBI collects information nationally, whereas the FDC can only account for those reincarcerated in Florida.

Using the Florida reincarceration measures as the baseline, we note that approximately 70.7 percent of the offenders have also been reported as being reinstitutionalized by the FBI. (It should be noted that the numbers of recidivists for the two measures are almost the same: 75 and 76.) Although the first finding of only 69.7 percent overlap was expected, this second finding was not. Theoretically, the FBI measure should be more comprehensive, but the figures show that only 70 percent of the people reincarcerated in the Florida prison system showed up as reincarcerated on the FBI rap sheets.

The senior author's experience on another project is relevant to this issue. Waldo and Chiricos (1970) attempted to develop a uniform data system in corrections across four states and decided to use the FBI number rather than generate a new identification number. They were somewhat surprised to find that (varying by state) 5–15 percent of the inmates did not have an FBI number. These findings tend to indicate that the Florida measure may be more valid, even though it is restricted to those who recidivate in Florida. In view of these findings, different measures of recidivism were examined to compare several different operational definitions. Three general types of data are compared— FBI, FDC, and self-reported contact with the criminal justice system. The FBI data were obtained from rap sheets for a follow-up period of 39 months, which gives some indication of whether or not the individual

TABLE 2 Comparisons of Percentages of Persons Recidivating Using Different Baseline Measures

Baseline Measures	n	Comparison Measures							
		1	2	3	4	5	6	7	8
FBI	311[a]								
1. Reincarceration (only felons)	76[b]			100.0	100.0	69.7	50.0	63.2	68.4
2. Reincarceration (for more than 30 days)	105			100.0	100.0	53.3	38.1	57.1	61.0
3. Recharged	208				100.0				46.2
4. Rearrested	208								46.2

	N[a]								
FDC	311								
5. Reincarceration (only felons)	75	70.7	74.7	78.7	78.7		46.7	60.0	65.3
Self-report	146								
6. Reincarceration	48	79.1	83.3	93.8	93.8	72.9		93.8	100.0
7. Rebooked	104			80.2	80.2				100.0
8. Rearrested	111				86.5				
Percentage of recidivists		24.4	33.8	66.9	66.9	24.1	32.9	71.2	76.0

[a] Total in sample under consideration.
[b] Number recidivating.
SOURCE: Griswold (1977, p. 96).

241

had recidivated anywhere in the United States during that time. In addition, reincarceration data were obtained from the FDC for the same follow-up period. Lastly, self-reported recidivism data from interviews of former inmates were collected about 2 years following release from prison; approximately half of those in the original sample were interviewed.

The percentages of recidivism vary considerably for the different measures (see Table 2). Proportions of those recidivating range from about one-fourth and one-third reincarceration—using FBI and FDC (felons only) and self-report measures—to about two-thirds and three-fourths for rearrest—using FBI and self-report measures.

Rather than correlate recidivism measures with one another, only percentage comparisons are made in this analysis. Percentage comparisons allow us to determine how closely two measures correspond, given a particular baseline measure. Simple correlations do not permit this kind of comparison. (For example, if FDC reincarceration is the baseline measure and 80 percent of the individuals are also reincarcerated according to the FBI, this may give us different information than an associational measure.)

As Table 2 shows, there are substantial discrepancies among the measures. Which measure is most appropriate? This question cannot be readily answered, but the findings do indicate that various measures have their limitations and that they are not necessarily equally valid or reliable.

The findings also demonstrate that recidivism measures are hierarchial. For example, if the FBI reported that an individual was reincarcerated, in all cases the individual was also included in the rearrested and recharged statistics. To a lesser extent, this same generalization applies to the self-report measures. In addition, as expected, a slightly larger proportion of individuals are defined as recidivists if we rely on the self-report rearrest or reincarceration measures rather than the FBI measures even though the follow-up period is shortest for the self-reports.

Table 3 illustrates the differences in results when models whose only difference is in reincarceration measures are compared. We have used log-linear regression because of the problem associated with ordinary least-squares regression when the dependent variable is dichotomous (Hanushek and Jackson 1977, Nerlove and Press 1973). Although it would also be possible to use multiple dimensional contingency table analysis (Bishop *et al.* 1975), Zahn and Fein 1974), we have relied on log-linear regression because we are only concerned with main effects

TABLE 3 A Comparison of Two Models When Only the Dependent Variables Are Different ($N = 261$)

	Model I,[a] FDC, Log-Linear Coefficient (B)[b]	Model II,[a] FBI, Log-Linear Coefficient (B)
Constant	−1.802	−1.549
	(3.08)	(2.61)
Ethnic origin	0.251	0.394
	(1.61)	(2.43)[c]
Grade completed	0.306	0.063
	(1.10)	(1.94)[c]
Age	0.043	0.024
	(3.21)[c]	(1.98)[c]
Marital status	0.090	0.235
	(0.53)	(1.36)
Working when arrested	−0.262	−0.085
	(1.64)	(0.51)
Age of first arrest	−0.025	0.009
	(1.68)[c]	(0.66)
Legal self-concept	0.321	0.130
	(2.59)[c]	(1.07)

[a] Values in parentheses are asymptotic T ratios.
[b] Comparable to b for ordinary least squares if multiplied by $[p(1 − p)]$ where p equals the probability of recidivating.
[c] Significant at 0.05 level.
SOURCE: Griswold (1977, p. 144).

and most of the variables have been measured at the interval level. The signs, significance, and magnitude of the coefficients vary to a large degree. (Unfortunately, a dummy variable for whether the individual was in the control or experimental group was not included in the models.) Regardless of whether the interest is in prediction or hypothesis-testing, the findings vary radically.[7] Clearly, one solution to the problem in this instance is simply to combine the two reincarceration measures.

[7] For example, if we compare coefficients for the two models, we find that for every year of school completed, the predicted probability of recidivating decreases by about 0.04 for Model I, but the coefficient for Model II is over 0.06.

PROPORTIONS OF RECIDIVISTS

As indicated above, it is difficult to discuss the proportions of recidivists in particular studies without specifying the characteristics of the sample under study, the length of follow-up, and how recidivism is measured; for these reasons, it is not possible to talk about an average recidivism rate. Glaser (1964) has argued that while studies often report that two-thirds of those released from prison return to crime, the proportion is probably closer to one-third. The overestimates result from two mistakes in computing rates. Frequently, offenders presently imprisoned are studied; this leads to overrepresentation of recidivists because recidivists are more likely to receive longer sentences and less apt to receive parole than first offenders. Inflation of recidivism rates may also be a consequence of selecting prisons where recidivists are concentrated.

Rates of recidivism have ranged from estimates of 5–8 percent for a sample of federal male parolees for whom recidivism was defined as reinvolvement in serious criminal activity within 1 year (Greenberg 1975) to over 80 percent reported by Canadian officials (Waller 1974). Some confidence may be placed in Glaser's estimate if the universe consists of studies of former inmates where the follow-up period varies from 1 to 5 years. And even Glaser's estimates may be inflated because some of the studies he cited used partial or total samples of parolees who could have been reincarcerated for technical violations; concomitantly, however, the proportion of successes in Glaser's study may be inflated because his sample consisted of federal inmates, who generally commit less serious offenses than state inmates (Levin 1971).

A tentative conclusion about the proportion of ex-inmates who recidivate does not seem warranted unless the definition of recidivism, the sample, and the follow-up period are specified, and such specifications would restrict the generalizability of such a conclusion.

CONCLUSIONS AND RECOMMENDATIONS

Although this discussion represents only an overview of some of the issues involved in the measurement of recidivism, several preliminary conclusions and recommendations can be made. Probably the greatest need is for the development of more uniform definitions and measures of recidivism, and several of our suggestions will focus on this point. It is only through such an endeavor that future recidivism studies will be more comparable than they have been in the past.

Recommendation One   At a minimum, future recidivism studies should use FBI indicators of recidivism.

At present, there are no common definitions or operational measures of recidivism, and it may be premature to arbitrarily accept any single definition as the best one. What is necessary is empirical analysis of the risk attached to the use of different measures. Clearly, different measures alter the probabilities that individuals will be defined as recidivists, but the effect that diverse measures have on program evaluations and policy decisions is less clear. Nevertheless, at the very least, future recidivism studies should use FBI rearrest and reincarceration information. Not only are these data readily available, but they have the advantage of allowing greater comparability among future studies. This suggestion does not preclude the further use of local or state information on recidivism; it does mean that for comparative purposes it may be preferable to include data on recidivism collected at the national level.

Recommendation Two   An appropriate group of experts should be convened to determine what kinds of offenses to include when measuring recidivism.

Although many might argue that the seven FBI index crimes should be incorporated in any recidivism measure, deciding what other types of crimes should be included is more problematic. Recidivism measures have ranged from those that incorporate only felonies to those that include all crimes except the most petty misdemeanors. One possibility would be to restrict the measure to only felonies, but a problem with this suggestion is that crimes are not always defined uniformly across jurisdictions (such as possession of marijuana). Technical violators of probation or parole should not be defined as recidivists, although they can be legitimately treated as failures in another context. Deciding upon what kinds of crimes to include is more difficult. Regardless of what crimes are included, the decision will probably not satisfy all researchers, but it is essential that there is a resolution to this issue in order to avoid continued confusion in comparing results. The National Advisory Commission on Criminal Justice Standards and Goals (1973) recognized this problem but offered no solution. It is necessary to establish a separate panel, subcommittee, or task force to resolve this issue and to offer future guidance for research.

Recommendation Three   The use of continuous measures of recidivism should be more fully explored.

Although there have been several attempts to develop indices of recidivism, it is questionable whether those currently available offer an improvement over dichotomous measures. This is not to suggest that attempts to measure recidivism as a continuous quantitative variable should be abandoned, but it is not clear that (for certain policy decisions) a continuous measure is preferable to a dichotomous one because the final decision may lead to a dichotomous outcome. In spite of these qualifiers, a continuous recidivism measure might allow determination of the relative success or failure of particular individuals and it might take advantage of available information that is ignored by dichotomous measures. The seriousness of an event could include such characteristics as: the level of involvement in the criminal justice system (rearrest, reconviction, etc.); the seriousness of the offense, the number of acts, and the sentence imposed. This type of index runs the risk of becoming so convoluted and complex that it might compound some of the problems discussed above, but it does have the advantage of allowing consideration of degrees of recidivism.

Recommendation Four   Follow-up periods in studies of recidivism should range from a minimum of 3 years to a maximum of 5 years.

A number of researchers have indicated that virtually all ex-inmates recidivate within 5 years. Some limit must be placed on the length of follow-up because at some point in time it is unreasonable to define individuals who commit further crimes as recidivists. In some instances a follow-up period of less than 5 years may be dictated by monetary or other constraints. Although it is known that the greatest proportion of individuals recidivate within a year or two following release, follow-up periods of less than 3 years may mask the extinction or delay-of-treatment effects. Until it has been demonstrated that shorter follow-up periods are adequate for evaluating programs, 3-year periods should be used. This, too, will permit greater comparability of various programs.

Recommendation Five   There should be a continued reliance on official measures, although self-report measures should be used when possible.

When self-report and official measures are compared, there are considerable variations in the proportion of people who recidivate, but self-reports do not appear to offer more constructive measures at present. While self-reports should be explored further before dismissing them completely, the experiences of the senior author are not encouraging. In addition to the problems of self-reports in general, some difficulties may become magnified in recidivism studies. Ex-inmates are not usually very cooperative, and they may perceive themselves as being in a more vulnerable position than other individuals. Coupled with these drawbacks are the difficulties of locating and gaining access to a rather elusive client population. One obvious bias is that those who are easiest to locate and interview are currently reincarcerated individuals. In spite of these shortcomings, self-reports should be employed when feasible.

Recommendation Six   Greater attention should be focused on the reliability and validity of recidivism measures.

There has been little consideration of the comparative reliability or validity of recidivism measures. In part, this is a reflection of the difficulties associated with the measurement of crime and the lack of adequate criterion variables that can be used to establish predictive or concurrent validity. (Unfortunately, social scientists have frequently focused on the development and utilization of more sophisticated statistical techniques rather than on problems in measurement, such as measurement error.) With regard to construct validity, findings concerning the failure of theories to explain and programs to rehabilitate may primarily reflect the lack of construct validity in operational definitions. In other words, it is unclear whether the problem lies in theory or in measurement. It will be difficult to place greater confidence in research findings until researchers can agree that recidivism measures are reasonably reliable and valid.

Recommendation Seven   At a minimum, studies of recidivism should only be compared within a context that considers: the sample, the length of follow-up, the quality of the research design, and how recidivism is measured.

The indiscriminate comparison of studies with diverse subjects, variable follow-up periods, research designs reflecting a wide range of quality, and disparate measures of recidivism will probably not advance understanding of the efficacy of correctional programs. The development of more uniform measures of recidivism is necessary in order to overcome some of the difficulties with past studies.

REFERENCES

Baer, D. J., Jacobs, P. J., and Carr, F. E. (1975) Instructors' ratings of delinquents after outward bound survival training and their subsequent recidivism. *Psychological Reports* 36:547–553.

Barnes, H. E., and Teeters, N. K. (1959) *New Horizons in Criminology.* Englewood Cliffs, N.J.: Prentice-Hall.

Berecochea, J. E., Himelson, A., and Miller, D. E. (1972) The risk of failure during the early parole period: methodological note. *Journal of Criminal Law, Criminology and Police Science* 63:93–97.

Bishop, Y. M. M., Fienberg, S. E., and Holland, P. W. (1975) *Discrete Multivariate Analysis: Theory and Practice.* Cambridge, Mass.: MIT Press.

Blumstein, A., and Larson, R. C. (1971) Problems in measuring and modeling recidivism. *Journal of Research in Crime and Delinquency* 8:124–132.

Cowden, J. E. (1966) Predicting institutional adjustment and recidivism in delinquent boys. *Journal of Criminal Law, Criminology and Police Science* 57:39–44.

Cymbalisty, B. Y., Schuck, S. Z., and Dubeck, J. A. (1975) Achievement level, institutional adjustment, and recidivism among delinquents. *Journal of Community Psychology* 3:289–294.

DiRenzo, G. J. (1966) *Concepts, Theory, and Explanation in the Behavioral Sciences.* New York: Random House.

England, R. W. (1971) A study of postprobation recidivism among five hundred federal offenders. In M. E. Wolfgang and L. Radzinowicz, eds., *The Criminal in Confinement.* New York: Basic Books.

Erickson, M. L. (1972) The changing relationship between official and self-reported measures of delinquency: an exploratory predictive study. *Journal of Criminal Law, Criminology and Police Science* 63:388–395.

Farrington, D. P. (1973) Self-reports of deviant behavior: predictive and stable? *Journal of Criminal Law and Criminology* 64:99–110.

Feinberg, W. E. (1971) Teaching the Type I and Type II errors: the judicial process. *American Statistician* 25(3):30–32.

Fox, V. (1972) *Introduction to Corrections.* Englewood Cliffs, N.J.: Prentice-Hall.

Glaser, D. (1964) *The Effectiveness of a Prison and Parole System,* Indianapolis, Ind.: Bobbs-Merrill.

Glaser, D. (1973) *Routinizing Evaluation: Getting Feedback on Effectiveness on Crime and Delinquency Programs.* Rockville, Md.: National Institute of Mental Health, U.S. Department of Health, Education, and Welfare.

Governor's Special Committee on Criminal Offenders (1968) *Preliminary Report.* Albany, N.Y.

Greenberg, D. F. (1975) The incapacitative effects of imprisonment: some estimates. *Law and Society Review* 9:541–580.

Griswold, D. B. (1977) Perception of Legitimate Opportunities, Legal Self-Concept, Adherence to Focal Concerns, Identification with Criminal/Non-Criminal Reference Groups, and Recidivism: A Multivariate Analysis. Unpublished Ph.D. dissertation, Florida State University, Tallahassee.

Hanushek, E. A., and Jackson, J. E. (1977) *Statistical Methods for Social Scientists.* New York: Academic Press.

Hempel, C. G. (1952) Fundamentals of concept formation in empirical science. In *International Encyclopedia of Unified Science.* Vol. 2, No. 7. Chicago, Ill.: University of Chicago Press.

Hood, R., and Sparks, R. (1970) *Key Issues in Criminology.* New York: McGraw-Hill.

Hopkins, A. (1976) Imprisonment and recidivism: a quasi-experimental study. *Journal of Research in Crime and Delinquency* 13:13–32.

Johnson, E. H. (1974) *Crime, Correction and Society.* Homewood, Ill.: Dorsey Press.

Kantrowitz, N. (1975) How to Shorten the Follow-up Period in Parole Studies from

Years to Months: A California Example. Paper presented at the American Sociological Association 70th Annual Meeting, San Francisco, Calif.

Korn, R. R., and McCorkle, L. W. (1966) *Criminology and Penology.* New York: Holt, Rinehart and Winston.

Laulicht, J. (1963) Problems of statistical research: recidivism and its correlates. *Journal of Criminal Law, Criminology and Police Science* 54:163–174.

Lerman, P. (1968) Evaluative studies of institutions for delinquents: implications for research and social policy. *Social Work* 13:55–64.

Levin, M. A. (1971) Policy evaluation and recidivism. *Law and Society Review* 6:17–46.

Lipton, D., Martinson, R., and Wilks, J. (1975) *The Effectiveness of Correctional Treatment: A Survey of Treatment Evaluation Studies.* New York: Praeger Books.

Mandel, N. G., Collins, B. S., Moran, M. R., Barron, A. J., Gelbmann, F. G., Gadbois, C. B., and Kaminstein, P. (1965) Recidivism studied and defined. *Journal of Criminal Law, Criminology and Police Science* 56:59–66.

Metzner, R., and Weil, G. (1963) Predicting recidivism: base-rates for Massachusetts Correctional Institution Concord. *Journal of Criminal Law, Criminology and Police Science* 54:307–316.

Moberg, D. O., and Ericson, R. C. (1972) A new recidivism outcome index. *Federal Probation* 36:50–57.

National Advisory Commission on Criminal Justice Standards and Goals (1973) *Report on Corrections.* Washington, D.C.: U.S. Government Printing Office.

National Advisory Commission on Criminal Justice Standards and Goals (1976) *Criminal Justice Research and Development: Report of the Task Force on Criminal Justice Research and Development.* Washington, D.C.: U.S. Government Printing Office.

Nerlove, M., and Press, S. J. (1973) *Univariate and Multivariate Log-Linear Logistic Models.* Washington, D.C.: Rand.

Nettler, G. (1974) *Explaining Crime.* New York: McGraw-Hill.

President's Commission on Law Enforcement and Administration of Justice (1967) *Task Force Report: Corrections.* Washington, D.C.: U.S. Government Printing Office.

Rossi, P. H., Waite, E., Bose, C., and Berk, R. (1974) The seriousness of crime: normative structure and individual differences. *American Sociological Review* 39:224–237.

Sellin, T. (1965) The significance of records of crime. In M. Wolfgang, L. Savitz, and N. Johnston, eds., *The Sociology of Crime and Delinquency.* New York: John Wiley.

Sellin, T., and Wolfgang, M. E. (1964) *The Measurement of Delinquency.* New York: John Wiley.

Stollmack, S., and Harris, C. M. (1974) Failure-rate analysis applied to recidivism data. *Operations Research* 22:1192–1205.

Tittle, C. R. (1975) Deterrents or labeling. *Social Forces* 53:399–410.

Trudel, R. J., Marcus, M., and Wheaton, R. J. (1976) *Recidivism: A Selected Bibliography.* National Institute of Law Enforcement and Criminal Justice, Law Enforcement Assistance Administration. Washington, D.C.: U.S. Department of Justice.

Unkovic, C. M., and Ducsay, W. J. (1969) An application of configurational analysis to the recidivism of juvenile delinquent behavior. *Journal of Criminal Law, Criminology and Police Science* 60:340–344.

Venezia, P. S. (1972) Unofficial probation: an evaluation of its effectiveness. *Journal of Research in Crime and Delinquency* 9:149–170.

Waldo, G. P., and Chiricos, T. G. (1970) Developmental problems in a regional data system for corrections. *Criminology* 8:215–237.

Waldo, G. P., and Chiricos, T. G. (1974) *Work Release as a Rehabilitative Tool: An*

Evaluation of Two State Programs. Southeastern Correctional and Criminological Research Center, Florida State University, Tallahassee.

Waller, I. (1974) *Men Released from Prison.* Toronto: University of Toronto Press.

Wilkens, L. T. (1969) *Evaluation of Penal Measures.* New York: Random House.

Zahn, D. A., and Fein, S. B. (1974) *Analysis of Contingency Tables Containing Non-Dichotomous Variables Using Log-Linear Cell-Frequency and Logit Models: Exposition and Interpretation.* (FSU Statistics Report M328.) Department of Statistics, Florida State University, Tallahassee.

Efficiency Considerations in Criminal Rehabilitation Research: Costs and Consequences

DAVID L. WEIMER *and*
LEE S. FRIEDMAN

Our objective in this paper is to suggest areas of economic research offering a potential for improving criminal justice policies that have rehabilitation as a major goal. We have been asked specifically to review the potential of benefit-cost analysis and cost-effectiveness analysis. While these tools of applied economic research can and should be used more frequently than they have been in the past, they have substantial limitations and, more importantly, only begin to scratch the surface of the potential contributions of economic thinking for correctional research. We begin by reviewing the basic purpose for such tools as benefit-cost analysis: to increase *efficiency* in resource allocation decisions. We will describe how benefit-cost analyses have been, and could be, applied to the institutional settings in which correctional resource allocation decisions are made. We hope this section will make clear the limitations as well as the conditions for more fruitful application of these tools. Then we will go on to discuss other methods of economic research that we believe offer potential for increasing the performance of the correctional system. Because some of the latter methods are less well developed, quick results with strong policy implications should not be expected; however, we believe it is essential that research of this type be encouraged.

David L. Weimer is an assistant professor, Department of Political Science and the Public Policy Analysis Program, University of Rochester. Lee S. Friedman is an associate professor, Graduate School of Public Policy, University of California, Berkeley.

EFFICIENCY: BENEFIT-COST ANALYSIS AND RESOURCE ALLOCATION DECISIONS

Despite the current debate over the effectiveness of correctional programs aimed at the rehabilitation of convicted criminals, rehabilitation remains a philosophically appealing goal for our correctional agencies. How might greater success be realized in the achievement of the rehabilitation goal? Three general approaches to improving decisions based on the notion of scarce resources can be envisioned. First, correctional agencies can alter their internal resource allocation pattern, i.e., the way they use the resources currently available to them. Resources may be shifted within an agency so that units of one correctional activity, such as security, are given up in order to concentrate on achieving more rehabilitation. Second, the level of resources available to correctional agencies can be increased so that they can attempt to produce more rehabilitation (and perhaps more of other outputs as well). Each of these two approaches depends on the possibility of using resources according to established methods, or what economists call technologies, to produce rehabilitation and other correctional outputs.[1] That is, it is known from experience that inputs X, Y, and Z can be combined in a particular way to produce outputs A and B.

The third approach for achieving more rehabilitation is to find and introduce new technologies that allow more to be produced at the same level of resource costs. The search for new correctional technologies is an economic investment in research and development. Such investments are typically characterized by a high risk of failure and are undertaken because of the possibility of a very large payoff. These investments include, for example, the contributions of academic researchers who develop and propose application of behavioral theories to the problem of rehabilitating criminals, as well as the initiation of actual demonstration projects and their evaluation.

There is no way other than one of these three methods to increase the rehabilitational output of the correctional sector. The fundamental concern of economics is that all these resource allocation decisions be made efficiently. While public attention has been focused on the definition of the problem as inadequate technology ("nothing works"), questions about the appropriateness of decision making given the state

---

[1] Nelson *et al.* (1967) define the economic concept of technology simply: "Technology is the operational part of a production function. If used with the inputs it specifies, the result will be an output of specified characteristics."

of knowledge about rehabilitational technology have been generally ignored. In other areas of public policy, the latter set of questions has become a central economic research focus as the limitations of traditional tools like benefit-cost analysis have become apparent. To understand the reasons for this (and the implications for research on correctional resource allocation decisions), we must first review the meaning of economic efficiency and the potential for benefit-cost analysis to help increase it.

Economists formally recognize resource allocations as being inefficient if and only if one or more individuals could be made better off (by another allocation) without making any other individuals worse off. When a more efficient allocation could be undertaken without harm to the equity of society's distribution of wealth, eliminating such inefficiency is clearly desirable to all but the malevolent. One of the economic rationales for the formation of governments with coercive powers is to reduce inefficiency in resource allocation: the entire government system of civil and criminal justice can be seen as an attempt to make us all better off than would be the case if we relied solely on private economic activity.

How can we determine if governmental activity is actually reducing inefficiency? Assume that we could measure the value to each individual of the outputs that would result from a particular government activity. Assume also that we could measure the costs of the activity to each individual in society. A necessary condition for the government activity to reduce inefficiency is that the sum of the value of the benefits that accrue to all individuals exceeds the value of the sum of the costs to all individuals. If the sum of the benefits exceeds the sum of the costs, it would at least be possible to make someone better off without making anyone worse off by fully compensating any whose costs are increased from the larger total benefit amount.[2]

The comparison of the anticipated aggregate costs with the anticipated aggregate benefits of an activity comprises the simplest description of benefit-cost analysis. Economists have devoted much effort to

---

[2] A sufficient condition for the activity to lead to a reduction in inefficiency is that the transfers to those realizing net costs actually be made. Some economists have recommended that activities be conducted if only the necessary condition for a reduction in inefficiency holds. One rationale for this recommendation is that each of many government activities will have a different set of winners and losers, so that as long as each activity gives more in the aggregate to the winners than it takes from the losers, the cumulative effect of all activities will make everyone better off. Harberger (1971) advances this recommendation as a basic postulate for benefit-cost analysis.

the development of systematic methods for measuring those costs and benefits. Methods for valuing inputs and outputs in the absence of competitive markets and methods for aggregating costs and benefits that accrue over time have been developed to permit the calculations of the net benefits (or costs) expected from the adoption of a project or program. Prest and Turvey (1965) provide a review of the major issues underlying the aggregation of costs and benefits for investment projects. Issues related to the application of the benefit-cost methodology specifically to correctional programs are presented by Holahan (1973) and Mahoney and Blozan (1968).

Often it is not possible to place a dollar value on some desired project or program output. Instead of attempting to analytically determine the efficient level of a particular output, we depend upon the political process to set the target level. To attempt to achieve efficiency, cost-effectiveness analysis is used to select the program that will produce the target level of output at the lowest cost. A variant of cost-effectiveness analysis involves choosing the program that produces the highest level of some output subject to cost constraints set by the political process. Blumstein (1971) provides a clear exposition of cost-effectiveness analysis in the context of the allocation of police resources. Singer and Bloom (1977) apply cost-effectiveness analysis to correctional programs in their comparison of the efficiency of the extensive inmate treatment programs provided by Maryland's Patuxent Institution with the efficiency of Maryland's conventional high-security prisons.

Benefit-cost (and cost-effectiveness) analysis can be used as a tool for program evaluation. While costs and benefits that have accrued in the past are not directly relevant to decisions concerning the efficiency of the allocation of currently available resources, costs and benefits that have occurred in the past can be used as guides for estimating costs and benefits likely to be realized from the program in the future. Historical operating costs can be used as a guide for estimating future operating costs. If the question one is trying to answer is whether or not to continue an ongoing program, the analysis should ignore start-up costs that will not be encountered in the future. On the other hand, if the question under consideration is whether or not to replicate a program in another location, the benefit-cost analysis would appropriately include the program's start-up costs to the extent they are expected to be incurred during replication. Clearly, the purpose of the evaluation will determine which of the historical costs and benefits should be included.

Benefit-cost and cost-effectiveness analyses are thus tools that can be used to assist decision makers in choosing programs that are likely to make the greatest improvement in efficiency. Can and should these tools be applied more frequently in the research and evaluation of correctional programs? Several correctional researchers have answered in the affirmative. Holahan has developed a framework for applying benefit-cost analysis in the evaluation of prison reform programs (Holahan 1973) and applied it to the evaluation of a pretrial diversion program (Holahan 1970a) and drug addict rehabilitation programs (Holahan 1970b). A number of publications by the Correctional Economics Center of the American Bar Association (1974a, 1974b, 1975) advocate the use, and illustrate the application, of benefit-cost analysis to correctional program evaluation. Veteran correctional researchers have advocated greater use of benefit-cost analysis as an evaluation tool: Glaser (1973) and Adams (1975) each devote a chapter in their respective monographs to the use of benefit-cost analysis in the evaluation of correctional programs. Young (1977) has suggested that benefit-cost analysis is not only a desirable component of criminal justice research (including correctional research) but also a stimulant to it.

While we agree that benefit-cost and cost-effectiveness analyses can be useful tools for correctional research, it is our opinion that more attention must be given to their limitations. Our discussion of these limitations is divided into two sections: the general limitations of benefit-cost and cost-effectiveness analyses as tools for program evaluation or the identification of promising innovations; and particular limitations related to the application of those analyses to the evaluation of correctional programs. After setting forth these limitations, we will suggest situations and procedures for which benefit-cost and cost-effectiveness analyses are likely to make major contributions to program evaluation and research in corrections.

GENERAL LIMITATIONS OF THE BENEFIT-COST APPROACH

The first general limitation of the usefulness of benefit-cost analysis as an evaluation tool is related to a characteristic of the analysis itself: a focus on inputs and outputs without explicit consideration of the process linking them. This limitation suggests that benefit-cost analysis alone will not be an adequate evaluation tool for correctional programs. The second general limitation is related to characteristics of the decision makers who direct its use and suggests that recommendations concerning the increased use of benefit-cost analysis should recognize the organizational position of the decision maker directing its application.[3]

Benefit-cost (and cost-effectiveness) analysis focuses on the inputs and outputs of programs. The process by which the inputs are converted to outputs is taken as given. When the question is whether or not to continue an ongoing program, neglect of the program's process of converting inputs to outputs may be justifiable. If one is interested in telling administrators how to improve their programs, however, one must go beyond the static comparison approach of benefit-cost analysis. Nielsen (1975) suggests that not only benefit-cost analysis but any evaluation procedure that ignores the process linking the inputs to outputs is unlikely to produce useful information for program administrators.

Lack of attention to process becomes a more serious limitation when one is evaluating programs with an eye toward finding candidates for replication or expansion. Focusing solely on inputs, outputs, and their economic valuation may, for example, lead one to ignore important factors peculiar to the program that are unlikely to be duplicated in replicating or expanding it. If such factors are overlooked, there is a risk that the benefit-cost analysis of the prototype will not correctly predict the magnitude of net benefits likely to result from its replication.

Benefit-cost analysis may also distract attention from the differential effects of programs on client subgroups. In commenting on Martinson's review of rehabilitation programs (Martinson 1974), Palmer (1975) suggests that the appropriate question is not "what works" but "which methods work best for which types of offenders, and under what conditions and types of settings?" Benefit-cost analysis of aggregate program inputs and outputs generally will not help answer those questions. One might begin to answer those questions by subjecting program components to separate benefit-cost analyses. Disaggregated benefit-cost analysis of this sort, however, presupposes that the evaluation design allows for the recovery of data that is disaggregated by

---

[3] It should be noted that benefit-cost analysis ignores the question of the distribution of the anticipated benefits and costs. The distribution of costs and benefits is not as central a question in evaluating correctional programs, which produce primarily a public good (crime reduction), as it is in the evaluation of capital investment programs, such as water resource projects, which often produce private goods (irrigation water) that can be used exclusively by individuals. For a discussion of the dominance of the efficiency goal in benefit-cost analysis, see Wildavsky (1966).

program units and categories of clientele. The use of benefit-cost analysis to evaluate program components may not be possible unless that application is anticipated during the design of the evaluation procedure.

Benefit-cost analysis was originally developed for the evaluation of prospective water resource projects in which there is little uncertainty concerning the functional relationship between inputs and outputs. In the evaluation of correctional programs, however, there is a much greater level of uncertainty concerning the functional relationship between inputs and outputs. In fact, a common objective of the evaluation is the identification of such functional relationships. We argue not that benefit-cost analysis is an inappropriate evaluation tool in the face of uncertain technology, but rather that it alone is inadequate. To the extent that benefit-cost analysis diverts analytical attention away from the investigation of the process by which inputs are converted to outputs, it can be considered counterproductive to the development of a clearer understanding of what will work best in which situations.

The second general limitation of the benefit-cost approach to program evaluation is related to the incentives facing correctional agency administrators, the decision makers. An implicit assumption behind the use of benefit-cost analysis is that decision makers have an incentive to increase efficiency. Because benefit-cost analysis is most appropriate for answering the question of whether or not to continue a program, its application may be threatening to program administrators who perhaps have little to gain from positive findings but much to lose from negative findings. One might therefore raise the question of the appropriateness of encouraging (perhaps through grant requirements) local correctional agencies to make greater use of benefit-cost analysis. On the other hand, it may be that enough programs are improved through such analyses that the benefits of requiring it outweigh the costs. It is ironic that the benefits and costs of requiring benefit-cost analysis are not known.

A major attraction of benefit-cost analysis is that it gives a "bottom line" on efficiency: net benefits are either positive or negative. However, by explicitly noting gains and losses in dollars, benefit-cost analysis may increase the self-evaluation problems in local correctional agencies. At least since Glaser (1965), correctional researchers have noted the tendency of local agency administrators to suppress negative program evaluations so as not to endanger funding. Evaluations in the benefit-cost framework are likely to be even more susceptible to administrative censorship than traditional impact evaluations because their results are in the language of the legislators—dollars. A report stating that a rehabilitation treatment under consideration provided only small reductions in recidivism might lead a typical legislator to say "try harder," but the same findings in a benefit-cost framework might be presented as resulting in net costs of X, triggering a more critical reaction from the same legislator.

We are not arguing that methodologically valid benefit-cost analyses would not be desirable as components of evaluations of local correctional programs. Obviously, we want state legislatures to look more critically at programs that appear to be inefficient. It should be realized, however, that the correctional agencies conducting benefit-cost analyses of their own programs may be tempted to either suppress findings of programmatic net costs or be overly optimistic in computing benefits and costs so that all programs will appear to have net benefits. Perhaps local correctional agencies should be encouraged to continue to concentrate their analytical resources on determining program impacts, leaving the responsibility for benefit-cost analysis to executive or legislative staffs, who have less to fear from the discovery of net costs, or to external researchers who are searching for promising programs for replication.

SPECIFIC LIMITATIONS IN BENEFIT-COST ANALYSIS OF CORRECTIONAL PROGRAMS

The general limitations of the benefit-cost approach do not discourage us from advocating its increased use. It is possible to recognize that benefit-cost analysis based on aggregate program inputs and outputs may lead to inadequate attention to differential effects of the program on various clientele groups, may divert attention from consideration of program implementation problems that may hinder replication, and may be subject to organizational bias, but still be a powerful evaluation tool. Several characteristics of correctional programs, however, make it difficult to satisfy the assumptions upon which benefit-cost analysis relies.

Benefit-cost analysis assumes that one can accurately predict program impacts or at least a probability distribution for program impacts. For example, in evaluating a proposed water resource project, engineers can with reasonable confidence estimate that the project will produce X acre-feet of water per year that can be used for irrigation. No such reasonable confidence estimates can be made about rehabilitation programs. In the absence of a strong theory for predicting the rehabilitative effects of various correctional programs, social scientists must base their predictions on empirical research. Even under the optimum conditions of a rigorous experimental design, researchers still face the problem of choosing a measure of recidivism that will accurately reflect the unobservable true incidence of criminal behavior for program participants and nonparticipants (controls). Correctional researchers are well aware of the difficulties involved in measuring the rehabilitation effects of correctional treatments.

In addition, rehabilitation is only one intermediate product of the correctional system that contributes to the goal of reduced crime in society. General deterrence and incapacitation effects are also intermediate products produced by the correctional system. Holahan (1973) explicitly recognizes that rehabilitation, incapacitation, and general deterrence contribute to crime reduction in his framework for the application of benefit-cost analysis to the evaluation of correctional programs. He notes that incapacitation and general deterrence may be important in comparing institutional-based with community-based correctional treatment programs. Unfortunately, incapacitation and general deterrence effects are difficult to measure. The measurement of the incapacitation effect is complicated by the problem of how to deal with crimes committed by inmates against other inmates. The measurement of general deterrence effects is at least as methodologically difficult as the measurement of rehabilitation effects.

It may be reasonable to assume that an experimental program reducing the burden of punishment for a small fraction of a jurisdiction's offenders will have a negligible effect on general deterrence. Continuing to ignore general deterrence effects—as does Glaser (1973) in his hypothetical benefit-cost comparison of prison and parole, regular probation, and probation with intensive services—in considering the expansion of a small-scale experimental program may lead to erroneous conclusions concerning the efficiency of correctional treatments. A program that provides 10 percent of first-time felony offenders with intensive-services probation (probation that includes intensive services) in lieu of prison terms is unlikely to reduce the level of general deterrence facing the unconvicted offender. Expanding the use of intensive-services probation to 90 percent of first-time felony offenders, however, may reduce the level of general deterrence to a point that the net benefits extrapolated from its experimental use might be offset by unanticipated costs associated with crimes committed by unconvicted offenders.

The use of benefit-cost analysis not only assumes that program effects can be predicted, it also assumes that dollar values can be placed on program effects. When inputs and outputs (effects) of a program are traded in markets, economists use the revealed prices as measures of the value of the inputs and outputs to society. Where markets do not exist (or are imperfect), economists must develop "shadow prices" to value program inputs and outputs. The shadow price of a unit of program output is an estimate of how much members of society would be willing to pay to obtain (or avoid) that output. The shadow price (and opportunity cost) of a unit of input measures the value of the unit of the input in its next best alternative use. The larger the portion of inputs and outputs that must be valued by shadow prices, the more sensitive the final estimate of the benefit-cost ratio to the skill (and biases) of the benefit-cost analyst. Despite the long history of the application of benefit-cost analysis to water resource projects, the shadow prices used to compute recreational benefits and environmental degradation costs are still subject to considerable controversy.

When benefit-cost analysis is applied to correctional programs, many of the costs and most of the benefits must be valued through the use of shadow prices. Crime avoidance, the major goal of most correctional programs, must be valued through the use of shadow prices. Friedman (1976a) discusses many of the issues involved in placing a dollar value on crime avoidance. What is the loss to society of stolen property? What is the dollar value of a human life (a recurring topic of debate among applied economists)? How can one value alterations in behavior that are in response to the fear of crime? Without clearcut answers to these questions, the range of estimates of the costs of crime will be very wide. In fact, the estimate of the shadow price of crime may be a major determinate of the benefit-cost ratio of programs that are expected to yield crime reduction as their major benefit.

Other questions need answering before benefit-cost analysis can be applied in a consistent manner. How can one value the opportunity cost of prisoners' time? How can one value the quality of life (including safety) within the prison? Do the wages of criminal justice system employees reflect the opportunity cost of their labor to society? The answers given to these questions will influence the costs and benefits of such program effects as the reduction in prison violence, the coercion of inmates into rehabilitation programs, and changes in criminal justice personnel levels.

Without a consensus on how program effects are to be valued, programs cannot be directly compared in terms of their benefit-cost ratios. Researchers trying to identify promising programs would be well advised to investigate the assumptions and valuation methods of programs that are reported to have a high benefit-cost ratio. Until a set of standard procedures is developed for applying benefit-cost analysis to correctional programs, the benefit-cost ratio will not be a reliable index of efficiency. Unfortunately, it is not clear how a consensus on a set of standard procedures could be reached, or once reached, how it could be determined if those procedures would lead to correct conclusions concerning efficiency. It could be a worthwhile undertaking to study the feasibility of developing some standardized set of guidelines to be used in correctional benefit-cost analyses when they are required by funding agencies.

CONTRIBUTIONS TO EVALUATION: COSTS, COST-EFFECTIVENESS ANALYSIS, AND BENEFIT-COST ANALYSIS

Should the use of benefit-cost analysis for the evaluation of correctional programs be encouraged? The preceding discussions of the general limitations of the benefit-cost analysis approach and the specific limitations of its application to correctional programs suggest the necessity of framing an answer to this question in terms of the circumstances of individual programs and the intended use of their evaluations. It should also be recognized that analytical effort is not unlimited: increased use of benefit-cost analysis may divert effort from other, perhaps more appropriate, analytical approaches. In light of current analytical limitations and resource constraints, we recommend that intensive benefit-cost analyses be conducted only under a restricted set of circumstances. We believe, however, that the conscious use of the benefit-cost analysis approach, particularly the systematic identification of the categories of program costs and benefits, can potentially increase the usefulness of many evaluations to decision makers and to the research community.

The benefit-cost analysis approach can serve as a framework for standardizing research in terms of its comprehensiveness. In their recent review of the evaluation of correctional programs, Gibbons *et al.* (1976) note: "Most correctional research has not described in detail what the program consists of or how different services produce different outcomes and has not identified the underlying assumptions." As the first step in increasing comprehensiveness, the benefit-cost analysis approach can help overcome some of those deficiencies. Program inputs (variously skilled labor, facilities, etc.) clearly fall under the heading of costs. Specifying these inputs helps define what a program being evaluated involves. Dividing all program impacts, including those that are not quantifiable, under either the "benefits" or the "costs" heading helps to elucidate the underlying assumptions of the evaluation concerning the effects of the program beyond those that are being statistically estimated. Producing an inventory of program inputs and impacts is only a first step toward increasing an evaluation's usefulness to the research community; an evaluation also should describe exactly how the program inputs were used and the assumptions concerning their relationship to the observed program impacts.

The second step in the benefit-cost analysis approach is to place dollar values on the inputs and negative impacts listed under costs and the positive impacts listed under benefits. We suggest three levels of comprehensiveness for valuing the entries under the "costs" and "benefits" headings: valuation of program inputs, valuation of all costs for closely related programs to facilitate cost-effectiveness comparisons, and valuation of all costs and benefits of closely related programs evaluated through an experimental design. The remainder of this section will elaborate these three approaches.

COSTS

Placing a dollar value on program inputs should be encouraged as a standard component of evaluations. It is important that program administrators and their budgetary sponsors be reminded that the operation of a particular program involves the use of resources that could be employed in other programs. A valuation of program inputs also produces useful information to the research community. A program that is reported to produce small gains in the reduction of recidivism might warrant further investigation if it involved small resource costs per inmate. Developing a bank of cost data from program evaluations would also facilitate the development of production functions for correctional programs that could be used to help identify functionally similar programs appearing to be either very efficient or inefficient in their use of resources. For example, if evaluations are available for 10 programs that are reported to be applying an identical behavioral theory and one of the programs appears to have a much lower per-inmate cost, investigative effort might be directed at determining if the low-cost program has involved a more efficient use of resources or if it did not actually test the theory in question.

Some models for the estimation of costs are available from researchers who have been involved in estimating the costs of implementing the corrections-related recommendations of the U.S. National

Advisory Commission on Criminal Justice Standards and Goals (1973). Singer and Wright (1976) provide a model for estimating the costs of institutional-based programs and parole. Thalheimer (1975) presents cost analysis for halfway houses. Similar studies are presented by Watkins (1975) for the cost analysis of pretrial diversion programs and by Weisberg (1975) for the cost analysis of alternatives to arrest.

COST-EFFECTIVENESS ANALYSIS

The efficiency of programs can be compared through a cost-effectiveness approach if certain conditions hold. The programs should be closely related so that the major unmeasurable effects of the program will be similar and thus cancel out during the comparison. For example, one community-based program can be compared with other community-based programs under the assumptions that they would have similar effects on incapacitation and deterrence. Such an assumption might not be valid in comparing a community-based program with an institutional-based program.

When the effects are unable to be valued as well as unmeasurable, cost-effectiveness analysis might still be used if the effects are likely to be highly correlated with other effects that can be reasonably valued. For example, consider two programs that are intended to reduce violence within prisons. One way to value reductions in prison violence would be to use the changes in the medical costs required to treat violence-related injuries among inmates. Clearly, such a measure underestimates the true value of avoiding prison violence. It might be a reasonable element in a cost-effectiveness comparison, however, if we believed that it would underestimate the true value of avoided violence by the same proportion for each program. Valuing more than one program effect in this manner may be inappropriate if the proportion of each effect is not the same in the two programs.

An analysis of gang rehabilitation techniques by Adams (1967) illustrates circumstances that allow reasonable cost-effectiveness comparisons to be made. Adams compared three alternative programs for encouraging the rehabilitation of youth gang members: assignment of a full-time counselor to work with gang members, assignment of a half-time counselor, and assignment of no counselor. The analysis could ignore possible program effects on deterrence and incapacitation because the three alternatives under consideration involved neither direct surveillance nor institutionalization. Only correctional system costs (costs of counselors and the costs of arresting, convicting, and punishing gang members who were suspected of committing offenses) were compared for the three alternatives. The analysis concluded that the assignment of a full-time counselor was most efficient because it involved the lowest criminal justice system costs. Inclusion of estimates of the social costs of gang crime would not have changed the results under the reasonable assumption that the social costs of crime are positively correlated with criminal justice system costs.

BENEFIT-COST ANALYSIS

Under what conditions should an attempt be made to conduct an intensive benefit-cost analysis as part of a program evaluation? As in the case of cost-effectiveness comparisons, the choice of programs for comparison should be such that unmeasurable effects will be similar. We suggest that an additional criterion be satisfied before analytic effort is invested in the production of complete benefit-cost comparisons: the programs under consideration should be evaluated through an experimental or strong quasi-experimental design.[4]

Our suggestion of this requirement is motivated by four characteristics of such designs. First, an experimental or strong quasi-experimental design facilitates the measurement of the magnitudes of program effects, an important consideration in determining how confident we are in our estimates of benefits and costs. Second, evaluations that employ an experimental or strong quasi-experimental design require that explicit attention be given to the process by which inputs are converted to program effects; the development of the design ensures that attention will be given to the program process, which is not directly dealt with by the benefit-cost approach. Third, because of the expense of the experimental design process, a program that is a candidate for such an evaluation is probably considered by at least part of the correctional research community as a candidate for replication. Benefit-cost analysis has a greater potential influence on resource use decisions when it is coupled with an evaluation directed at the question of program replication than when it is coupled with an evaluation simply asking if a single program should be continued or discontinued. Fourth, the use of an experimental or strong quasi-experimental design for evaluation is likely to involve the participation of researchers from

---

[4] Adams (1975, p. 82) makes an observation similar to ours concerning benefit-cost analysis and the evaluation design supporting it: "The technique is most easily applied in conjunction with experimental or quasi-experimental research designs and with costs and benefits calculated only in the period of follow-up."

outside of the correctional agency administering the program. Consequently, the subjective valuation of program effects required in the application of benefit-cost analysis to social programs is less likely to be subject to organizational biases.

An illustration of the application of benefit-cost analysis in conjunction with a controlled experimental design evaluation is provided by Friedman (1977b) in his interim evaluation of the New York supported work experiment. The supported work concept involves the subsidized employment of ex-addicts and ex-offenders on a contract basis in local public agencies. A reasonable wage, working with peers, and flexible length of time in the program are intended to create a low-stress, rehabilitative environment for program participants. An interim evaluation of the supported work program in New York City was facilitated by the random selection of a control group at the beginning of the program. Quarterly interviews with those in the control and experimental groups and reference to official records (for example, police, welfare, and social security files) permitted a measurement of program impacts after 2 years of operation. A summary of the benefit-cost analysis of the New York supported work experiment is presented in Table 1. The program appears efficient in the sense that each dollar of resources invested in the program yielded $1.64 in benefits.

Several comments on the program and the analysis are in order.

TABLE 1 Social Benefits and Costs (per Experimental Man-Year) of the New York Supported Work Experiment

Benefits	
1. Value added by program to public goods and services	$4,519
2. Postprogram experimental earnings	1,154
3. Savings from reduction of crime-connected costs	
System	86
Crime reduction	207
4. Drug program participation	0
5. Health	(285)
Total Social Benefits	$5,681
Costs	
1. Opportunity costs of supported work employees	$1,112
2. Staff and nonpersonnel expenses	2,362
Total Social Costs	$3,474
Benefit-cost ratio 1.64	

SOURCE: Friedman (1977b, p. 165).

First, the control group and experimental group consisted of individuals not originally held in custody. The analysis, therefore, applies to benefits gained from entering noninstitutionalized individuals into the program. The analysis would not be appropriate for estimating the net benefits of entering an individual in the program who would otherwise be incarcerated. Such an analysis would have to deal with the question of changes in the level of deterrence and incapacitation.

Second, despite the discovery of net benefits for the supported work program, only a small portion of the benefits (about 5 percent) resulted from savings due to reductions in crime-connected costs (case-processing costs and estimated victim costs). An evaluation directed solely at measuring the impact of the program on the recidivism rates of its participants would have found only small gains, especially in terms of the program's nominal budgetary cost. The narrowly focused evaluation might have discounted the program as ineffective. Expanding the analysis to include social benefits and social costs leads to the recommendation that the program be introduced (still on an experimental basis) in other jurisdictions. The combination of comprehensiveness and compactness is one of the strongest advantages of benefit-cost analysis relative to alternative evaluation techniques.

Another point of interest of this example is related to the aggregation of benefits from different sources. The dollar value of the benefits resulting from value added by the program to public goods and services, although involving discretion in its estimation, is probably subject to a lower percentage of error than the estimation of the dollar value of the benefits resulting from savings generated by avoiding crime-connected costs. If the savings generated by avoided crime-connected costs made up a larger portion of the benefits, we would reasonably be more skeptical of the finding that benefits exceed costs. When a large degree of uncertainty in the accuracy of dollar estimates exists, an analyst should investigate the sensitivity of the findings by recalculating the benefit-cost ratio using less optimistic estimates of the cost and benefit components.

The interim evaluation of the supported work experiment demonstrates the use of benefit-cost analysis as a positive as well as a normative tool.[5] In addition to computing the social benefit-cost ratio, which answers the normative question "Is the program efficient?," a

---

[5] For an exposition of the use of benefit-cost analysis as a positive tool for aiding in the anticipation of implementation problems, see Luft (1976).

benefit-cost ratio can be computed from the point of view of several important segments of society as a guide in predicting how the segments would react to the program. A benefit-cost ratio computed for tax payers as a group can help determine if the program is likely to continue to be politically feasible. In New York, a benefit-cost ratio was computed for the welfare department, which contributed funds to the program. If the benefit-cost ratio for the welfare department had been found to be less than one, continued administrative feasibility might have required different funding arrangements. The benefit-cost ratio was also estimated for a typical program participant. If the participant benefit-cost ratio had been less than one, it would have suggested that problems might be encountered in attracting additional participants on a voluntary basis and additional pecuniary rewards for participation should be considered.

Finally, the interim evaluation of the supported work experiment identifies factors related to program success that might be peculiar to New York City. An evaluation aimed at determining if a program should be replicated cannot stop at the computation of the benefit-cost ratio: thought must be given to problems that might be faced in attempting to realize the anticipated net benefits from the operation of the program in other jurisdictions.

NEW DIRECTIONS FOR RESEARCH TO INCREASE THE EFFICIENCY OF THE CORRECTIONAL SYSTEM

In the beginning of our paper, we outlined the three possible ways of improving resource allocation in the correctional system. Each way depends on the decisions made in various parts of the correctional system. To some extent, these decisions depend on the state of knowledge about the technologies that might be used. We hope it is clear that the economic evaluation techniques discussed in the main part of the paper can contribute to important ways to this state of knowledge if they are used appropriately.

Now we would like to clarify the importance of developing other techniques of economic policy analysis as a means of improving resource allocation in the correctional system. There is no evidence that correctional decision-making, given the state of knowledge, is as good as it can be. For resource allocation to be efficient, correctional agencies have to make efficient internal resource allocation decisions, funding sources have to provide the agencies with the appropriate amount of resources to allocate, research and development must be undertaken at an efficient level, and the results of research and development efforts must be used efficiently. The last point means that efficient new technologies must be diffused successfully throughout the correctional setting, and even more importantly, that inefficient demonstration programs must be prevented from spreading (this is more important because of the expected high frequency of failure). The correctional industry must be organized to make these decisions appropriately, or put differently, the various agencies must have incentives to make appropriate decisions.

Charles Schultze (1977) forcefully argues that the perceived failures of the government's social programs of the 1960s were not primarily failures of ideas but failures of organization. Schultze argues that those failures were due primarily to a lack of understanding of public organizational phenomena on resource allocation. As he puts it (p. 15):

[T]he formal models of cost-benefit analysis, for the purpose of determining whether [government] intervention is worthwhile, have been constructed with rigor. But the effort that has gone into theoretical and applied analysis of how to create or utilize decentralized mechanisms for social intervention has been, with a few exceptions, rather limited.

One very interesting way of studying the effects of economic organization is to trace the effects of an innovation as it diffuses through the system.[6] In terms of correctional resource allocation, what is known about the introduction and diffusion of innovations? When the Law Enforcement Assistance Administration (LEAA) selects projects as "exemplary," do jurisdictions throughout the country adopt them? Do they work as intended, and do they survive when LEAA funding is used up? What would explain the answers to these simple questions? Perhaps jurisdictions considering new programs would make different decisions if the funding arrangements were changed (e.g., from block to matching grants or by changes in the matching rate). How is the funding offering decided, and by what criteria should it be set?

Organizational questions also need to be asked in other ways. Most correctional services are provided by government agencies. Perhaps some of these services could be better provided through a regulated private market or through the increased use of nonprofit agencies.

---

[6] Friedman (1976b) has used this approach to study the mutation of the own recognizance bail reform during its diffusion among local court jurisdictions. Weimer (1977) has used the approach to study the advantages and dangers of programs of the Law Enforcement Assistance Administration (of the Department of Justice) designed to induce the diffusion of prosecutorial management innovations.

Without systematic exploration of the efficiency levels that can be achieved under alternative organizational arrangements, the best chances for learning how to improve the correctional sector may be foregone.

The economic tools for exploring and answering these questions are still primitive, but some recent work shows a potential for allowing substantial advancements. In particular, the techniques of McFadden (1976a, 1976b) for predicting the decisions of government bureaus might be used to study aspects of the resource allocation decisions of correctional funding agencies. The evolutionary models of economic growth developed primarily by Nelson and Winter (Nelson 1972, Nelson *et al.* 1976, Nelson and Winter 1977) have recently been extended by Friedman (1977a) to explore the determinants of production efficiency in decentralized public sectors. Similar studies could be done of local correctional institutions. The methods used by Rhodes *et al.* (1977) in studying the Des Moines community-based corrections innovation and its diffusion are in the spirit of the framework suggested earlier.

We conclude by noting that a failure to identify highly successful rehabilitation programs has led to a review of research efforts to date. It is fitting that we reexamine the research methodologies that have been employed in the search. Under certain circumstances, well-known procedures such as benefit-cost analysis may improve the process by which promising correctional technologies are identified or existing programs continued. The research questions we have outlined in this section could be important in generating and translating promising experimental programs into operational technologies in correctional agencies, as well as in eliminating existing inefficiency. The design of effective organizational mechanisms for regulating the growth and development of the correctional system can make an important contribution to improved resource allocation, and we encourage research aimed at building and using the tools of economic policy analysis to do this.

REFERENCES AND BIBLIOGRAPHY

Adams, S. (1967) A cost approach to the assessment of gang rehabilitation techniques. *Journal of Research in Crime and Delinquency* 4(1):166–182.

Adams, S. (1974) Evaluative research in corrections: status and prospects. *Federal Probation* 38(1):14–21.

Adams, S. (1975) *Evaluation Research in Corrections: A Practical Guide*. Washington, D.C. National Institute of Law Enforcement and Criminal Justice, U.S. Department of Justice.

Blumstein, A. (1971) Cost-effectiveness analysis in the allocation of police resources. Pages 87–98 in M. G. Kendall, ed., *Cost-Benefit Analysis*. London: English University Press.

Commission on Correctional Facilities and Services (1974) *Cost-Benefit Analysis: Three Applications to Corrections*. Washington, D.C.: American Bar Association.

Commission on Correctional Facilities and Services (1974) *Community Programs for Women Offenders: Cost and Economic Considerations*. Washington, D.C.: American Bar Association.

Commission on Correctional Facilities and Services (1975) *A Handbook of Cost-Benefit Techniques and Applications*. Washington, D.C.: American Bar Association.

Cook, P. J. (1975) The correctional carrot: better jobs for parolees. *Policy Analysis* 1(1):11–54.

Friedman, L. S. (1976a) *The Economics of Crime and Justice*. Morristown, N.J.: General Learning Press.

Friedman, L. S. (1976b) The evolution of a bail reform. *Policy Sciences* 7:281–313.

Friedman, L. S. (1977a) Evolutionary economic growth in a public sector. Paper presented at the 1977 Annual Meeting of the American Economic Association, New York.

Friedman, L. S. (1977b) An interim evaluation of the supported work experiment. *Policy Analysis* 3(2):147–170.

Gibbons, D. C., Lebowitz, B. D., and Blake, G. F. (1976) Program evaluation in corrections. *Crime and Delinquency* 22(3):309–321.

Glaser, D. (1965) Correctional research: an elusive paradise. *Journal of Research in Crime and Delinquency* 2(1):1–11.

Glaser, D. (1973) *Routinizing Evaluation: Getting Feedback on Effectiveness of Crime and Delinquency Programs*. Washington, D.C.: National Institute of Mental Health, U.S. Department of Health, Education, and Welfare.

Harberger, A. C. (1971) Three basic postulates for applied welfare economics. *Journal of Economic Literature* IX(3):785–797.

Holahan, J. (1970a) A Benefit-Cost Analysis of Project Crossroads. Prepared for the Manpower Administration, U.S. Department of Labor, under contract 82-34-68-15. National Committee on Children and Youth.

Holahan, J. (1970b) *The Economics of Drug Addiction and Control in Washington, D.C.: A Model for Estimation of Costs and Benefits of Rehabilitation*. Washington, D.C.: Office of Planning and Research, District of Columbia Department of Corrections.

Holahan, J. (1973) Measuring benefits from prison reform. Pages 491–516 in *Benefit-Cost and Policy Analysis 1973*. An Aldine Annual on Forecasting, Decision-Making, and Evaluation. Chicago, Ill.: Aldine.

Leslie, A. C. (1972) *A Benefit-Cost Analysis of New York City's Heroin Addiction Problems and Programs*. New York: Health Services Administration.

Lipton, D., Martinson, R., and Wilks, J. (1975) *The Effectiveness of Correctional Treatment: A Survey of Treatment Evaluation Studies*. New York: Praeger Publishers.

Luft, H. S. (1976) Benefit-cost analysis and public policy implementation: from normative to positive analysis. *Public Policy* 24(4):437–462.

Mahoney, M., and Blozan, C. F. (1968) *Cost-Benefit Evaluation of Welfare Demonstration Projects: A Test Application to Juvenile Rehabilitation*. Prepared by the Research Management Corporation for the U.S. Department of Health, Education, and Welfare.

Martinson, R. What works?—questions and answers about prison reform. *Public Interest* (35):22–54.

McFadden, D. (1976a) The revealed preferences of a government bureaucracy: empirical evidence. *Bell Journal of Economics* 7(1):55–72.

McFadden, D. (1976b) The revealed preferences of a government bureaucracy: theory. *Bell Journal of Economics* 6(2):401–416.

McKee, G. J. (1970) Cost-benefit analysis of vocational training in the California Prison System. *Western Economic Journal* 8(3):324.

Nelson, R. R., Peck, M. J., and Kalachek, E. D. (1967) *Technology, Economic Growth and Public Policy.* Washington, D.C.: Brookings Institution.

Nelson, R. R. (1972) Issues and suggestions for the study of industrial organization in a regime of rapid technical change. In V. Fuchs, ed., *Policy Issues and Research Opportunities in Industrial Organization.* New York: National Bureau of Economic Research.

Nelson, R. R., Winter, S. G., and Schuette, H. (1976) Technical change in an evolutionary model. *Quarterly Journal of Economics* 90:90–118.

Nelson, R. R., and Winter, S. G (1977) In search of useful theory of innovation. *Research Policy* 6:36–76.

Nielsen, V. G. (1975) Input-output models and the nonuse of policy analysis. In M. J. White, M. Radnor, and D. A. Tansik, eds., *Management and Policy Science in American Government: Problems and Prospects.* Lexington, Mass.: Lexington Books.

Palmer, T. (1975) Martinson revisited. *Journal of Research in Crime and Delinquency* 12(2):133–152.

Prest, A. R., and Turvey, R. (1965) Cost-benefit analysis: a survey. *Economic Journal* 75:685–705.

Rhodes, W., Blomberg, T., and Seitz, S. (1977) The Des Moines Project and Replication. Unpublished paper, School of Criminology, Florida State University, Tallahassee.

Schultze, C. L. (1977) *The Public Use of Private Interest.* Washington, D.C.: Brookings Institution.

Singer, N. M., and Wright, V. B. (1976) *Cost Analysis of Correctional Standards: Institutional-Based Programs and Parole,* Vol. II. Washington, D.C.: American Bar Association.

Singer, N. M., and Bloom, H. S. (1977) A Cost-Effectiveness Analysis of Patuxent Institutions. Unpublished paper, Department of Economics, University of Maryland, College Park.

Thalheimer, D. J. (1975) *Cost Analysis of Correctional Standards: Halfway Houses.* Vol. II. Prepared for the National Institute of Law Enforcement and Criminal Justice, U.S. Department of Justice. Washington, D.C.: American Bar Association.

Thurow, L. C., and Rappaport, C. (1969) Law enforcement and cost-benefit analysis. *Public Finance* 24:48–64.

U.S. National Advisory Commission on Criminal Justice Standards and Goals (1973) *Corrections.* Washington, D.C.: U.S. Government Printing Office.

Watkins, A. M. (1975) *Cost Analysis of Correctional Standards: Pretrial Division.* Vol. II. Prepared for the National Institute of Law Enforcement and Criminal Justice, U.S. Department of Justice. Washington, D.C.: American Bar Association.

Weimer, D. (1977) Federal Intervention in the Process of Innovation in Local Public Agencies: A Focus on Organizational Incentives. Unpublished discussion paper 78-22, Public Policy Analysis Program, University of Rochester, Rochester, N.Y.

Weisberg, S. (1975) *Cost Analysis of Correctional Standards: Alternatives to Arrest.* Vol. II. Prepared for the National Institute of Law Enforcement and Criminal Justice, U.S. Department of Justice. Washington, D.C.: American Bar Association.

Wildavsky, A. (1966) The political economy of efficiency: cost-benefit analysis, systems analysis, and program budgeting. *Public Administration Review,* 26(4):292–310.

Young, D. R. (1977) Cost-Benefit Analysis: A Component and Stimulant to Criminal Justice Research. Unpublished paper. Prepared for the Fourth Annual Research Exchange Association for Criminal Justice Research, Albany, New York.

Appendix:
Conference on
Rehabilitation,
July 25–27, 1977

PANEL ON RESEARCH ON REHABILITATIVE TECHNIQUES

LEE SECHREST, *Chairman*, Department of Psychology, Florida State University

NATHAN AZRIN, Department of Psychology, Southern Illinois University and Anna State Hopsital

EUGENE EIDENBERG, Deputy Undersecretary for Intergovernmental Relations, U.S. Department of Health, Education, and Welfare

STEPHEN FIENBERG, Department of Applied Statistics, University of Minnesota

JACK GIBBS, Department of Sociology, University of Arizona

ALAN KAZDIN, Department of Psychology, Pennsylvania State University

SAMUEL KRISLOV, Department of Political Science and School of Law, University of Minnesota, and Chairman of the Committee on Research on Law Enforcement and Criminal Justice

RICHARD SCHWARTZ, Law School, State University of New York at Buffalo

GRESHAM SYKES, Department of Sociology, University of Virginia

CLAUDEWELL THOMAS, Department of Psychiatry, College of Medicine and Dentistry of New Jersey

ANN WITTE, Department of Economics, University of North Carolina

273

PARTICIPANTS

STUART ADAMS, Criminal Justice Consultant

ALFRED BLUMSTEIN, School of Urban and Public Affairs, Carnegie-Mellon University

JOHN CONRAD, Academy of Contemporary Problems, Ohio State University

ALLYSON ROSS DAVIES, RAND Corporation

RAYMOND FOWLER, Department of Psychology, University of Alabama

LEE FRIEDMAN, Graduate School of Public Policy, University of California at Berkeley

GARY GOTTFREDSON, American Psychological Association

PETER GREENWOOD, RAND Corporation

DAVID GRISWOLD, School of Criminology, Florida State University

PAUL LERMAN, School of Social Work, Rutgers University at New Brunswick

RICHARD LIGHT, Kennedy School of Government, Harvard University

MICHAEL MALTZ, Department of Criminal Justice, University of Illinois at Chicago Circle

ROBERT MARTINSON, Center for Knowledge in Criminal Justice Planning

EDWIN MGARGREE, Department of Psychology, Florida State University

ALDEN MILLER, Center for Criminal Justice, Harvard Law School

KENT MILLER, Institute for Social Research, Florida State University

JOHN MONAHAN, Program in Social Ecology, University of California at Irvine

JOAN PETERSILIA, RAND Corporation

HERBERT QUAY, Applied Social Sciences, University of Miami

EVA REZMOVIC, Department of Psychology, Northwestern University

WILLIAM RHODES, School of Criminology, Florida State University

STANTON SAMENOW, Program for the Investigation of Criminal Behavior, St. Elizabeth's Hospital

STAFF

SUSAN O. WHITE, Study Director

ELIZABETH BROWN, Research Assistant

DOROTHY E. JACKSON, Administrative Secretary